WOMEN VOLUNTEER TO GO TO PRISON

A History of the Elizabeth Fry Society of B.C. 1939 -1989

WOMEN VOLUNTEER TO GO TO PRISON

A History of the Elizabeth Fry Society of B.C. 1939 -1989

LEE STEWART

ORCA BOOK PUBLISHERS

First edition

Canadian Cataloguing in Publication Data
Stewart, Lee Jean, 1944-
   Women volunteer to go to prison

   Includes bibliographical references and index.
   ISBN 0-920501-93-1

1. Elizabeth Fry Society of British Columbia — History. 2. Female offenders — Rehabilitation — British Columbia — History. I. Title.
HV8992.C2S84 1993   364.3'74'060711   C93-091115-6

Publication assistance provided by The Canada Council
Cover design by Susan Fergusson
Printed and bound in Canada

Orca Book Publishers
PO Box 5626, Station B
Victoria, BC   Canada
V8R 6S4

Orca Book Publishers
Box 3028, 1574 Gulf Road
Point Roberts, WA   USA
98281

This book is dedicated to the memory of the remarkable women, the founders of the E. Fry, who took up an unpopular cause when they first volunteered to go to prison

CONTENTS

FOREWORD

The Honourable Madam Justice P.M. Proudfoot
Court of Appeal for British Columbia

This book spans fifty years of the development of the Elizabeth Fry Society of British Columbia, an organization made up substantially of volunteers. Its members, without question, had an enormous influence on the prison system for women in British Columbia and, for that matter, in Canada.

When an initial handful of women became involved in this worthy pursuit, little did they realize just how important a role they would play in making life, both inside a prison and outside on release, just a little more tolerable and kinder.

The Elizabeth Fry Society had its beginning in British Columbia in 1939. Its object was to assist women in conflict with the law. Since that time, many of the vast improvements in the field of corrections can be attributed to this organization.

From the outset they were pioneers in what was, predominantly, a male world. Their perseverance soon convinced those in authority that the Elizabeth Fry Society was seriously committed to helping women in trouble with the law. This book documents that progress.

Initially, the members of the Society spent their time visiting the prisons, such as British Columbia's Girls' Industrial School and Oakalla Prison for Women. However, it did not take long until their services expanded to cover a wide variety of needs such as public education, supervision of community living, homes for adolescents, emergency receiving homes, a very effective counselling service for shoplifters, court work service, and pre-release planning.

One of the significant aspects which had to be dealt with by the Society over and above prison reform was to alter public attitude. Once women were sent to prison they were forgotten. They were considered to be lost to the community. The Elizabeth Fry Society did not believe this and felt that that attitude had to be changed. They worked hard at changing the public's perception. It is fair to say that over the years they have had some success in promoting both reform within the institution and within public attitude.

One of the key concerns that faced the Society was the amount of inactivity in the institutions. Women were spending hours on end doing absolutely nothing, or, alternatively, doing uninteresting institutional chores. The educational facilities available, initially, were abysmal. When I was involved in the *Royal Commission on the Incarceration of Female Offenders* (1978), it was obvious that the educational facilities at the prison for women were at a bare minimum. During the hearings, the Elizabeth Fry Society made two recommendations:

1. That every inmate who is capable be required to work or attend school and that idleness and lack of gainful activity not be permitted.

2. That the facilities and courses offered within the institution be publicized and inmates be encouraged to participate in them.

Fortunately, with the opening of a new facility in January 1991, facilities have greatly improved, and interesting courses of training are now offered. The Elizabeth Fry Society had much to do with this progress in recognizing the potential, and doing something about it.

This organization can be satisfied with the lasting contribution it has made towards implementing change in the field of corrections for women. The Elizabeth Fry Society realized more could be done for women than locking them up to spend their time in inactivity and idleness. While the organization has grown more sophisticated and influential in government planning for corrections, the Society has never stopped caring for women who have been separated from society as a result of their conflict with the law.

This dedication to the cause has continued. This book is a fine history of that dedication.

The Hon. Madam Justice Proudfoot
Vancouver, British Columbia
December, 1991

PREFACE

Lee Stewart

It was a rainy day in late November, 1986, when I first became acquainted with the Elizabeth Fry Society of British Columbia. I had been invited by Grace Black to meet with herself and Maida Duncan, members of the history committee, to discuss the possibility of my writing the history of the Society to commemorate the upcoming fiftieth anniversary of the EFSBC in 1989. The women on the E. Fry History Committee (they always referred to their Society as the E. Fry) knew very little about me—just that I was an historian with an interest in women's history in British Columbia. Similarly, I had only a vague understanding that the Society aided women in prison, and I only knew that because my husband recalled that his grandmother, Ida Matoff, had been a Fry volunteer in the 1960s.

This first meeting at Grace Black's home was an opportunity for us to look each other over, to assess the task at hand, and determine if we could work together. It was an interview disguised as a social occasion. Sitting in Grace's living room, we drank tea from a matched set of china cups and ate homebaked cookies and cake. We exchanged brief outlines of our lives, laughed politely, appeared to agree on the methods and objectives of compiling a history of a women's organization, and arranged a second meeting to include Marie Legg and Beth Weese, the other members of the History Committee.

At this second meeting we got down to business. Seated around Grace's kitchen table, we drank coffee from an assorted collection of mugs and ate packaged biscuits. The biscuits told me these were busy women who did not normally combine their volunteer work with entertaining. All four women had been longtime volunteers in other organizations before they became involved with the EFSBC. They had a great deal to say about the role of women, the role of government, and the role of the private sector in corrections. Most of all they had much to say about the E. Fry. Yet they unfolded their experiences cautiously, watching for my reactions, searching for my sensitivity to their stories.

As an historian, I had previously researched the social and educational reform work of clubwomen in British Columbia in the late nineteenth and early twentieth centuries. Listening to Grace, Maida, Marie, and Beth, I was conscious of the voices of women both in the past and present. I was fascinated by the views they held in common with their predecessors and intrigued by the differences. I wanted to understand the work they did with the E. Fry and why they did it. They wanted me to write that story, not to immortalize themselves but to explain women's voluntary tradition to those who will follow them.

Several months passed before I was formally engaged by the EFSBC to commence this book. In the meantime, I read all the biographies of Elizabeth Fry that I could find and began to make a dent in the corrections literature. I travelled to the University of Toronto, Robarts Library, to examine the criminology holdings and found there was an empty space in the collection where the history of the Elizabeth Fry Society should have been. Despite the many references to the Elizabeth Fry Society, little had been written about its appearance in Canada. Surveys of the criminal justice system in Canada could only surmise the beginnings of Elizabeth Fry and guess at its origins in British Columbia. Scholars called for more histories of prisoners' aid societies and for clarification of the role these societies have played in correctional change.

I was excited, although somewhat overwhelmed, at the variety of ways I might approach this topic. Preliminary research made it apparent that the focus would be guided by my own expertise and training in women's history and by my sources — the EFSBC records and oral testimonies of Fry volunteers. The history would not, therefore, tell the stories of prison inmates or attempt to assess the clinical aspects of their treatment but would endeavour to explain women's work for penal reform in the twentieth century. The EFSBC accepted my proposal to write a history of the Society that examined its role in effecting correctional change for girls and women.

From the outset, I had numerous concerns related to my being able to juggle the demands of the Fry history project with my continued employment as a college history instructor, to the state of the EFSBC records which would be the source for my research, to the proposed deadline for the completion of the history, and to the freedom I would have to interpret the E. Fry history — nothing unusual for an historian up for hire! All of these factors did pose their share of difficulties, except for the last one. The women who made up the history committee — all past presidents — wanted neither a hagiographic nor a popular treatment of their history. They only wanted me to *get it right* — to project the real story of the E. Fry. To this end they offered vigorous and painstaking criticism of each chapter that,

I believe, strengthened the writing without compromising the analysis. I have learned this scrupulosity is the process by which the Fry women achieve their objectives.

This history, then, is the result of several years of research, which included months of reading through the EFSBC records, newspapers, and government documents; visiting provincial and federal women's prisons and talking with the inmates; and interviewing many past and present Fry volunteers and executive directors. It examines the history of the first fifty years of the EFSBC from 1939 to 1989 and is organized thematically within a chronological framework.

The title of the book is derived from the headline of a column in *The Vancouver Province* which announced the original organization of the Elizabeth Fry Society in 1939 by several women in Vancouver. The first two chapters discuss the beginnings of the Society in British Columbia, the first in Canada. These chapters review women's historic interest in penal reform from the voluntary efforts of Elizabeth Fry in the nineteenth century to the women who organized for social reform and to advance the status of women in British Columbia before the Second World War. Chapter three examines the EFSBC's work with female inmates in Oakalla to the mid-sixties; the next chapter looks at the Society's efforts to improve conditions in the provincial industrial schools for girls. Chapter five explores how and why the EFSBC established its group homes. The sixth chapter looks more closely at collective identity and the work of the volunteers — called the "Lizzie Frys" by the women they visited in prison — who gave the Society its direction. Chapter seven documents the various ways the Society attempted to bridge the distance between prison and the outside community, especially for discharged inmates. The penultimate chapter examines the historical efforts of the EFSBC and the national organization, CAEFS, to close the federal prison for women in Kingston and return the inmates to prisons in their home provinces. The concluding chapter brings the history into the present and reflects on the patterns of both continuity and change that characterized the Society's first fifty years. It shows some startling parallels between the EFSBC's efforts and the work of Elizabeth Fry, in the previous century.

In the final analysis, this is a book about the process of change in corrections and the role played by the voluntary, or private, sector. It is, not surprisingly, a history of women's work. Although many individual women are named in these pages, the emphasis in this history has been on the collective efforts of the volunteers who constitute the life's blood of the EFSBC. This was the wish of the women on the EFSBC history committee, who guided this project, and echoes the perspective voiced by the first president of the society in 1939 when she refused to have her photograph taken for a

Vancouver newspaper claiming, "that it is the Society and its work that is important, not the individual."

On a personal note, I wish to express my admiration for the women on the EFSBC history committee, Maida Duncan, Marie Legg, Beth Weese and Grace Black. They have envisioned much for the EFSBC and each played important parts in its history. They have long awaited this book and it is their belief in this project, their support, and their patience that has made it possible.

I greatly appreciate the time and energy contributed by B.C. historian, Dr. Jean Barman, who read the manuscript as it neared completion and offered constructive criticism, editorial advice, and collegial encouragement.

I must also express my gratitude to my husband, John Levin, who has shared with me his expertise on organizational behaviour, lent his services as a proofreader, and tolerated my obsession with the Elizabeth Fry for (he would say) too long.

It seems appropriate that the members of the history committee have the last word. It was, after all, their idea to write the history of this, the first Elizabeth Fry Society in Canada, and to this end they formed a committee to plan and carry out the project nearly a decade ago. After many months of reading and sorting through board minutes, annual reports, budgets, and associated documents, they came to understand not only the complexities of writing a history but also the purposes it might serve. Although, in the final chapter, I suggest, philosophically, that in preserving the past this history provides a legacy for future Fry volunteers, the women on the history committee had somewhat more practical aims in mind. They hoped to reveal the evolution of women's voluntary activity and to acknowledge the role played by the community at large in supporting the initiatives of the EFSBC. The committee wants to take this opportunity to make special mention of the financial help given to the Society, often at very crucial moments in its history, by philanthropic foundations, community organizations, businesses, church groups, and individuals who showed their confidence in the work of the EFSBC.

Lee Stewart

1. AN INTRODUCTION TO ELIZABETH FRY: A NAME FOR PENAL REFORM

. . . the attraction of the Elizabeth Fry — its purpose (as I understood it) — was to do what was possible to assist women in conflict with the law. And that had to do not only with getting them new glasses or underwear, it had to do with having the wit and the wisdom to do something for women who were deprived of their freedom and, therefore, their dignity. . . . The public didn't care what happened to the offender after she was sentenced. The Elizabeth Fry Society cared.

Marie Legg, EFSBC volunteer. November 9, 1987.[1]

From its formation by a few women in 1939, the caring of the Elizabeth Fry Society of British Columbia (EFSBC) has taken many forms in its attempts to provide aid and assistance to female offenders, to shape public attitudes towards their treatment, and to refine the philosophy of corrections.[2] Fry members not only visit women in prison and sponsor rehabilitation programs, but since the 1960s the Society has been concerned also with preventive and after-care. Fifty years after its inception, in addition to public education, the wide variety of services offered by the EFSBC include: community living homes for adolescents; emergency receiving homes in Vancouver and Burnaby; counselling programs for shoplifters; courtwork services for women and men; pre-release planning for inmates at the Burnaby Correctional Centre for Women (formerly Lakeside and Twin Maples); specialized treatment programs in family therapy and life skills; transition homes; programs for the Willingdon Detention Centre; and parole supervision. In the process of expanding services to meet the needs of its clients, the Elizabeth Fry Society of British Columbia has undergone changes in its structure to ensure its viability in a changing world. No longer an exclusively volunteer organization, the EFSBC remains, however, a Society with a predominantly female membership that has established a nearly unique model of partnership between its volunteer and professional workers. (See Charts 3 and 4, pages 171 and 172.)

Fraudena Eaton was one of the founders of the Elizabeth Fry Society of British Columbia in 1940. Committed to women's issues, Eaton helped organize a self-help group for unemployed women in Vancouver in the 1930s. In 1942 she was appointed director of the Women's Division of the National Selective Service Agency to oversee recruitment of labour during the war. To this end, Eaton established daycare services for the children of working women. In British Columbia, she was active in the Local Council of Women; president of the Provincial Council of Women, 1951-53; appointed to the B.C. Labour Relations Board, 1953-54; awarded the Garnett Sedgwick Award for outstanding contribution to furtherance of civil liberties in B.C. in 1954 and an LLD from UBC in 1958. Eaton became president by acclamation of the National Council of Women, 1956.
(photo courtesy of Canada Wide Photo)

The EFSBC is one of nineteen such societies across Canada, but in 1939 it was the first to be founded and named after the woman who had worked so diligently, over a century ago, for penal reform in Great Britain.[3] In choosing Elizabeth Fry's name, women in Vancouver ensured that her goals and ideals would reverberate through the decades to guide and strengthen the commitment of contemporary reformers. Fry's work is also testimony to the ability of a woman, without legitimate political power, to alter public opinion and move governments. Thus the name Elizabeth Fry serves to link the women in the twentieth century Society to women's own history of noble deeds and significant endeavours.

Perhaps it was a need to establish the Society in British Columbia as a legitimate heir, both to a tradition and a heroine, that led members over the years to establish communication with descendents of Elizabeth Fry.[4] In 1954 these members were successful in locating a great niece who sent, as a gift to the British Columbian Society, a portrait of her famous aunt. In 1982, Michael Fry, a great nephew who had written a biography of Elizabeth, forwarded a cash donation to aid the EFSBC in its work.[5] At the EFSBC's fiftieth anniversary dinner in 1989, a great great granddaughter living in Port Alberni on Vancouver Island was an honoured guest.[6] Although Fry relatives have, over the years, given their blessing, so to speak, to the B.C. Society, and confirmed its place in the Fry family tree, the Elizabeth Fry Society of British Columbia proved, by its own record of caring, that it was, indeed, entitled to carry the name of Elizabeth Fry.

It was Fraudena Eaton, one of the founding members in 1939, who suggested naming the Society after Elizabeth Fry. An energetic, educated wife and mother, Fraudena Eaton, was committed to women's rights and social reform. Over the next several decades she would become a prominent clubwoman in Vancouver working to ensure equality for women on legal and employment issues.[7] In the years when she was homebound with young children, Eaton had read Fry's memoirs and had been moved and impressed by her interest in society's most neglected women, women in prison. Eaton urged her colleagues who were interested in this area of social service to read about Fry's ideals for a women's prison and her methods of reform.

In the first fifty years of the British Columbian Society's existence, the story of Elizabeth Fry's prison work has been part of every member's informal initiation. "Who was Elizabeth Fry?" and "What did she do?" are questions that are asked by most individuals and groups who want to know more about the EFSBC. For speakers wanting to introduce the work of the Society, telling the story of Elizabeth Fry has served as a basis for making the Society's purposes meaningful both to its members and its supporters.

Contemporary studies of organizational culture suggest that the stories, historical or mythological, which are repeated within the organization help to create its identity. They are often the "glue" that binds the people in the organization together and provides them with a sense of mission.[8] For many years in the EFSBC, the Elizabeth Fry stories contributed to a distinctive ethos that pervaded the whole organization. This ethos was characterized by its members' outstanding commitment to service, their perseverance against the odds, and their commitment to innovation.[9] A brief recounting, then, of Elizabeth Fry's work to improve the lives of women in prison is an appropriate, even essential, introduction to the history of the Elizabeth Fry in British Columbia.

Elizabeth Fry was a nineteenth century English Quaker who, acting according to the tenets of her beliefs, sought to ensure humane comforts and provide spiritual guidance to society's most forgotten souls, the female prison population. In a reforming age in which Quakers were prominent in their work to liberalize attitudes and institutions, Elizabeth Fry's mission was, nevertheless, remarkable because its success depended almost entirely on her own devotion to the cause. Undeterred by middle-class conventions that constrained women's public or political interests, especially in such inhospitable quarters as a jail, Fry drew her strength from divine principles, not earthly practices. Her inspired resolution, gentle dignity, and personal charisma opened doors that were ordinarily closed to women with neither wealth, education, nor political connections.

Fry did not, however, eschew women's primary social responsibilities nor was she exempted from personal anguish. The daughter

Elizabeth Fry, a Quaker, had been one of the first women to become active in prison reform in England in the early 1800s. In this period, both male and female inmates were housed together in despicable conditions. Fry formed "ladies' committees" to assist female offenders and was instrumental in establishing separate institutions for women. Nearly a century later, Vancouver women interested in the welfare of female offenders housed at Oakalla Prison Farm formed a prisoners' aid society and named it after Elizabeth Fry. This organization in British Columbia was the first Elizabeth Fry Society in Canada.

of a well-to-do merchant and banker, Elizabeth Fry married a London tea importer. She managed a large household in addition to her various charitable activities, while continually in a pregnant or postnatal condition. Elizabeth Fry suffered in her delivery of eleven infants into the world and she mourned her loss when a daughter, her namesake, died in childhood. She endured the social humiliation that accompanied her husband's bankruptcy. Although her own religious convictions had not been untested, Fry's determination to serve God and humankind in some meaningful way never faltered.

Elizabeth Fry drew public attention to the appalling conditions in London's Newgate Gaol when she made her first visit to the female inmates in 1812. Fry reported the wretched state of the confined women who had neither adequate clothing, blankets, coal nor candles to warm them in their damp and filthy surroundings. In an institution built for 500 prisoners there were over 800, of which 300 were women. Many had no choice but to make their beds on the floor. Whatever amenities were wanted, whether a pail for refuse, nourishing food, or garments to replace rags, had to be paid for by the prisoners and brought to the jail by friends from the outside. These necessities, or, as was often preferred, alcohol to merely dim the reality of their condition, relied on bribery and prostitution. This was not difficult in conditions that did not segregate women, or where doors between the men's and women's side of the prison had been conveniently left open to facilitate the transaction of sordid business. Moreover, many of the women shared these unsavoury circumstances with their children, often born in the prison.

Fry's immediate response was practical. With the aid of other Quakers, who were wives and mothers like herself, she returned to the prison with food and clothing for the destitute women and children. On successive visits, Elizabeth Fry read aloud from the Bible in her attempt to occupy the idle hours of the inmates with some spiritual comfort and moral instruction. After consulting the women about their own wants and needs, Fry organized a school in the prison to teach the children and their mothers how to read. Later she set up a prison library. Fry believed that both the human body and the human spirit required nourishment. She also recognized that not even this combination of practical and inspired responses to the individual human need would ever be sufficient without more permanent reforms to penal institutions and the law.

Her reputation as a prison reformer established, Elizabeth Fry appeared in 1818 before a Parliamentary Committee examining evidence concerning the London prisons. Her presence before a chamber that would not elect or be elected by women for another hundred years was as unusual as her visits to Newgate Gaol. Fry's testimony, based on her observations of the causes of the deplorable conditions that continued to characterize women's lives behind bars, articulated the standards that she believed to be essential to the humane treatment of women in prison. She was adamant that all of the physical necessities be provided without the prisoners having to pay for them; she pleaded for more space for the inmates and spoke against the use of solitary confinement except for the sleeping arrangements. Fry also wanted education for those who could not read. In addition, Elizabeth Fry stressed that women inmates should be supervised only by women, ideally, in a women's prison; that they should be gainfully employed; that all prisoners should be classified according to their crime, character, previous record, and current conduct; and that non-denominational religious instruction should be provided.

Many of these ideas had been started, and even financed, on a voluntary, experimental basis at Newgate by Elizabeth Fry and her Ladies' Committee.[10] Fry was as firm an advocate of the formation of ladies' committees, to administer and perform practical social work, as she was of prison reform. She, herself, organized the first ladies' committee to visit Newgate with her on a regular basis. Her advice to the women visitors going into the prison was to be quiet, to submit to decrees which they could not alter, to observe the rules of the prison and not try to mitigate prisoners' sentences. Fry counselled also that the visitor should not be too familiar with the inmates, or refer to their past crimes, but should always make deci-

sions in consultation with them. Fry's aims had been to treat the
prisoners like human beings instead of animals, to give them hope
for their future, and to help their children. Although her efforts improved the atmosphere of order, industry, and sobriety within the
jail, permanent changes were slow to implement because prisons
were not centrally administered. Nevertheless, most of Fry's measures for the physical well-being of women in prison were
introduced in a Parliamentary Act in 1825.[11]

In Victorian England the new middle class was beginning to
re-examine laws, institutions, and social conventions. Quakers, generally, were in the forefront of movements for the abolition of
slavery and capital punishment, and the reform of prisons and the
penal code. Their belief that a divine spark resided in all human
beings giving them the potential to choose a moral existence meant
that Quakers like Elizabeth Fry felt compelled to improve prison
conditions in the hopes that the prisoners might have the opportunity to reform.

Although not the only humanitarian to be concerned with prison
reform, Fry was the first to insist that women prisoners required different treatment from men, preferably in segregated facilities supervised
by women. She was aware that the presence of male staff and inmates offered the potential for the abuse and exploitation of the
women. However, Elizabeth Fry articulated the separation of male
and female inmates for reasons other than the prevention of sexual
contact. Fry saw that, even in prison, women were still mothers who
had responsibility for their children. To Fry, the needs of these
women and their offspring were clearly different from those of the
male prisoners and could best be interpreted by other women—female staff and "ladies' committees." Fry argued that the constructive
rehabilitation of women relied on their being tended by women who
would be both friends and models to the inmates.

Fry recognized also that there were different causes for women's
crimes. In the nineteenth century, both men and women were convicted more often of unlawful personal behaviour than of serious
crimes against person or property. There was, however, almost a
subcategory of moral or sexual offences that applied almost exclusively to women. Prostitution was the most obvious example of
these women's crimes. Fry saw a relationship between "moral de-
pravity" – the majority of so-called female criminality– and poverty.
Limited opportunities for wage earning and the low salaries paid to
working women placed them in the most marginal economic position in society.[12] In some instances, prostitution might seem the
only alternative to starvation. Although she did not question the
justice of incarceration, Fry believed that an end to this cycle of
despair could be found if female inmates were to receive payment

for honest work, instead of punishment in the form of ten hours on the treadmill.[13] Fry was convinced that employment for female prisoners could aid in their reform, and provide them with earnings and saleable skills on their release.

These two recommendations for the treatment of women prisoners not only challenged the Victorians' attitudes toward crime and punishment but also their ideas about womanhood and work. Some Victorians objected to the idea of employment for prisoners on the grounds that they would be taking work away from the "industrious poor." A few may have been concerned about the exploitation of prison labour.[14] But the great majority of the public was simply unwilling to believe that female inmates warranted any extraordinary consideration of their sex in their treatment. Women in prison were not only criminal offenders, they were outside the bounds of "true womanhood."[15]

In the nineteenth century, a woman convicted of any moral or sexual offence suffered not only the penalty of a prison sentence but also the lifetime label of "fallen woman." There was little social redemption possible for such a woman. Any woman who was unchaste, whether as a result of a sole indiscretion or her occupation, bore the stigma of moral impurity. She had forfeited all that was valued in the primary social role for which she was regarded: that of wife and mother. These were the real ideological barriers that faced Elizabeth Fry's recommendations to treat female inmates primarily as women capable of redemption, and not as base creatures.

It may have been their religious convictions that brought Fry and her Ladies' Committee into the prison but it was the bond of common motherhood that enabled them to empathize with their "fallen sisters." Concern for the children helped to focus the efforts of the Quaker women and win the trust of the inmates. Ultimately, Elizabeth Fry and the Ladies' Committee were able to hire a female staff member—a matron to supervise all aspects of prison life—and to introduce work programs into the prison. The first employment of the women at Newgate was to knit stockings by arrangement with a large company that still depended on a cottage system of manufacturing. It was deemed successful when, after a year of its operation, over 20,000 articles were produced, and the habits and morale of the inmates visibly improved.[16]

Fry is remembered as the heroine of penal reform in the nineteenth century. However, Elizabeth Fry understood that, ideally, the implementation and success of reform measures relied on the cooperation of the prison authorities, the women prisoners, and the Ladies' Committee. In fact, Fry regarded the Ladies' Committee as the most essential body for reform and she urged women to form a society rather than making individual efforts. She observed that a duly organized society made for greater continuity and a variety of members contributed different areas of competency. Fry wrote, also, that a committee often had better judgement than an individual; had greater order, method and regularity; reached sounder decisions; and held more weight with the authorities.[17] Nor did Elizabeth Fry over-estimate the importance of the social position of the members of the Ladies' Committee. In her view, women of status had the time to devote to useful charity work, the means to financially support the endeavours of their committees, and the influence to command respect from parliamentarians, prison officers, and prisoners alike.[18]

From 1813 to 1830, Elizabeth Fry was a public figure who, like Florence Nightingale, became legendary as much for her capacity to direct light in dark corners as for her being a "lady" who dared even attempt such a thing. However, Elizabeth Fry was never without opposition and although she retained her reputation as a reformer, after 1830 she began to lose her influence with the prison authorities. The popular tide of humanitarian concern, which had previously been sympathetic to her efforts, retreated in the face of an apparent increase in crime. Another parliamentary committee, in 1831, was critical of Fry and her committee's methods at Newgate. The public mood had shifted to demand hardship and privation for convicted criminals and was less tolerant of treatment that appeared "too soft" in prisons "reformed by narrow sentiment and blind zeal."[19]

After the "professional reformers"[20] came into power in 1832, Elizabeth Fry's brand of penal reform was regarded as belonging to the old order. The new breed of reformer was not guided by Christian principles but by the more fashionable and more secular "scientific" methods of controlling prisoners' behaviour pioneered in the United States. In this new spirit of reform, penitentiaries were designed to prevent any communication amongst the prison population. Indeed, prisoners were to be housed in single cells and expected to maintain total silence to encourage continuous reflection on their transgressions and inspire penitence.[21] Inmates who spoke would have their meal rations reduced as punishment. With the advent of this strict prison discipline, the Ladies' Committees were discredited as well-meaning but ineffectual.[22]

In her last years of visiting the women in Newgate, Elizabeth Fry was increasingly criticised for her continued Scripture readings.[23] In fact, there was little else she could offer now that "efficient, professional service" had replaced the "amateur goodwill" of the Ladies' Committee. Elizabeth Fry always believed she worked under divine guidance; nevertheless, she had been a practical reformer whose primary concern had been the rehabilitation, not the punishment, of the prisoner. To her death in 1845, she deplored what she considered to be the cruelty embodied in the ideas of the new penal reformers.

She continued to proclaim the best discipline was the one which was most successful in preparing the prisoner for a return to active life and to earn an honest living, and refuted arguments that these ends could be achieved through fear and deprivation.

When Elizabeth Fry forced Victorian society to examine the conditions of its penal institutions, she opened a new chapter in what is now known as the history of corrections. Although Fry could not reconcile her own beliefs with the new penal philosophy being implemented in the final years of her life, it had been her recommendations and innovations that caused many of the concepts surrounding crime and punishment to be reconsidered. Governments began to take a more responsible role in the maintenance of prisons and inmates. However, Elizabeth Fry's most enduring legacy was to be the creation of separate prisons for female inmates, and the conviction that female personnel were necessary to protect women from abuse, and conducive to their rehabilitation.[24]

The legendary experiences of Elizabeth Fry still serve to fortify women working to improve conditions for female offenders. Irrespective of changing values in correctional philosophy, the caring and commitment that made Fry a heroine in the last century are still the qualities that are essential to both volunteers and professionals in social service work. Elizabeth Fry symbolizes the bonds of sisterhood that enjoin women on both sides of the law.

Although a hundred years separate the work of the first Elizabeth Fry from her counterparts in British Columbia, the guiding principles of the EFSBC bear some surprising similarities and continue to sustain a sense of mission for Fry volunteers and staff. The following chapters will recount the history of the Elizabeth Fry Society of British Columbia and its work to promote the development of constructive attitudes, procedures and rehabilitative programs at all levels of the correctional process, and within the general community. This account will document the growth and development of the Society, an independent community-based voluntary agency, and try to explain its continuity amidst changing attitudes toward the nature of social work and public responsibility for social services. The history of the Elizabeth Fry Society in British Columbia is, then, a history of social reform in the field of corrections but it is also a study of organizational expansion that has been directed and managed almost exclusively by women.

Concepts of crime and punishment, as well as attitudes toward women, depend very much on social values. The social environment, in turn, is shaped and influenced by a vast array of factors including politics, economics, religion and philosophical movements.[25] This social context will be explored in the following chapter to account for the historical beginnings, in 1939, of the Elizabeth Fry Society of British Columbia.

2. THE PROVINCIAL MOTHERS OF REFORM

The [EFSBC] President called on Mrs. Rex [Fraudena] Eaton who spoke briefly of the value of the work Judge Helen Gregory MacGill contributed to penal reform and to many other branches of welfare endeavors. She said she felt very happy to have the opportunity to pay tribute to the late Judge MacGill for her driving force in all matters where she took an interest. Mrs. Eaton said that when she herself was first associated with Judge MacGill and she felt discouraged and ready to quit, Judge MacGill told her in no uncertain words to go on and [Mrs Eaton said] it was perhaps due to this power that our beloved departed had of forcing others to carry on, that she herself did not stop.

EFSBC Minutes of Annual Meeting, March 27, 1947[1]

This extract from the minutes of the annual meeting of the Elizabeth Fry Society of British Columbia in 1947 indicates how consciously the tradition of philanthropic caring was passed from one generation of women to the next. It was a tradition that had its origins in the cohesive women's culture of the pre-suffrage era and was perpetuated through the bonds of female friendships. The EFSBC officially dates its founding from 1939, but its history properly begins in the years prior to the First World War when British Columbian women such as Helen Gregory MacGill first identified penal reform as an issue in need of women who cared.

From the early years of settlement in British Columbia, women's interests extended beyond their domestic responsibilities to social, economic and political issues in the public sphere. Although individually constrained by social conventions and civil inequalities, through their collective efforts women (who were actually a minority of the population in B.C.) achieved some influence in matters concerning the education and welfare of women and children, legal and urban reform, municipal government, and public health. From the 1880s, middle class women established a network of organizations in British Columbia that were committed to shaping a humane society. In 1883, B.C. women who saw alcohol as the cause of much human misery formed a branch of the Women's Christian Temperance Union (WCTU) to campaign against the sale and use of liquor. The WCTU focused its practical attention on the most helpless victims of alcoholism when in 1892 it established the Alexandra Orphanage. In 1894 and 1895 three local Councils of Women formed in Vancouver, Victoria and Vernon to further the work of the National Council of Women of Canada to "conserve the highest good of the Family and the State." Numerous organizations—the Young Women's Christian Association (YWCA) in 1896, the Victorian Order of Nurses (VON) in 1898, the Children's Aid Society in 1901, the Imperial Order of the Daughters of the Empire (IODE) in 1902, the University Women's Club in 1907—attracted the energies of women who felt the need to be involved not only in the making of their community but also in promoting social justice. Within these female societies, bonds of friendship and support formed among women that served to encourage a tradition of philanthropic caring, voluntary social work and increased involvement in the conventionally male domain of public policy.

Women derived their confidence to pursue their civic-minded endeavours from their maternal roles. They reasoned that as mothers they were accustomed to the caring and nurturing of children and were therefore well prepared to look after the public welfare. Nevertheless, women realized that many of their reformist goals would remain unfulfilled as long as they had no legitimate voice in governments or the electoral process. Thus, by the turn of the century, women's philanthropic organizations were involved in promoting feminist causes, particularly the suffrage movement. In this era the goals of feminists, often described by historians as "maternal" or "social" feminists, were aligned with the goals of women's philanthropic endeavours: to produce a better, more humane world.

Prior to the First World War, married women had few outlets outside the domestic sphere and they relied on their club associations to legitimize their community activity and provide a network of support, both personal and formal. During the First War, women apparently gained new means by which to express their public concerns and demonstrate their social usefulness. Women were enfranchised in British Columbia in 1917 and the shortage of manpower and the increased production needs of the war provided opportunities for middle class women to work outside the home. In the post-war period, many of the organizations, which women had established to lend credibility and encouragement to their social work in the pre-suffrage era, experienced a decline in membership. However, the inspiration and friendship derived from female associations continued to sustain a tradition of women's voluntary work and women's clubs did not disappear. For some women, their club affiliations remained a key ingredient to their individual success in public life. Other women simply recognized that many of women's concerns and humanitarian causes would continue to be overlooked without the caring and commitment that had been the practice of women's voluntary societies.

Since the early 1900s women in Vancouver felt that the status of women and children under the law and the treatment of girls and women in conflict with the law required particular vigilance from women's organizations. The University Women's Club (UWC) and the Local Council of Women (LCW) both championed the legal rights of women and children and formed committees to investigate the treatment of female prisoners and delinquents. In 1911, after members of the UWC discovered that there had been little change to domestic legislation in British Columbia since the mainland became a crown colony, Helen Gregory MacGill, a Vancouver clubwoman, journalist, mother and homemaker, became the convener of the UWC's committee for better laws for women and children. MacGill undertook a study and reading of the law as vigorous as any law student and published her findings so that women might be well informed about the laws affecting their lives. A member of several organizations, including the LCW, MacGill led delegations of women to petition the provincial government for changes to the laws affecting women's property and guardianship rights.[2]

MacGill also spent many hours in the police court where she observed the cycle of female delinquency: "young, neglected and ill-treated girls charged with prostitution, their fines paid by their male 'friend,' and their subsequent return to the streets."[3] In keeping with the beliefs and objectives of the maternal feminists MacGill formulated probation policies for their protection. She emphasized the role of the Juvenile Court in assigning preventive and rehabilitative treatment for young offenders and was critical of the court's inefficiency and impracticality.[4]

MacGill was not the only woman to write and agitate for the reform of laws affecting women and children. Mary Ellen Smith, Alice Townley, Janet Kemp, Anne Spofford, Laura Jamieson and many others, all active in one or more of the LCW, the WCTU, and the UWC, helped to win the vote for women and effect other changes in the law that brought women closer to civil equality with men. It was a measure of the esteem in which the work of Helen Gregory MacGill and the women's organizations was held that, after women were enfranchised, MacGill was appointed judge of the Juvenile Court of Vancouver in July 1917. With her constituency of collective support from the female societies and some individual aid from friends (and husbands of friends) in high places, Judge MacGill was able to ensure the drafting and passage of new statutes for the protection of children and the increased use of probationary services.[5] As a result of women's organized efforts and their new-found power at the polls, British Columbia emerged in the 1920s a leader in social legislation in Canada.

Nor did Vancouver clubwomen neglect the welfare of girls and women in conflict with the law. Institutional care for male juvenile delinquents, the Juvenile Reformatory, had been established by the province in 1890. In 1905 the reformatory was disbanded and re-placed by a different facility and concept evident in its new name: the Provincial Industrial School for Boys.[6] Changing attitudes as to the causes and treatment of delinquent behaviour were responsible for the new institution that would try to eliminate the harsher aspects of a prison environment. Ideally, school discipline and industrial train-ing would impart conscientious habits and skills to the boys and prevent their returning to dubious friends and dissolute pastimes after their release. To ensure that delinquent girls would not continue to have their treatment neglected, in 1911 the Vancouver Local Coun-cil of Women took up the cause to establish an institution for girls. In keeping with the value the maternal feminists placed on domes-ticity it would be a "Home for Wayward Girls."[7]

Council member Alice Ravenhill, a notable reformer and recent immigrant from England, advocated the "Home" be built for delin-quent girls some distance from the city "to afford outdoor occupation and make the outward appearance of restraint unneces-sary." Social reformers generally perceived that a rural environment was a naturally restorative context for the treatment of delinquency. Ravenhill advised further that the Home should be "supervised by a female physician to assure the mental and physical health of the inmates and to advise on the period of detention." Also, "facilities should be provided in the Home to enable the girls to learn occupa-tions to keep them self-supporting and to raise their self-respect."[8]

The Local Council of Women (LCW) was successful in its peti-tions to the city and provincial governments. In 1914, the Provincial Industrial Home for Girls opened on Cassiar Street in what was then a semi-rural area of Vancouver. The LCW was doubtful, how-ever, about the suitability of the appointment of a man as the first superintendent of the Home.

Feminists in this era promoted the employment of women in areas of social work and the administration of justice not so much because they believed in equal opportunities for women in all occupa-tions but because they believed that women were best suited to understand and remedy the needs and problems of girls and women. Women's representation in the public sphere advanced initially be-cause social feminists insisted on a separate but equal status for women. The LCW and the UWC recommended that all public institu-

tions having women and girls as inmates should be officered by
women, and in institutions for both sexes, women should administer the women and girls' department.[9] It was at the insistence of
Vancouver women's groups that the first female police officer was
appointed. The UWC had even urged the establishment of a
women's court with a woman magistrate and women officers. In the
Juvenile Court, Judge MacGill tried the girls' cases while a male
judge heard the boys'.[10] Female appointments were victories for feminists and generally resulted from the continuous lobbying of
women's organizations. It was public pressure from women and
clergy that forced City Hall to reconsider its refusal to vote a salary for
a female probation officer appointed by Judge MacGill for the Juvenile
Court.[11] The members of the LCW would not, therefore, count the establishment of the Girls' Home as a success until they saw it directed
by a woman.

As anticipated by the LCW, the first superintendent of the Industrial Home for Girls did not establish the model institution of
reform that the LCW had envisioned. He seemed to regard the
Home as a prison and applied the provincial "Gaol Rules and Regulations" to its operations.[12] In 1918, a female appointee, Margaret
Bayne, formerly a school teacher and suffragist, was more acceptable; Bayne's policy to create "a harmonious home"[13] atmosphere
was more in line with the LCW's thinking about the ideal setting for
the education and moral reclamation of the errant girls.

The UWC's interest in civic institutions that housed women had
led them in 1913 to recommend to the Attorney General's Department that in addition to fresh air and disinfectant, proper diet,
clothing, and medical inspection by a female physician be provided
for women in prison.[14] A few years later, in 1916, a complaint from
a young school teacher, who had been held in custody as a material
witness for a trial, brought to light the squalid conditions shared by
both the accused and convicted in the women's quarters of the provincial jail—Oakalla Prison Farm.[15] A joint committee of women
from the University Women's Club, the Local Council of Women
and the Women's Christian Temperance Union formed to investigate the conditions for women prisoners at Oakalla. This joint
committee marked the beginning of a detailed study of the prison
and recommendations for its reform.

The committee members were horrified by their visit to the
women's section of the provincial jail. They found all of the female
inmates housed together in one long room furnished only with cots
and two open toilets. In this room the women ate, slept, and sat. If
the weather was favourable they were allowed outside once a day
but there was no organized exercise program or any kind of activity
except the cleaning of their room. The inmates' days were spent in

idleness without any diversions of reading, writing or handicrafts. They had not even a place to sit other than their beds. Security regulations meant the women were deprived of their corsets and garters and looked a bedraggled sight with their drooping stockings and underwear. Women on their way to receive medical treatments had to pass through the men's quarters where they were greeted with jeers and coarse language.[16] The committee protested these conditions and set about researching a proposal for a new prison for women.

In this area of penal reform, B.C. women took an early lead in linking medicine and social work to reformative measures in prisons. Sub-committees studied health, diet, sanitation, medical services, the special needs of pregnant inmates and those with tubercular or venereal infections, and the segregation of classes of prisoners for their more effective training and rehabilitation.[17] The study took two years to complete and twenty-four years before it was even partially implemented.

Despite the painstaking work of Vancouver women to improve the treatment of women in prison, conditions in the provincial jail, Oakalla, got worse before they got better. The University Women's Club kept the issue of penal reform alive throughout the 1920s with repeated resolutions to the Attorney General's Office. In 1922 the UWC's Social Service Committee made several recommendations for the classification of offenders, for improvements to their diets, for a daily wage to be made available on their release, for classes and recreation, and for psychological examinations. In 1923 the UWC began a campaign for a building for women prisoners, entirely separate from the men's quarters at Oakalla, "where occupations suitable to women could be established with a view to their reform and re-establishment in society."[18] However, there were no permanent improvements made in the housing and treatment of women prisoners in this decade.

Of the many causes demanding provincial resources, inmates, and it seems female inmates particularly, commanded the least interest. In the ten years following the end of the First World War, British Columbia's economy had steadily strengthened and prospered. The Liberal government led by Premier John Oliver had been responsive to the reform forces in the province, especially now that women were empowered with the vote, and piloted much progressive legislation through the legislature. The social climate was generally favourable to the civic reform measures introduced by the maternal feminists; newly enfranchised, well-connected, organized women, with one of their own — Mary Ellen Smith — now an MLA, had been able to mobilize public support to effect major changes to family law and child welfare. Penal reform did not attract a similar constituency and failed to gain any priority with the government. It proved to be a last cause, and a lost cause in this era.

The ideas of penal reform conceived amidst the fertile visions of the progressive twenties took root in the barren realities of the depressed thirties. The effects of the Depression in western Canada were far-reaching. Families of all classes experienced the now commonplace traumas of unemployment, poverty, even conflict with the law. The increased and visible incidence of personal misfortune caused major shifts in popular attitudes towards economic, political and social issues. Many western Canadians found traditional solutions were no longer adequate to cope with the larger scale of social distress and unrest. Private philanthropy was regarded as treating only the symptoms of an inequitable society and the public mood now questioned the causes. The new reformers, some modelling their views after the British Fabians and others preaching the social gospel, wanted to make fundamental changes to society and increase the role of government in regulating the economy and administering relief in order to ensure a greater degree of social security for every citizen. They wanted political decisions to reflect a greater concern for the masses. Reformers began to examine the functions and beneficiaries of various public institutions that were founded to protect or enhance the public welfare, with the view of reforming the ones that were ineffective and discarding those that were outmoded. Along with other hidden and neglected corners of public responsibility, penal institutions and their habitually forgotten inhabitants came under renewed scrutiny, initially at the federal level.

Under Canadian law, the responsibility for incarceration was split between the federal and the provincial governments. The federal government in Ottawa had authority over correctional institutions — penitentiaries — that housed offenders sentenced to two years or more; those sentenced to less than two years were held in provincial jails. Across the country, there were several penitentiaries built for men but only one for women, in Kingston, Ontario. Similarly, there were few provincial prisons built for women.[19]

In the 1930s there was some evidence that the conventionally harsh regime in federal prisons might be undergoing a review. The widespread adversity and social unrest manifested during the Depression, along with new socio-political ideologies, demanded revisions to correctional philosophy and renewed interest in correctional innovations. Federal prisoners of good conduct could now have some lighting in their cells and were permitted to write a letter every three months to their families. There was also some modification to the Auburn system's strict rule of silence that was the model in effect in the Canadian penitentiaries.[20]

The inauguration of the First Canadian Penal Congress in Montreal in 1935 suggested that penal reform was an idea whose time had come. Attended by individuals in corrections, judicial officers, and social workers, the Congress discussed the most pressing problems that faced the penal system; some had been previously identified in the Penal Inspector's Report of 1928. The Congress adopted resolutions that supported new institutions for young offenders modelled on the British Borstal type, probation services and government subsidies for prison after-care networks.[21] Prompted by the recommendations of the Canadian Penal Congress, disturbances in federal prisons, and repeated calls for a public enquiry by Agnes Macphail, the first woman elected as a Member of Parliament who made some of the earliest efforts to advance the cause of Canadian penal reform, a Royal Commission was struck. It was chaired by Mr. Justice Archambault, who was appointed in 1936 to investigate the Canadian penal system.[22] The report of the Archambault Commission in 1938 revised the goals of incarceration and placed a greater emphasis on the transformation of reformable criminals into law-abiding citizens.[23] The Archambault Commission also considered women prisoners and drew attention to their needs. In effect, the report broadened the base of support for reformers' demands for innovation in correctional treatment.

Along with new socio-political ideologies, the Depression served to focus attention on social science as a study that could also rationalize the approach to social problems. An address to the Penal Congress in 1935 by Frank R. Scott, a founder of the League for Social Reconstruction and professor of law at McGill University, indicated the promise social science held for penal reformers. Scott declared, "Modern penology is a science, one of the new social sciences. It is not philanthropy."[24] He urged further that penology, being a science, must work by scientific method and be divorced from politics; thus he armed reformers with an empirical authority that transcended righteous goodwill. Psychology, sociology and social work gave new impetus for a treatment model in corrections and the increasing professionalization of reform.

All of these forces for correctional change on the national scene had an impact at the local level. In British Columbia a nucleus of noted sociologists and social workers, pioneers in the field of penology, would nurture and renew the efforts begun by women. The School of Social Work at the University of British Columbia would not be established until after the Second World War, but the Vancouver Branch of the Canadian Association of Social Workers formed in the late 1920s with eleven members. Not all the members had a diploma or a degree in social work but they had made a special contribution in the field and several of them later provided the foundations of the UBC social work program.[25] Dr. Coral W.

Topping was one of these early social scientists who taught the fledgling courses in sociology at UBC in the thirties. His primary interests were family welfare and criminology. Topping had published one of the first critical assessments of the Canadian correctional system in a study of penal institutions in 1929.[26] His expertise was an available and valuable asset to penal reformers in British Columbia; he was particularly supportive of prisoners' aid societies that would form in Vancouver in the 1930s – the John Howard and the Elizabeth Fry Societies.

In British Columbia, as elsewhere, the welfare of prisoners inside the provincial institutions had been left to religious societies and women's organizations. Unlike the eastern provinces that had an historic tradition of prisoners' aid societies, which offered help to inmates in the critical period after their release, the only agency in British Columbia to assist discharged prisoners was the Salvation Army. The chaplain at the B.C. Penitentiary in New Westminster often gave men a place to sleep for a night or two following their release but no agency provided specific after-care services. At the suggestion of the warden of the B.C. Penitentiary, the Vancouver Ministerial Association launched a group to assist prisoners and their families.[27] This society was named after the British penal reformer John Howard and its appearance in Vancouver in 1931, during the Depression, was timely. With unemployed men from all over the west sleeping on the streets, the difficulties facing discharged prisoners and their families were greater than usual.

Under the direction of Rev. J. Dinnage Hobden, a Methodist who gave up his ministry to serve as the Executive Secretary, the John Howard Society of British Columbia assisted prisoners, primarily male, in a variety of ways. In addition to making regular court and prison visits, helping families to adjust, offering advice, spiritual counsel and temporary relief, the Society arranged transportation, and secured shelter, employment, and medical treatment for inmates on their release. The John Howard Society was also helpful in securing and supervising parole, a relatively new and little-used remission procedure for inmates.[28]

The founding of the John Howard Society served to redirect the energies of the women in the University Women's Club, the Local Council of Women, and the Provincial Council of Women (formed in 1921), all of whom had a long-standing interest in female inmates and penal reform. The UWC established a delegate to the John Howard Society to keep informed of its work. Gradually all of the UWC's efforts on behalf of the women prisoners were conducted through its representative to the John Howard Society.

The UWC was made aware that the conditions for women in the provincial jail, Oakalla, were deteriorating. As a result of the increased prison population during the worst years of the Depression, the women's quarters were converted to emergency hospital accommodation for the men. The women were now housed in the oldest part of the jail, built in 1912. In 1936 and again in 1938 the UWC approved resolutions presented by their John Howard representative that protested "the hopelessly inadequate, overcrowded, and unsanitary conditions of the women's quarters . . . and the lack of any reformatory program," and demanded the government direct its attention to these matters.[29] The Provincial Council of Women had conducted its own study in 1934 and made similar criticisms. In 1938, the Provincial Council of Women sent a delegation to meet with the provincial cabinet to press for the immediate construction of a new building for women at Oakalla along the lines recommended by women's organizations before the First World War.

The efforts of women who had argued for penal reform for so many years finally met with success. In the 1930s there was some evidence that the conventionally harsh regime in federal prisons might be undergoing a review. The Provincial Council of Women extracted a promise from the provincial cabinet that a new building for women at Oakalla would commence the following year. Helen Douglas Smith, the second woman to be elected to the provincial legislature and former president of the Provincial Council of Women, introduced the bill to proceed with the new prison.

A new building for female inmates had been a goal of organized women for a quarter of a century; its construction concluded an era of feminist politics and of penal reform but it did not signify an end to the tradition of women's caring. At the annual meeting of the Provincial Council held in March 1939 in New Westminster, a women's auxiliary was formed to work on behalf of the women's section of Oakalla Prison in cooperation with the John Howard Society. Thus the torch of caring was passed to another generation of penal reformers who within a year would establish a new identity as the Elizabeth Fry Society of British Columbia.

3. THE FIRST TWENTY-FIVE YEARS IN OAKALLA 1940-1965

In those early days, women as members of the Council of Women and the Elizabeth Fry Society had to prove themselves. We were looked at askance — as interfering in man's domain. We were pioneers in the field of social reform, and we had to convince politicians and those in authority that we knew what we were talking about.

Hilda Collins, EFSBC President, 1953-57[1]

In 1939, the decision of the Provincial Council of Women to form a "women's auxiliary" to aid inmates in the new women's prison at Oakalla represented a continuity of women's interest in penal reform that began before the First World War. However, the women who met in December, a few months after the declaration of the Second World War, were determined to extend this interest, which had finally succeeded in ensuring a new facility for women, into more active involvment in assisting female inmates. They knew that in the following months, perhaps years, as the country increasingly focused on the war effort, the treatment of women in prison would not be a national priority; they feared that the recommendations of the Archambault Commission, urging a change in the philosophy of corrections from the punishment model to a greater emphasis on rehabilitation, could be easily forgotten.

The Council women envisioned a new voluntary organization that might surpass the "watchdog" and lobbyist functions conventionally performed by social reform committees of women's clubs, and be more practically oriented. Women interested in social work of this nature proposed a prisoners' aid society that would work in cooperation with the John Howard Society but would establish its own identity.

In choosing to blaze their own trail, these founding members had recognized the pitfalls of establishing a society for women that was merely "auxiliary" or "helpful" to the pre-existing Society and not of separate status. Although the John Howard Society exerted some efforts on behalf of female inmates, the Society's limited resources were directed primarily at men, the majority of the prison population. It was clear to the Council women that a women's organization was needed to address the equally compelling needs of the minority. Early in 1940, at the suggestion of Fraudena Eaton, the new organization was named after the nineteenth century Quaker penal reformer who had made such an impact on the treatment of women in British prisons. It was the first Elizabeth Fry Society in Canada.[2]

From the beginning the Elizabeth Fry Society of British Columbia (EFSBC) pursued a different course from its sibling, the John Howard Society. With funds raised by the Welfare Federation, the John Howard Society had established an office and employed a Methodist clergyman, Rev. J.D. Hobden, as Executive Director, and a teacher, Jean Wilton, as a case worker. Under Hobden's direction, the John Howard Society concentrated on providing practical services to discharged prisoners and in securing and supervising their parole. Hobden was the key figure in the organization which was modelled on the lines of a social welfare agency with a board of directors. The Elizabeth Fry was formed as a female voluntary society with elected executive officers responsible to the membership. The Society relied on well-connected female patrons to attract public interest and financial support.[3] Its volunteers worked collectively toward the rehabilitation of female inmates at Oakalla and their re-establishment after their release.

While holding similar purposes, the missions of the Elizabeth Fry and the John Howard societies reflected different reformist traditions. The legacy of the social gospel was evident in the combined sectarian convictions and practical applications that characterized the John Howard Society.[4] The first objective cited in the original constitution was "to seek to remove the conditions which lead persons into crime"; the objectives "to befriend the first offender," "to help the dependents of men in prison," and "to aid in the establishment of discharged and paroled prisoners" followed.[5] The idea underlying these objectives, that crime and criminality (like poverty) were the by-products of an inequitable and uncaring community, had informed the thinking of many social reformers in the west since the Methodist Minister J.S. Woodsworth had founded the All Peoples' Mission in Winnipeg's North End before the First War. The effects of the Depression in the 1930s had fashioned a new left-leaning political party—the CCF led by Woodsworth —seeking social justice and reconstruction on economic and political fronts. It was in this political climate of protest and reform that the John Howard Society was established.

The Elizabeth Fry Society of British Columbia was an offspring

of the Provincial Council of Women and, in the tradition of organized women, looked to a collective model of voluntary social work
directed by and in the interest of women. Although, in the words of
Hilda Collins, the third president of the EFSBC, these women were
"pioneers" in penal reform and venturing into unfamiliar territory,
as active Council women they were quite used to "interfering in
man's domain."[6] Indeed, it was the conviction of at least three of the
founding members of the Elizabeth Fry Society of British Columbia
—Marguerite Rines, Fraudena Eaton, and Helen Douglas Smith,
MLA,[7] all of whom were energetically involved in issues of public welfare and government—that the Canadian penal system had remained
"man's domain" for too long. The unhappy result was the neglect in
the housing and treatment of female offenders. Like their predecessors,
the earlier "maternal" or "social" feminists, the founders of the EFSBC
believed that women required different but not unequal treatment
under the law and in public institutions, and resolved to provide female inmates with special aid and assistance. This mission was stated
in the preamble of an early draft of the constitution of the EFSBC.[8]

The initial aim of the EFSBC —"to reclaim as many as possible
of the girls and women who are committed to prison . . . through
rehabilitation and education" —suggested that the Society perceived
that the plight of women in prison was the result of incomplete or
improper socialization and a lack of marketable skills; hence they
held the view that education and rehabilitation could restore these
women and girls "as useful citizens." Whereas the John Howard
Society attributed criminal behaviour to an inequitable community,
the Elizabeth Fry Society narrowed the source of the problem to the
individual's upbringing —to deficiencies in her family life and a lack
of caring in the home. It was natural for those early Fry members
who identified themselves as "women interested in philanthropy, religion, education and social reform" to share the belief that, if given
care and instruction, the "girls" in prison could be returned "to normal and happy existence" (as stated in the EFSBC constitution).

Throughout the first twenty-five years of the EFSBC's work in
Oakalla, all of the female inmates were regarded by both staff and
visitors as "girls." Today, to call a grown woman a "girl" would be
viewed as undermining her autonomy, individuality, and her accountability. This appellation, as a substitute for "woman," would be
regarded as unsuitably paternalistic in corrections, as in other fields.
Inmates are now termed "clients" of agencies such as the EFSBC.
However, in the 1940s and 1950s, it was precisely the qualities of
immaturity that were being defined when the Fry visitors and prison
staff referred to the female inmates as "girls." With this designation
Fry women and the prison matron were also defining both their
relationship to these inmates and an explanation for their criminal

behaviour. These definitions were not only compatible with current correctional philosophy but in some ways formed it.

Fry women and staff attempted to be guardians, surrogate mothers, or elder sisters to "girls."[9] They worked to improve the prison environment in a way that would positively affect the girls' future lives and perhaps overcome the inadequacies of past parenting. They believed it was, after all, deficiencies in the girls' families and home life that led to their current difficulties. "Girls" were still in need of care and nurture. Elizabeth Fry women believed it was their responsibility as members of the community to respond to these needs.

Whatever traditions informed the organization and mission of the two prisoners' aid societies in the early 1940s, both the John Howard and the Elizabeth Fry societies were directed by progressive reform philosophies that regarded an inhumane and punitive penal system as a waste of human resources, and sought realistic correctional change. In their emphasis on rehabilitation for prison inmates they attempted to alter the public's attitude toward the causes and the treatment of crime in the community. More important, the prisoners' aid societies ensured that the community recognize its responsibility for correctional treatment. Many of the innovations emphasized by the Archambault Commission were delayed or interrupted by the Second World War. For example, an alternative to prison for young male offenders, the New Haven Borstal Training School for Boys, was established in Burnaby in 1937 and then closed in 1942, and not reopened until 1947.[10] But the John Howard Society's insistence on the increased use of parole and the Elizabeth Fry's efforts to promote constructive activities and a humane environment for the women at Oakalla continued throughout the 1940s and 1950s.

The Provincial Council of Women regarded its success in convincing the provincial government to build new quarters for the women at Oakalla as a first positive step in bringing rehabilitative measures to female inmates. The old cells for women on the top floor of the south wing of Oakalla were rat-infested and draughty. A walk on the roof provided the only exercise, and darning the socks of the male inmates constituted the main activity. The Doukhobor women who required vegetarian diets were allowed to cook their own meals but there were no other concessions.[11] In the latter part of the 1930s, the women's quarters were needed for hospital wards for the men and the female inmates were moved to the ground floor of the original jail — a red brick building constructed early in the century. The upper floor was used by the Mounted Police as a training facility and the inmates called this structure "the crumb joint" or "the horse barn" because the Mounted Police horses were tethered outside.[12] The women remained in this outdated accommodation until the new building was opened in November 1940.

Apart from being uncomfortable and inadequate, the conditions that faced women at Oakalla did not allow for any instructive programs to fill the inmates' time. Not only did the women's proximity to the male inmates subject them to verbal abuse, women were such a minority of the prison population that their welfare was easily overlooked even though they shared the same premises. The Provincial Council of Women had wanted a modern facility for female inmates that would be separate from the men, preferably in a setting more conducive to their own rehabilitation. It had been rumoured in 1937 that property in Burnaby had been purchased to house women prisoners from Oakalla. However, this "Home for the Friendless" became the site of the Borstal Training School for Boys. Instead, the new women's building was constructed on property adjoining Oakalla, and the various women's organizations that had urged this project on the provincial government for many years rejoiced that their demands had been partially met.

When the new women's "house of corrections" opened at Oakalla, at a cost of $64,000, *The Daily Province* newspaper reported that it provided "cheerful and comfortable quarters, bright dormitories, and a modern kitchen and laundry."[13] The facility had been modelled on the American plan for moderate security with all outside cells and no bars on the windows. Its completion in 1940 signalled the beginning of the EFSBC's regular association with the women at Oakalla. The president of the Society, Marguerite Rines, announced to *The Daily Province* that the EFSBC would now go ahead with its plans to hold monthly concerts, establish some form of arts and crafts, and introduce a program of vocational training.[14]

Prior to the formation of the Elizabeth Fry Society there had been few visitors to the women's jail. Delegates from church groups and women's organizations, motivated by their own altruistic purposes, periodically had assessed the deficiencies in the jail and made some effort to offer spiritual or material relief. But these early visitors did not attempt to respond to the day-to-day needs and problems of female inmates. The Society wanted to establish a more regular relationship with the women's prison and be an effective agent for reform and rehabilitation. Members recognized that they had to forge bonds of trust not only between themselves and the inmates but also with the prison staff, who had to be convinced of the benefits of allowing Fry visitors into the institution.

Initially fortified with little more than the courage of their convictions, Elizabeth Fry volunteers in the 1940s ventured somewhat cautiously through the prison gates. Like the first Elizabeth Fry, they drew on their own strengths and beliefs and sought to provide some moral guidance by means of a religious education committee. The

Society arranged for different churches to hold Sunday services in the prison throughout the year; also the WCTU showed films and made monthly presentations. It seemed like a constructive beginning, to introduce eductional and rehabilitation programs into the prison, but within the decade the Fry Society advised their members against using their visits to proselytize. Although always a minor aspect of the Fry's approach, and perhaps not unappreciated by the inmates who welcomed any diversion, religious instruction was left to the church missionary societies in coordination with the prison chaplain, appointed by 1953. The Fry wished to emphasize more practical aspects of its involvement with the female inmates and align its activities with the more progressive strategies of social work. This ability of the Fry to redirect its focus in consideration of both its clients' needs and trends in correctional philosophy accounted for its viability as a volunteer agency over the next several decades.

The new women's building at Oakalla improved the physical conditions of women's detention but the problem remained of how to fill the useless, idle time of imprisonment. Darning men's socks could hardly sustain the spirit let alone the mind, and the EFSBC had as its goal the reclamation of the women in Oakalla. The Society resolved to initiate work projects that gave the inmates a sense of pride in their own accomplishments while simultaneously making a contribution to the war effort. The Fry volunteers organized a Red Cross room where the inmates cut bandages and knitted helmets and socks. They sewed navy jackets from old felt hats and mended garments for refugees. The EFSBC brought in materials for other handcrafted items and taught the women how to hook rugs. Many of these items were displayed at the Pacific National Exhibition and later sold with the proceeds used to keep funding the arts and crafts program.

The intention of the EFSBC was to inaugurate occupational therapy for the female inmates. Arts and crafts programs were introduced on an experimental basis to provide more constructive ways for the women to spend their time and to convince both the prison staff and the provincial authorities that these programs were effective. These tactics of initiating social reforms and later turning the responsibility over to government were the means, historically, by which women altered attitudes about the public responsibility for social welfare. Through these methods the Fry women embarked on their campaign to convert the women's prison from a holding cell to a treatment facility in order to show the government "the value of occupational therapy in segregating those who are willing to try from those whom nothing will help."[15]

After exhausting the talents of their membership to oversee the making of largely decorative items, members of the Arts and Crafts

Committee decided to hire a crafts instructor for the women at Oakalla. The women on the committee tried to determine what kind of handiwork might provide a marketable product and thereby a potentially useful skill to the inmates. They decided upon small leather goods: gloves, belts, change purses, billfolds, watch straps and luggage tags. It proved more difficult to find an instructor to go to the prison. The EFSBC approached a number of occupational therapists and educational institutions before the UBC Extension Department sent them a McGill graduate and trained nurse who was skilled in leatherwork, weaving and clay sculpture. For a weekly visit to Oakalla the Society paid their first crafts instructor a salary of $2.50 per week plus expenses for travelling and materials (not to exceed $10) per month.[16]

By 1950, the EFSBC had increased the hours of the handicrafts instructor to five afternoons a week. After six months of this schedule, with the approval of the warden, the matron in charge of the women's prison, and the Fry membership, the EFSBC formally approached the provincial government about taking over the salary of the instructor on a permanent basis. In this way, the Society was able to establish the place of occupational therapy within the women's prison.

The EFSBC, by necessity, had to receive the approbation of the staff of the women's prison. In fact, the relationship that formed between Miss Bessie Maybee, matron, and the Society grew to mutual respect. After her retirement from Oakalla concluded a thirty-year association with the Fry, Maybee wrote about the early years in the 1940s: "I listened to and learned from the volunteers and gradually became convinced that such a program [occupational therapy] was the answer to a new look in prisons. From that time on I have never missed an opportunity in promoting the aims of the Society and never lacked for moral backing sorely needed at times."[17] Maybee was supportive, therefore, when she was asked in 1950, by a commission newly established to organize a Department of Corrections, to implement the occupational therapy program in the women's prison and carry out the Society's ideas of handicrafts and vocational training. With the backing of the Society, a large room was constructed in the prison, above the kitchen and the dining room, and equipped with a loom, power sewing machines, a household sewing machine, a large stock of handicraft material, two typewriters and an ancient hairdryer.[18]

The arts and crafts program that had begun with knitting and leather work at the EFSBC's expense became in the 1950s a full-fledged occupational therapy program supported by the new Department of Corrections. Moreover, the program had expanded to include some vocational training. Although previously the Society had arranged correspondence courses in shorthand and typing, this method of study was not preferred by the majority of inmates. Not surprisingly, the occupational therapy program outgrew the allotted space within a short period of time. From 1952-1954, Maybee was appointed matron in charge of work and training. The occupational program, which began in a small way, began to encompass the entire institution and included quantity cooking, homemaking, dressmaking, power sewing, laundry, hairdressing, home nursing, handicrafts and carpentry. Some basic schooling was offered and recreational exercise, group living and counselling were emphasized. Once a week a teacher from UBC's Pro-Rec (Professional Recreation Department) took interested inmates to the Quonset hut gymnasium and showed them the fundamentals of basketball, volleyball, and badminton. The EFSBC had successfully challenged the old philosophy that one must not disturb the inmates or make demands on them.[19]

For those who preferred outdoor work the Society organized the landscaping of a rockery—a victory garden—to involve inmates in beautifying the prison grounds. This turned out to be an immense project that commenced in 1943 under the supervision of volunteer Constance Girling, who worked on the rockery until 1949. Girling began with $25 from the EFSBC's budget to purchase shrubs, and when the money ran out she managed to get plants donated from a variety of sympathetic horticulturalists around town. Without a car Girling traipsed all over the Lower Mainland to pick out shrubs and had to rely on her ingenuity to transport them out to Oakalla. After one such foray to North Vancouver she managed to pack her plants on the ferry. After disembarking, she depended on the good will of a Vancouver restaurant owner to look after them until Kelly, the policeman who transported prisoners from downtown to Oakalla twice a week, could rescue them in the paddy wagon.[20] Girling befriended gardeners at other public institutions, such as the psychiatric hospital where the patients raised plants as part of their therapy, and she eagerly accepted any superfluous plants. Another gardener friend who worked at the Ocean View Cemetery went out to Oakalla for a day or two to help with the rockery. There was much work for the Fry volunteers that did not involve going into the prison but supported the aims of the prison visitors.

In the interests of providing some entertainment for the women at Oakalla, the EFSBC arranged Sunday music concerts and movies. Fry volunteers also formed a library committee and Mrs. J.D. Hobden, the convener, attempted to build up the inadequate collection.[21] Initially, volunteers recruited donations that tended to be "the right sort" of magazines, as well as Bibles from the Gideon Society, but neither prompted a great deal of enthusiasm from the prison readers. To help organize the prison library, the Fry hired, on a part-time basis,

In the 1940s, one of the first projects of the Elizabeth Fry Society of British Columbia was to establish a library for the women of Oakalla. The EFSBC hired a librarian on a part-time basis to organize library services. As with other initiatives taken by the EFSBC, for example the hiring of an arts and crafts instructor to provide "occupational therapy" for the inmates, library services became accepted as an essential aspect of prison programs aimed at education and rehabilitation of the inmates.

Winifred Clucas – a librarian from the Vancouver Library – and asked the Public Library Commission to establish a travelling service to the women's prison. The commission thought that the prison should establish its own library but agreed to support the Society in its negotiations with the Attorney General's Department. There was little headway made until the attorney general himself visited Oakalla in 1943 and the inadequacy of the make-shift library was apparent. Within a few months $800 was granted for the purchase of books and in the following year, $1,480 was allotted for library services for the men's jail and $350 for the women's. The Public Library Commission was responsible and the Vancouver Library organized the administration of the service and the processing of the books.[22]

The active role taken by the EFSBC to establish library services for the prison population meant that by 1948 the prison library had 2,000 volumes and the inmates could borrow books three times a week. The Fry had endeavoured to make the prison library an essential part of the educational and rehabilitation program of the institution before this became the accepted policy of either the provincial administrators or professional librarians (who later became great advocates of "bibliotherapy" in "the reclamation of the citizen").[23] As a result of the EFSBC's initiative the attorney general appointed a full-time librarian in May 1949 to take charge of the libraries at Oakalla, New Haven Training School, and the jails at

Prince George and Nelson.[24]

By the end of their first decade in Oakalla, the EFSBC had introduced many changes into the prison routine in the hopes of improving the conditions of women's incarceration and, perhaps, the outlook of the inmates. In addition to making the grounds more attractive, establishing an arts and crafts program, and a library service, Fry women had extended their caring to provide entertainment for holidays, and gifts at Christmas. The Society also took care of more mundane matters, whether it was providing shoes, sweaters, layettes for the pregnant women, eye glasses or dental work. Donations of needed articles came from both church groups and city merchants. In 1954 the Society tried, unsuccessfully, to convince the Dental Association to formulate a cost-sharing plan in cooperation with the EFSBC to provide dentures—not included in the dental work paid for by the government—for needy patients in Oakalla.

Guided by the precedents of the John Howard Society, the EFSBC initiated an after-care committee that helped women to find a boarding house or a job on their release from prison. Volunteers might drive a released inmate to the bus depot if their home was out of town. Fry members were also available as "big sisters" if the former inmate needed to talk or sort out problems that might arise on the "outside." The Fry women often responded to the call from the prison staff and the John Howard Society to accompany women from prison on a daily outing. Thus the EFSBC, along with the Howard Society, became advocates of the use of day parole to re-introduce the inmate into society.

In addition to the EFSBC's practical attention to the needs and rehabilitation of the inmates throughout the 1950s, the Society continued its commitment to raise public consciousness about matters of penal reform. The Society's activities and concerns received publicity in the local newspapers and on radio broadcasts. Much of the financial support that was donated for the Society's work was raised by the public speaking of Fry patrons and members. However, the support of public opinion was equally important to the EFSBC, who wanted to ensure a climate more receptive to its ideas that treatment, not punishment, should be the aim of correctional institutions.

Within ten years of its completion, the women's building at Oakalla was again overcrowded due to the increase of drug and alcohol offenders; its potential to fulfill the new aims of treatment and rehabilitation was thus significantly impaired. Originally designed for forty women, the prison now housed seventy-eight, leaving little space for recreation, study, or the segregation of first offenders. Vigilant about the problems that remained unsolved at Oakalla, the EFSBC continually brought resolutions to remedy the situation to the attention of the Provincial Council of Women and the provincial government. In 1951 the Elizabeth Fry urged that steps be taken immediately to improve the conditions for female inmates, noting that the present number of staff should be increased from twelve to twenty-five, and that more space was needed to eliminate beds currently located in the corridors, the laundry room, and the basement. The Society also protested that money spent transporting the overflow female prisoners to the makeshift accommodations in the army detention barracks in Prince George would be better applied to building a new women's prison. Moreover, the EFSBC was adamant that a prison for women should be modelled on the cottage plan, which permitted inmates to cluster in "family" groups and work units and be built on property separate and removed from any proximity to the men's prison. The Society further insisted that the new prison should provide for the segregation of first offenders, repeaters, and drug addicts.

The Fry's recommendations were punctuated by a riot in October 1952 in the men's section of Oakalla that spilled over into the women's jail. Although to some extent this activity was part of a continental pattern of prison unrest, local factors provided ample cause for the violent outburst. The overcrowding of over 900 male inmates (daily average) in an institution designed for half that number gave rise to problems of segregation and inadequate work and recreational activities. Conditions in the women's jail were similarly affected, with an average daily population of 65 and a monthly population of 1,984.[25]

The EFSBC was not successful in its bid for a new women's prison but the government did comply with their immediate demands to provide more staff, additional facilities for group participation in occupational therapy and work programs, segregation of the prisoners, and subsidies to cover the costs of transporting discharged inmates to their homes, if out of town. These victories did not end the Society's persistence about the necessity for a new prison for women and an increase in social and psychiatric workers, but the construction of a vocational training room and two small cottages temporarily alleviated some of the overcrowding.[26]

The effects of the EFSBC at Oakalla were also felt in that distant outpost of the women's jail in Prince George. Miss Maybee had been moved to Prince George to convert the former army barracks — a wooden H-shaped building that contained thirty-eight bedrooms, a large rotunda, a dining room, a laundry, and a kitchen — into a women's prison. From 1947 to 1950, Maybee found herself in charge of "twenty-five of the oldest recidivists and a very green staff of six women." Years later, Maybee wrote that although the Elizabeth Fry women were not present, their ideas were, as she purchased bedspreads and cotton for curtains to hide the chicken wire on the windows, and made the tough old army barracks look like a home. Maybee recalled that "a jail with frills and white table cloths for Sunday dinner caused the then-rigid, old-time B.C. Police [the jail's supervisors] to shudder." Furthermore, Maybee established programs in homemaking, cooking, sewing, laundry, gardening (very large and successful), handicrafts, a beauty parlour, and religious observances on Sundays. Maybee also welcomed various services — Public Health, the Salvation Army, and the National Film Board — from the community into the jail.[27]

The surge in the prison population without any corresponding expansion of the women's division at Oakalla actually aided the call of the prisoners' aid societies — the John Howard and the Elizabeth Fry — for the increased use of probation by the courts. The societies had urged alternatives to incarceration, especially for the many women who appeared in the courtroom on charges of intoxication. (For example, from September to December in 1953, there were 150 women.)[28] With an increase in the number of probation cases, the EFSBC was gratified. However, the responsibility for the supervision of the female probationers from the Vancouver courts fell to Major Francis Wagner of the Salvation Army and Jean Wilton, the women's worker of the John Howard Society, both of whom attempted to deal with these duties on a part-time basis. The EFSBC now prepared a number of arguments in favour of the appointment by the government of a full-time female probation officer. Their efforts were rewarded when, in June 1954, the first Women's Probation Officer was appointed to the Provincial Probation Service. The Society did not hesitate to reiterate the request for more female appointees as it deemed necessary in subsequent years.

Although by 1954 the conditions in Oakalla Women's Division were far from ideal, they were sufficiently improved, as a result of the new additions and the efforts of the EFSBC and Bessie Maybee who had returned from Prince George, that an "open house" was arranged. The opening of the prison in October to eighty invited representatives from church, welfare, and service clubs was the idea of Maybee, now matron in charge, who asked the Society to organize the occasion in an effort to win public support for their work in the women's prison. It was important to the matron and her staff that the institution be regarded as a vital facility in the community, and that the public recognize that all who live and work in the prison were in need of acceptance.[29]

Despite the constraints of the prison architecture, the administration had implemented the "group system" whereby the inmates, in designated groups, worked, slept, ate, and took part in recreational activities in distinct parts of the building under the supervision of the group's matron. For the open house, displays of the inmates' work were set up and group members acted as hostesses, showing the visitors how they lived and worked. The invited guests were surprised at "the extreme youth of the girls" in custody. They did not fail to notice the cleanliness of the institution or the quality of the inmates' sewing, weaving, leatherwork, copperwork, shellwork, and knitting handicrafts that were for sale. The guests toured the newly built, small, self-contained cottage units where up to twelve first offenders—the younger girls—lived in a nearly "normal" family-style setting and did cooking, housework, and day jobs for the institution. While taking tea served by "neatly-aproned young girls," members of the press recorded comments made by the visitors that they "had no idea prison could be as nice as this." The open house was judged by everyone to be a success. Maybee reflected that "it was heart-warming to see the pride they [the inmates] took in their involvement and how gracious they were to all." Only Jean Wilton, the case worker, ruefully noted that what the visitors could not see was the bitterness and frustration which arise in conditions of deprivation of personal freedom.[30]

Maybee and the Fry women were pleased with their achievements to date but by no means complacent. They wanted the public to see the beneficial effects of occupational and work programs on the appearance and atmosphere in the prison, but at the same time they did not want to hide the deficiencies. The EFSBC repeated the open house twice in the following two years. As the overcrowding and understaffed conditions in the prison worsened, the event called attention to the harsh reality that could not be softened by chintz curtains in the dining room. The inmates were again unclassified and unsegregated due to the lack of a senior social worker and sufficient space. Rehabilitation programs were curtailed for the same reasons. After the Doukhobor women had burned the Quonset hut used as a gymnasium there was nowhere for the inmates to have any physical exercise in inclement weather.[31] There was no treatment for the increasing number of very sick addicts. Maybee's report of the operation of the women's jail for 1954-55 emphasized the problems faced in the recruitment and holding of staff due to the exacting nature of the work, the necessity for shifts, and the inequality in wages.[32]

In 1955, the EFSBC again took both its extensive criticisms of the women's jail and its demands for a new prison to Victoria. Within a year the government revealed that it had purchased land at Whonnock for a new women's jail and a committee had been appointed to plan the new building. In the meantime, more improvements would be made to the women's facility at Oakalla. By 1957, an increase in staff helped to bring individualized attention to the first offenders and allowed for their segregation from the older women (considered habitual offenders) and drug users. A Panabode cottage accommodated ten "girls" from the addict group in a full work and study program. A new wing, opened in December, enabled the educational and training programs to expand, and provided a bright and airy laundry and a large gymnasium in which church services, concerts, films, games, square-dancing and physical training classes could be held.

Ironically, the success of the EFSBC's ventures into Oakalla temporarily distanced the Society from their primary initiative—that of prison visiting. The establishment of a Department of Corrections in 1957 emphasized the role of the professional social worker and criminologist in the initiation of formal programs. Volunteerism in the prison was regarded increasingly with suspicion by professional workers who needed, perhaps, to establish their own credibility and justify their specialized training and expertise. For several years in the mid-1950s, faced with the achievement of their original goals and the assurance that, subsequently, the new professionals would determine the directions of treatment, the EFSBC left prison visiting to the case workers. In this period, the role of the volunteer in prisons was redefined, and in the words of the EFSBC president, "We looked for new ways to be useful." By 1959, however, convinced that a need still existed for members of the community to reach out to women in prison, the Society was anxious to recommence their visits. Encouraged by the chief matron of the Women's Division at Oakalla, who agreed that there was a place for volunteers within the prison routine, the EFSBC prepared to renew its work with the female inmates in the turbulent 1960s.

From its inception, the Elizabeth Fry Society recognized that education was vital to the process of correctional change. Moreover, the attempt to teach and instil reformed attitudes was a threefold commitment of the Society. The EFSBC believed that it was as important to educate the public to view prisons as institutions for the rehabilitation of the offender, and not merely their punishment, as it was to educate, and thereby rehabilitate, the inmate herself. The EFSBC also recognized the importance of educating its members to ensure their ability, in the words of Hilda Collins, "to convince politicians and those in authority that we knew what they were talking about."

Throughout this pioneer period, as in its later history, the Society invited qualified persons to instruct its volunteers about innovations in the field of corrections, changes in the law that affected women, and ways to increase their own effectiveness as penal reformers and prison visitors. At meetings of the EFSBC, its members had the opportunity to learn about recent publications on prison reform and correctional treatment.

Fry women attended conferences held by the Canadian Penal Congress, and researched many issues as the EFSBC was invited to submit briefs to Royal Commissions and recommendations to the provincial government. The EFSBC also advised women intending to establish Elizabeth Fry Societies elsewhere. For example, in 1949 the EFSBC assisted women in Kingston, Ontario, where the only federal prison for women in Canada was located, to organize the second Elizabeth Fry Society in Canada. At the instigation of Agnes Macphail, Canada's first female member of parliament and noted penal reformer, an Elizabeth Fry Society had been formed in Toronto in 1952. Although the Toronto EFS was financed and organized differently from the EFSBC—it received public funds and hired an executive director—the EFSBC welcomed another society in eastern Canada. These activities kept the Elizabeth Fry members well informed and made the Society an integral player in the developing field of corrections in the post-War period.

The Society also enjoyed a long-standing association with educators in the School of Social Work at the University of British Columbia. Penologist Dr. Coral W. Topping remained a patron of the EFSBC for many years and gave Fry members an open invitation to sit in on any of his classes at UBC. In turn, his students frequently enlisted with the Fry to acquire volunteer experience in the field. Most significant to the education of the Fry members were Topping's contributions as a speaker at the Society's meetings. Topping spoke on a variety of topics that kept the Fry women informed about the most recent trends in penal reform and treatment—for example, community-based alternatives to incarceration, the social causes and cures for crime, and the prison as a centre for rehabilitation. Many of the Society's ideas and ideals in its formative years were seeded by Dr. Topping and researched under his guidance.

Throughout the years, speakers representing the different preventive and treatment services spoke at EFSBC meetings on such subjects as the Western Remission Service, the Alcoholism Foundation, probation services, transition houses, and programs for drug addicts. The conscientious effort to keep abreast of the issues made the EFSBC a reliable advocate for prison reform. It was equally important to the Society that it remain an agency of respected volunteer workers. Marjorie J. Smith, who became the head of the UBC School of Social Work, and Hugh Christie, warden of Oakalla, frequently addressed meetings of the Fry and were highly supportive of the role of volunteers in penal reform. But the EFSBC recognized the need to continually update its volunteers' capabilities in order to maintain their status in the prison and assist the inmates.

In their attempts to ensure the viability of the volunteer in corrections and to better inform prospective members about the work

of the Elizabeth Fry Society, the executive officers initiated prepara-
tory lectures in the fall of 1961. A series of talks by women working in
the fields of law and corrections focused on women, children and families and the law; delinquency; probation and the female offender; and
finding jobs for "problem girls." This six-week series held at the YWCA
was open to anyone in the community who was interested in the work
of the EFSBC and served to attract new members, particularly those
interested in the welfare of young offenders. The lectures also signified
a more formal attention to the training of the volunteer to maintain
the standard of competence and credibility that had been established by the Society.

However, the actual experience of working within the prison
and becoming personally connected with the women on the inside
provided the Fry volunteers with an education of a different kind.
On a personal level, Fry women confronted the great distance between freedom and confinement each time they entered and left the
prison. As one volunteer recalled, after her first visit to the women's
unit at Oakalla:

> You walk into the building . . . and then you know a terrible thing.
> There are people kept in confinement and I was free. It hits you
> like that. By simply appearing in the hall, the matron would un-
> lock the door for me to leave. In my mind, this was emphasized
> and re-emphasized every time I went to Oakalla. . . . [33]

Fry visitors reflected on the accident of birth, or the grace of
God, that explained the differences between their lives and those of
the women they went to visit. They wrestled with the implications of
being regarded as "ladies bountiful," even questioning their right to
invade the privacy of inmates. But their visits reaffirmed their belief
that a prison sentence did not end the community's responsibility
for the individual or the penal institution.

When the Fry volunteer followed a convicted woman into
prison, she learned that they shared similar concerns, even common
frustrations, as wives, girlfriends, and mothers trying to solve the
problems of being female. But Fry women saw also that their shared
gender identity did not entirely bridge the gulf between their different expectations and experiences. In their attempts to assist inmates,
Fry women sometimes volunteered to retrieve a woman's personal
effects left in her boarding house at the time of her arrest. They
found themselves in parts of town unfamiliar to them and saw conditions in boarding houses they never imagined could exist.

> . . . I went down to that Cobalt Hotel, which was the worst place in
> town. Really, I was shocked at first to see how they lived. I felt
> they didn't have a chance with their problems. [They had] no-

where to go but their rooms with their drugs and their alcohol . . .
if you haven't seen those rooms and the corridors leading to them
. . . it was quite devastating really![34]

The prison matron thought the Fry women sometimes risked
their personal safety in running errands in these parts of town but re-
sourceful Fry volunteers learned how to cope with unnerving situations.

> I would go several times to a place on Cordova Street—an addict's
> place—because she needed clothes when she came out [of jail].
> How else would she get them? These places belonged to Chinese . . .
> and they never acknowledged they knew what you were talking
> about. I went one day with Mabel because the matron said I
> shouldn't go alone. I didn't mind going alone—didn't bother me—
> but I took Mabel and she followed me upstairs and we ran into
> him [the landlord] so I put on a hard voice. I knew I had to sound
> fierce and commanding or we would never get anywhere . . . finally
> we got the room and the clothes and marched (not walked!) out.
> That's the way it was in those days![35]

The Fry volunteers felt the discomfort of being out of place in
these impoverished surroundings but it served to help them better
understand the vulnerability of many female offenders. A volunteer
sent to retrieve a coat from an inmate's apartment found herself lost
while searching for the address in an unfamiliar part of town. She
recalled the insight she gained from this experience.

> I went into a restaurant to ask for directions . . . you know, I used
> to ask the girls [in Oakalla], "Why do you always go down to that
> bad part of town? Why don't you come up to Granville Street?"
> They said, "Because everyone looks at us." Well I knew then how
> they must have felt. That restaurant was full of prostitutes, you
> know, and every single eye was on me. I stood out like a sore
> thumb . . . it was the same thing.[36]

Through their work at Oakalla, women in the EFSBC became
aware of the common and often tragic pattern of circumstances that
inevitably led to a woman's serving time in prison. Poor economic
backgrounds, also their ethnicity, might compound their problems.
It did not go unnoticed by the Society that a disproportionate number of girls and women in conflict with the law in British Columbia
were Native Indians. (See Table 4, page 164.) The EFSBC was continually incensed that Native girls were committed to Oakalla for
vagrancy and drunkenness and were further corrupted—"learning
things they would never otherwise know"—by their mingling with
older inmates. The Fry women held the view that Native girls were
particularly vulnerable to bad influences in the urban areas because

of their incomplete schooling and their unworldliness. Not surprisingly, the Fry volunteers felt quite custodial toward the Native girls sentenced to Oakalla. With the aid of old primers and first grade texts donated by schools, they undertook to teach the illiterate girls to read and write, and encouraged the other inmates to similarly tutor the Native girls. The EFSBC had the interests of the Native girls in mind when they requested that the government cover the cost of transporting discharged inmates to their homes elsewhere in British Columbia. They felt they had a better future away from the temptations of the city. The EFSBC endeavoured, with the cooperation of the Native Indian Service Council, to establish supportive after-care for the discharged Native prisoners —often taking them into their homes until they found employment. It was, perhaps, a measure of the Society's growing reputation in this area that, in 1956, its president, Hilda Collins, was asked to address the Provincial Advisory Committee on Indian Affairs on the Society's work to assist in the after-care and rehabilitation of Native girls and women.

By the mid-1960s, the Fry volunteers —now familiarly called Lizzie Frys by the women they visited—were established as an accepted part of the prison routine and unlike other visitors they did not upset the inmates or precipitate any disturbance. Their visits served to break the tension and mitigate the bitterness that thrived in conditions of confinement. They increasingly won the trust of the female inmates and were respected and relied upon both by the warden and the matron at Oakalla. Nevertheless, the EFSBC volunteers often felt their caring was helpless to counteract the effects of years of drug and alcohol dependency on the older inmates in Oakalla, and they looked more hopefully to preventive care to divert the younger girls, already in trouble but not yet habitual offenders or addicts. Fry women recognized that the young girls were often themselves victims, and suffered from neglect, lack of self-esteem, and suitable role models. Thus, in the 1950s, the EFSBC began to exert efforts on behalf of the "delinquent" girls housed in the reformatory, or the girls industrial school.

4. REFORMING THE REFORM SCHOOL

*It is an accepted fact that young girls have learned the elementary
steps in a life of crime in an institution where there is no segregation. . . .
Underwear has been made on the premises of hard unbleached cotton
and nightgowns of ugly white flannelette. In this respect the [Girls'
Industrial] school is way behind modern trends in rehabilitation.*

Report of EFSBC on conditions in Girls'
Industrial School, January 1954[1]

The Elizabeth Fry Society of British Columbia had spent its first
decade familiarizing itself with current trends in prison reform and
rehabilitation and promoting the practical application of these ideas
for the benefit of the women at Oakalla. Although the Society continued to work with the inmates in Oakalla, in 1954 it turned its
attentions to the institution that housed the younger girls in conflict
with the law. Through their prison visiting, the Fry workers became
increasingly aware that time served by girls in the Provincial Industrial School—the detention centre for the juvenile court system in
British Columbia—did not divert them from Oakalla but rather ensured they would end up there. The EFSBC realized that the Girls'
Industrial School (GIS) was in need of extensive reform if it was to
provide any rehabilitative function. The Society also hoped that its
work might have a greater influence on the lives of the younger girls
who had not yet become habitual offenders.

Even without any first hand knowledge, it would have been easy
to have been a critic of the school's inadequacies. In 1954, the
school at 800 Cassiar Street in Vancouver had occupied the same
building since the Local Council of Women celebrated its construction in 1914. Its substantial Spanish Mission-style structure made
the remodelling that was necessary to modernize its treatments and
facilities both difficult and expensive. What had been originally an
ideal semi-rural site was deemed, forty years later, "a most unsuitable location within a stone's throw of the city's lights and
attractions."[2] Despite its thirteen-and-one-half acres, the school's

The Provincial Industrial School (originally called "Home") for Girls, built in 1914 at 800 Cassiar Street in Vancouver, was the result of years of lobbying by the Local Council of Women (LCW). The LCW wanted to ensure that "wayward girls" would have the same opportunities for rehabilitation as delinquent boys for whom the Juvenile Reformatory was built in 1890. By the 1950s, the Girls' Industrial School was inadequate and outdated; the Elizabeth Fry Society attempted to reform the school's programs and advocated the construction of a new facility. (photo courtesy of British Columbia Archives and Records Service)

proximity to a populous residential district and the downtown core necessitated strict measures of supervision. The opportunities for inmates to escape or smuggle forbidden goods into the institution meant that the girls had no freedom of movement between the building and the grounds.

Not only the building but also its administration belonged to another era. Responsibility for the school was divided between the Director of Industrial Schools, who was in fact the head of the Boys' Industrial School, and the on-site superintendent of the Girls' School. Working conditions that required employees to work eleven out of every fourteen days and salary schedules that paid men and women unequally made it difficult to recruit and retain suitable personnel. With its record of runaways and recidivism the institution was clearly unable to fulfil its purpose "for custody and detention, with a view to the education, industrial training and moral reclamation" of the girls, as defined by the Industrial Schools Act.

Although the EFSBC had a number of concerns about the Girls' School, based on the heresay of the female inmates at the provincial jail, the Society was not content to launch an uninformed attack. The Society recognized that if it was going to have any long-term impact on the school, the Fry had to be accepted by the staff as an ally in their common interests in the rehabilitation of the delinquent girls. It was in this spirit of cooperation that the Elizabeth Fry Soci-

ety sought an invitation from the superintendent of the Girls' Industrial School to visit the premises early in 1954 in order to identify
ways in which the Fry might be of some assistance to the staff.

As it happened, the first visit to the Girls' Industrial School by a
delegation from the Elizabeth Fry Society followed in the wake of a
series of riotous protests by the girls in the school, and subsequent
press publicity. On December 20, 1953, mattresses in a basement detention room had been set on fire and the police and fire departments
had to be called to restore order. Again, shortly before New Year's
Day, some of the girls rioted in the dormitory, ripping their nightgowns, smashing glass and furniture, and finally setting fire to the
curtains. The next morning the Christmas tree was set on fire and
more windows were broken before the police arrived to put nine of
the girls in the detention cells.[3]

On January 18, 1954, the Fry delegation was conducted on a
tour of the GIS building by the Treatment Director and Acting Matron, Doreen Aylward. Fry members were discomfited by the bleak
and neglected conditions of the young girls' confinement. The institution had three floors of accommodation. On the top floor there
was a medical room, a bathroom, three admission rooms, and stor-
age. Poor access to exits and the customarily locked doors on this
floor presented serious obstacles to the girls' safety in the event of a
fire. Flights of stairs and limited toilet facilities made the use of the
sick bay and the weekly routine of medical treatment both awkward
and exhausting for both inmates and staff. The second floor contained four dormitories, two dressing rooms, two bathrooms, a
school room, and staff rooms. With twelve to fifteen girls in each
dormitory, equipped with only a cot and a wooden chair for each
girl, there was no privacy and no space for any personal effects. An
insufficient library, a common locker for all of the girls' belongings,
a small sewing room, a craft room with unsuitable equipment, a
dilapidated and uncomfortably furnished lounge, and a dining hall
made up the main floor. The laundry, kitchen, storerooms and detention cells were located in the basement. A separate gymnasium
equipped with well-meaning but ill-conceived donations was apparently little used.

The delegation of Fry women saw little in the school to suggest
that this facility could provide any form of social rehabilitation. The
institution certainly failed to achieve the home-like atmosphere that
the maternal feminists had envisioned for these girls forty years earlier. Nor did it fulfil the promise of its name "Industrial School."
Despite the trend in the treatment of delinquency toward a model of
re-education to counteract the effects of the deprived environments
thought responsible for anti-social behaviour, the girls spent much
of their time in idleness. School subjects were offered only by corre-

spondence and there was no significant program of vocational training. The GIS provided neither an exemplary standard of living for
the girls in residence nor the opportunity to learn how to take and
keep a place for themselves in society. The lack of care and understanding in planning the girls' treatment was reflected even in the
issue of their clothing. No self-esteem or dignity could be encouraged by the uniform cotton print dresses that were institutionally
made all of one pattern, or the rough and ill-fitting underwear and
nightgowns designed to subdue any expression of vanity. These latter garments were so detested they had been the object of the girls'
wrath in the recent riot.

When the Fry women visited the school in January 1954, they
found the drab and outdated facility, the lack of screening or segregation of the girls with their varying behavioural disorders, and the
archaic policies regarding the girls' clothing reasons enough for the
violent outburst of the girls in the previous month. Indeed, the superintendent of the school, Ayra Peck, was on leave of absence due
to a breakdown of her health caused by the strenuous and unsatisfactory working conditions within the school. Without any clear
authority to do more than observe obvious deficiencies and shortcomings of the institution, the Society nevertheless reported its
findings and recommendations to the Provincial Minister of Health
and Welfare, and to the chairman of the committee recently appointed by that minister to enquire into the operations of the
Provincial Industrial Schools.

The number of serious and obvious disturbances in the Provincial
Industrial Schools during 1953 had precipitated the Government's appointment of the committee to enquire into their operations. In
particular, increased escapes and behaviour problems had resulted
since the introduction of new treatment programs in 1952. (These
programs were barely in evidence in the Girls' Industrial School.)
The old policies that merely maintained order and cleanliness were
being replaced by a more constructive approach to the needs of the
individual child. The public, not surprisingly, wanted to know why
so-called improved treatments had resulted in confusion, inconsistency, and unhappiness in these schools.

The EFSBC report preceded by nine months the more elaborate
report of the provincial committee, but it first brought to light the
grim and appalling surroundings which housed together girls, ages
eight to eighteen, from the wayward child to the prostitute, drug
addict, alcoholic, and the mentally ill. (See Tables 10 and 11, pages
167 and 168.) The members of the Elizabeth Fry were particularly
dismayed that almost half the inmates were Native girls who had
left their own communities and fallen victim to seducers and alcohol in the city. Although the adult men who used and abused these

young girls were seldom taken into custody, the girls were sentenced to the industrial school.

It was frequently the Indian girls, rebellious and hostile at their confinement in such foreign and inhospitable surroundings, who found themselves secluded in the basement detention cells. These dungeon-like quarters consisted of concrete cells, each with a prison toilet and reinforced windows. The cell contained neither chair nor bed, only a mattress and blanket on the damp concrete floor. A member of the Fry delegation recalled the shock of her first encounter with this form of punishment.

> You know in those days they used to turn the hoses on the girls, those fire hoses, to quell them. And this one Indian girl . . . she was downstairs in one of the isolation rooms, there were two of them down there . . . and they turned the hose on her. When I went to see her she put her arms round my knees and said please . . . get me out of here. I felt so dreadful. I was helpless. I couldn't do a thing. She just begged me . . . but I couldn't do anything . . . and you know the pressure [of the fire hoses] it's terrific . . . and icy cold water. They'd be left like that.[4]

As one-time visitors, the volunteers were helpless to stop treatment methods they knew to be cruel and damaging. But if the EFSBC could gain the confidence of the school's staff, they felt hopeful that changes to improve the school and rehabilitation of its charges would be possible. Consequently, the EFSBC report made some stern recommendations to begin the screening of the girls as was done at the Borstal School for Boys, and to improve the basic accommodation for the girls along with the school's cooking and laundry facilities. If the EFSBC was tempted to criticize the administration of the school it held back, preferring to report within the limits of its mandate. A return invitation and the opportunity to offer some immediate and practical assistance to the staff and the girls in detention was the Society's first objective at this stage. The EFSBC left the detailed indictment of the school's inadequacies to the provincial committee empowered by the government to fully assess the schools' operations.

After an extensive investigation of the buildings, personnel, and programs, the provincial committee concluded that the sources of the disorder in the industrial schools did not lie in the new treatment programs but in the circumstances related to staff, overcrowding, and the particular problems presented by the boys and girls committed to the schools. Since the end of the Second World War, all the correctional institutions in British Columbia had experienced overcrowded conditions. New treatment programs recommended by the schools of social work could not be accommodated by outdated facilities, and senior personnel in these institutions were seldom willing to embrace change. Although a new Boys' School was being built at Brannan Lake on Vancouver Island, both the Young Offenders' Unit at Oakalla and the Boys' Industrial School in Coquitlam remained plagued by discontent which surfaced at the levels of both the administration and the inmates.

The greater numbers of delinquent boys and complexity of the problems associated with the senior personnel of the Boys' Industrial Schools might have predisposed the committee to make the boys' school the main focus of its enquiry. However, the outbreak of violence at the girls' school immediately following the formation of the provincial committee, and the subsequent recommendations made by the EFSBC, ensured that the plight of delinquent girls would be given equal consideration. In fact, the gross inadequacies of the girls' school were emphasized throughout the provincial committee's report. The necessity for a new, and newly named, "Training School" for Girls was chief among the conclusions of this report because the investigators recognized that, without a redesigned facility, other changes to the girls' treatment and education would be impossible.

In the course of its enquiry, the provincial committee had consulted with juvenile court judges, social workers, and educators in order to place the operations of the industrial schools within an appropriate context of treatment of the young offender. Magistrates and judges who were familiar with the GIS confessed that they had been unwilling for some time to commit offenders to this institution. (Judge Helen G. MacGill had not been reappointed by the new Conservative Premier Tolmie in 1928 because of her refusal to sentence female offenders to the provincial juvenile home.)[5] A brief presented to the provincial committee by the B.C. Branch of the Canadian Association of Social Workers advocated the careful screening of all children prior to their committal to determine their medical, psychiatric and social backgrounds, and urged that this information should be considered by the court before the disposition of the child to ensure her most beneficial placement. Educators from the University of British Columbia's School of Home Economics assessed the use of space, equipment, and the education of the girls in the industrial school. Taking these submissions into account, the provincial committee's report thus confirmed what had been apparent immediately to the Elizabeth Fry Society: that current conditions in the Girls' Industrial School did not warrant girls' confinement there for purposes of rehabilitation. A new building and a complete revision of personnel and practices were required.

Aware that it could take years for the recommendations of the committee's report to be considered and implemented, the EFSBC

urged the government to begin hiring additional, well-trained staff
as a first step to improving the treatment of the girls in the GIS. The
Society stressed that attractive salaries would ensure the calibre of
social workers that were needed. In the wake of the report there
were, in fact, numerous resignations and a new administrative staff
was appointed to make such alterations as were possible to the old
Girls' Industrial School situated on a busy city corner. One of the
first programs to be updated was the basic education of its residents.

The responsibility for the education and vocational training, believed to be key factors in the rehabilitation of the girls, was in the
hands of the provincial authorities. The investigative committee had
been severely critical of the methods of schooling that had been
offered heretofore at the school. The report argued that the
correspondence courses, which were the only means of instruction
available to girls in detention, were unsatisfactory on a number of
accounts. Firstly, these courses were designed for the average or
"normal" child with a desire to learn, whereas most of the children
in the Industrial Schools had a history of failure and showed a ten-
dency toward language and reading disabilities. The correspondence
courses were perhaps the least effective method of instruction. Children past the compulsory school age of fifteen rarely were
sufficiently motivated to enlist in learning by correspondence. Moreover, the varying lengths of the child's stay in the school seldom
allowed a course of study to be completed.

In September of 1955 a newly remodelled classroom with modern blackboards, new desks and lighting was opened in the school.
A teacher appointed by the Department of Education organized a
suitable program of instruction on the basis of a rural ungraded
school. The girls were so eager to participate in the new school
program that the first classroom had to be limited to the elementary
grades which accommodated about sixteen girls. Two more classrooms were constructed on the third floor by tearing out partitions
and installing better lighting. These rooms were used for crafts and
high school correspondence work.[6]

Definitions of what constituted an appropriate education for
girls considerably reduced the options available in the industrial
school. The authors of the report stated that the education to enable
a girl "to take her place in normal society upon being released" was
to be accomplished "through instruction in all phases of housekeep-
ing with practice in all departments of the school, and through
formal instruction in the subjects normally taught in the schools of
the province plus some vocational training." The report stated also that
"all girls should be given instruction in the rudiments of hairdressing
and personal care" with advanced training for those who could profit-
ably use it. Vocational training was limited to classes in flower

arrangement, corsage making and horticulture. A few hair dryers, sewing machines and typewriters represented the selection of mechanical skills that a girl might acquire in the Industrial School.

The belief that domestic education, alone, constituted rehabilitation for the wayward girl who ended up in the Industrial School was not accepted by all the Elizabeth Fry volunteers. Although the Society supported the school's pleas for more equipment to set up a "beauty parlour" and recognized that traditionally female trades were the most likely areas of employment for the graduates of the Industrial School, privately the Fry women often became irritated with the public's expectation that the girls' future would be assured if they were trained to be housemaids or hairdressers.

One volunteer, herself a university science graduate in the 1930s and equipped with her own experience at sidestepping gender expectations, encountered this view when she spoke of the need to expand vocational training in the school in the 1960s.

> We used to address women's groups, church auxiliaries. We needed their donations and support for our work . . . but many of them made the assumption that the only work the girls could be trained for was domestic work. But this was really an old-fashioned attitude and it annoyed me very much.[7]

However, the EFSBC's primary purpose was not to revolutionize the educational curriculum. The Society recognized that schooling formed a significant aspect of the treatment of the girls in detention and was encouraged that a more energetic commitment had been made by the province when the correspondence courses were replaced by personal instruction. The chief attitudes that the EFSBC wished to alter had to do with the causes, treatment, and prevention of delinquency and, to this end, members continued to promote reform of both the institution and public attitudes.

Immediately following their first visit to the school, the Society began a correspondence with the Provincial Minister of Health and Welfare to keep his office informed of the Fry's interest and work in the Girls' Industrial School. During the remainder of the decade the Elizabeth Fry Society continually forwarded their recommendations to the government regarding the need for a new building to facilitate modern treatment methods and suggested alterations that might be made to improve the existing School in the meantime.

The EFSBC was informed by its own research into the ideal and necessary conditions for the rehabilitation of delinquent girls. Its conclusions, sent to the minister in August of 1955, suggested that a new girls' school must make changes in the educational and recreational programs, the physical accommodations, and the personnel.

The EFSBC maintained that in any new construction both space and facilities should be provided for educational instruction – including vocational training in the skills and trades of dressmaking, cooking, laundry, hairdressing, gardening and waitressing. Although these subjects still trained girls for traditionally female occupations, this program recognized that these services had expanded from a home environment to an institutional and potentially more remunerative context for female employment. The Society's recommendations also called for facilities to allow a recreational program of organized sports, games, and handicrafts. In addition to instructional programs, however, the EFSBC was concerned that a new building provide suitable private space for sleeping and reflection. The Society recommended bedrooms to accommodate no more than four girls, and a small chapel or quiet room. Another of the Society's chief concerns was that a new building take into account the modern standards of treatment and discipline applied to delinquent behaviour. The Society wished to ensure that there would be separate units within the institution to allow for the segregation of the girls, such as a reception room for new arrivals; a self-contained, maximum security wing for difficult girls; a self-contained unit for young, emotionally disturbed girls; and a general unit. The Society also urged the government to consider building smaller industrial schools in different parts of the province to avoid transferring the girls away from their own communities and to reduce the problems associated with administering a large institution in the lower mainland.

The EFSBC launched a determined and persistent campaign to win the interest and understanding of public opinion on the issue of the GIS and the needs of the young offender. It sought to publicize some of the ordinary, less sensational activities of the school. Members spoke to various community and church organizations about the emotional insecurity of many of the girls in custody, the need for treatment of the mentally disturbed girls, and the causes of delinquency. The Society appealed to the network of women's groups which had traditionally supported penal reform in British Columbia. Local Councils of Women responded to the EFSBC's efforts to make the existing conditions more comfortable with donations which included a television set that was much appreciated by the girls in the school. The Provincial Council of Women strengthened the EFSBC's petitions to the government by endorsing its resolutions calling for the construction of a new training school for girls to be built outside the city.

Not yet a powerful voice on its own, the EFSBC still looked to the traditional methods employed by organized women to sway public opinion and influence government decisions. Although the EFSBC was beginning to establish an identity as the watchdog on issues relating to women and the law, the success of the Society's proposals relied on the support of women's organizations like the Provincial Council of Women and its politically connected women.[8]

The combination of strategies – the tact and determination of the EFSBC with its specific proposals and the public support provided by women's networks – would have an impact. Within five years of receiving the incontrovertible evidence contained in the reports of the Elizabeth Fry Society and the provincial committee's enquiry into the Industrial Schools, the government built a new facility to replace the forty-five-year-old structure on Cassiar Street. The Provincial Training School for Girls, to be known as the Willingdon School for Girls, opened in the fall of 1959 at 3655 Willingdon in the municipality of Burnaby, east of Vancouver.

The new school conformed to many of the EFSBC's specifications for a modern institution that would allow for segregation and rehabilitation programs. Built according to the cottage plan, the current model for correctional institutions, the Willingdon School provided accommodation for seventy-five girls in individual bedrooms. A medical unit of ten rooms was designed to receive new admissions and keep girls in isolation in times of illness; an additional ten rooms held inmates who could not be controlled in the more open setting.

The purpose of the Willingdon School was to hold and rehabilitate children and youth committed to its care for the mutual protection of themselves and society. The objectives of the training school were to provide a regulated environment in which to provide treatment, training, and re-education for each individual committed to the school; to improve the girl's self-concept, her relationships with others, her attitudes toward authority, and moral and spiritual values; to develop self-control; and to prepare for re-adjustment upon re-entry into the community.[9] In effect, the training school combined the responsibilities of the home and school to socialize and prepare the individual for an independent and law-abiding future.

The facilities and their physical arrangement were designed to reflect the school's purpose and goals to reform girls who were ill-equipped to measure up to the legitimate demands of society. The organization of learning and living space at Willingdon attempted to meld the community of the boarding school with the intimacy of the family unit. A main building supported classrooms for elementary, high school and commercial studies, space for arts and crafts, a library, training in sewing, homecooking and hairdressing, and a regulation size swimming pool. In addition to staff facilities and a main kitchen, there was a chapel, a tuck shop, and a joint auditorium/gymnasium. Within each of the three duplex units on the grounds, there were two cottages where ten girls lived and ate their meals under the supervision of five staff members who occupied the upstairs apartments.

To the EFSBC, the opening of the Willingdon School in 1959 represented a renewed commitment to the reclamation of girls in conflict with the law. However, the Fry women were all too aware that the new School for Girls would not immediately guarantee the restoration of girls' lives that had suffered years of neglect and abuse. The EFSBC could easily detect a direct link between a deprived, often a depraved, home life and a girl's propensity for the charges that resulted in her committal: so-called incorrigibility, intoxication, sexual immorality, theft, vagrancy and breaking and entering. (See Table 10, page 167.) When the new school drew some criticism about the cost of the high ratio of staff to inmates in the institution (one to two) the Society was quick to its defence, arguing that the reclamation of human lives must not be measured in dollars and cents.

Late in 1960, the president of the EFSBC, Thelma P. Ayling, voiced further objections to a Vancouver newspaper's accounts of the recent fire and escape by several girls from the Willingdon School. Ayling was concerned that "readers get the mistaken impression that taxpayers support young 'thugs' in luxury who wreck the new building rather than appreciate it." Clearly, public opinion was looking to some justification for the amenities provided at the training school and was disillusioned by this example of the girls' vandalism and repudiation of the state's accommodation. Ayling chastised this narrow view of the costs of rehabilitation:

> ... it is bad sense and worse economics to keep sending offenders
> ... to prison. The new system seeks to rehabilitate and must offer
> worthy goals and a sense of achievement. As any sensible mother
> knows, one does not lock offspring in a gloomy room. ... Does
> any mother really believe that these youngsters in the school, aged
> eleven and up, having ... known little but drab and unhappy homes,
> can be spoiled by pleasant surroundings and orderly living?[10]

Ayling went on to correct the newspaper's estimate of the damage at $1,000 to the more realistic figure of $260 and deplored the thoughtless slant of the reporting of the incident.

The Elizabeth Fry Society regarded public criticism of the modern, humane approaches to correctional treatment as being generally detrimental to inmates and ignorant of current trends. The EFSBC's own critical assessment of conditions at Willingdon, such as there not being enough psychiatric and psychological service for assessment and therapy purposes and a need for more cooperation from welfare branches and other agencies, was aired rarely in a public forum. The Society's methods were to make direct recommendations to the appropriate governmental authorities and not to rouse public indignation. Even the EFSBC's promotion of the new Girls' Industrial School had relied on a program of public education as to the benefits of reform and did not seek to sensationalize the inadequate conditions of the outdated building.

Aside from the objectives of the Elizabeth Fry Society to ensure the construction of a new facility for the GIS and to enlighten public opinion about delinquency, the most significant endeavours of the Elizabeth Fry Society were its direct involvement with the girls in the Industrial School. The Society's earliest reception at the Girls' Industrial School on Cassiar Street had convinced Fry members that whatever improvements might be looked for in the long-term, the staff and inmates could benefit from some practical assistance immediately. Two months after its initial visit to the school in 1954, the Society had formed a rehabilitation committee to plan a program, with the approval of the staff, that would provide diversions to ease the boredom and restore a sense of childhood fun to the inmates of the GIS.

The Elizabeth Fry Society introduced a number of events to enliven the routine of institutional life. The Society sponsored monthly parties at the Girls' Industrial School. Under the direction of two square-dance callers, Marjory McCarthy and her husband, the parties became the most popular activity at the school. The McCarthys reported that often when they arrived the girls seemed depressed but they brightened up after a Virginia reel.[11] On a regular basis the Fry volunteers also showed films and brought in candy, clothing, and shoes that had been donated to the residents. The girls were always very excited about the cakes that Fry women took to the school each month for girls who had birthdays. Those whose birthday it was frequently shed tears of joy at being remembered and receiving what was often their first birthday cake.

In the summers the EFSBC held picnics for the girls' school at a member's summer home at Boundary Bay. The Society rented a bus and took the girls and social workers for a day of games and feasting on hot dogs, homemade pies, ice cream, soda pop and cookies. The highlight of the winter months was the Fry Christmas party where the girls were treated to presents and refreshments. Gifts of personal items were donated by a variety of benevolent community organizations such as the Rotary, the Lions, the Kiwanis, the Soroptimists, and church groups who took an interest in the Fry's work. From time to time these organizations also donated tickets which enabled volunteers to take girls from the GIS to concerts, theatrical performances, and the Ice Capades. Managers of Famous Players and Odeon Theatres similarly donated movie tickets.

While the special group events uplifted the spirits of both the staff and inmates of the industrial school the Fry women saw their most important function was to respond to the girls with love and friendship. They understood clearly that volunteers could provide a kind of caring, distinct from that of social workers and counsellors. It was with a knowledge of their own strengths and limitations that Fry volunteers developed a visiting program that emphasized an affective, accepting approach to their relationships with the girls.

The volunteers did not try to solve the girls' problems, give them advice, or make judgements about their behaviour. Instead the Fry women strove to establish trusting friendships through personal correspondence and visits with the girls. Interested volunteers began by writing letters to some of the girls who received no visitors and were lonely. Gradually the Fry women began to make regular visits to individual girls and arranged to take them on outings, for a drive, or to the volunteer's home for lunch. The staff at the school advised the Fry women when girls were admitted to hospital or were in confinement in "the lower regions" so that they could visit them there.

The Elizabeth Fry Society held a series of lectures at the start of each year to interest and initiate new members and provide them with guidelines for visiting the girls at the school. In time, "rules for visitors" became more formalized into a document containing twenty-one points outlining the "dos and don'ts" of the volunteers' relationship with the girls. The volunteer was advised to see the girl on a regular basis. She should seek a common topic of interest for conversation, rather than ply the girl with questions, give praise and encouragement and be a good listener. Pity, criticism, and preaching were to be avoided while poise, dignity, and tolerance were to be maintained. The volunteer was counselled not to believe everything she heard, not to be shocked, and to let the girl know that all information would be treated confidentially unless it appeared in her best interests to inform her social worker. The girl should be informed, therefore, not to tell the volunteer anything that she would not want discussed with her social worker.

The volunteer was advised, also, about her legal obligations to pass on information to the authorities, and the safety and permissibility of certain gift items she might be tempted to bring to the school. Knowledge of an escapee's whereabouts, or breach of terms of a provisional release must be reported. No perfume, nail polish remover, glue, cola drinks, unsmoked cigarettes or matches should be left with the girls, and financial aid should not be given. The list of rules concluded with some encouragement to the volunteer that might have deterred the faint of heart! "Do not be afraid of being a visitor. It is as easy as is any other relationship with a teenager, and is usually a satisfying experience."[12]

In fact, the relationships that Fry women established in the girls' industrial schools on Cassiar and Willingdon did provide some of their most engaging and rewarding experiences as volunteers in the Society. Fry women recalled their work with the girls "in the old days" with enthusiasm, some wistfulness, and always with good humour. One former Fry volunteer admitted with great passion, "You've no idea how happy I would be if I were twenty years younger and I could go back. I really enjoyed it."[13] The Fry women were seldom sentimental in their attachments. They were very realistic about what could and could not be accomplished, but all were profoundly affected by their friendships with the girls.

The Fry volunteer was assigned to one or more girls at the School and undertook to spend at least an hour a week visiting each girl. It was not unheard of for the volunteer to consider this a full-time commitment that meant her visiting at the school four or five days a week. Most often the volunteer helped the girl with her homework, wrote letters to her family, or simply shared a cigarette and a friendly chat.

> Usually we went on a Sunday afternoon. If it was nice we went for a walk around and chatted...sometimes it was difficult to find a common ground. I took them some chocolate bars. . . . They were allowed to smoke . . . given four cigarettes a day, but they thought that was not enough, so I took cigarettes. I didn't smoke but I would puff on a few. Two or three girls would gather round to smoke. I took my big dog out to see them and I could really make contact with them with the dog.[14]

Volunteers who went into the old Cassiar school preferred to take their girls away from the oppressive environment of the school. Remembers one: "I took the Indian girls to Lynn Valley to run on the trails in the woods . . . they loved this."[15] Another Fry visitor laughed as she recalled: "The girls would vie with each other about who would get me. I was popular because I had a car!"[16]

Apart from outings to relieve the monotony of the institutional confinement, the Fry women assisted the girls in practical ways. They would accompany the girls to the outpatient department at the hospital where they might be going for pre-natal check-ups, outfit their babies, or, as happened on at least one occasion, take a girl to visit her sick mother.

An enduring relationship between the Fry volunteer and the girl from the training school often began with her release. This was a crucial period for the girl whose period in detention was finished. Seldom was there a family waiting to welcome her home. Somehow she had to find a job and a place to live. The Fry volunteers worked hard to establish contacts who would be potential employers for the girls. It was vital that the girls found suitable accommodation, pref-

erably away from the old influences that contributed to their recent
conflict with the law. Many of the volunteers who had established
close friendships with their girls took them into their own homes to
give them a chance to get their lives in order after their discharge.

> One Indian girl released from Willingdon in June was to go to the
> Mission School in Cranbrook in September. I asked my husband
> about having her here. We knew her quite well [from her previous
> visits]. The social worker came out and looked us over. We were
> alright so she was with us all summer. . . . We all got along well . . .
> she was very close to us.[17]

The girl, Pam (pseudonym), who went to live that summer with
her Fry volunteer, Judith Babb, kept in touch for over twenty years.
Recalls Babb: "She wrote the most beautiful letters . . . had a whimsi-
cal way of putting things . . . I've kept all her letters and she told me
she saved all of mine." Babb proudly displays photographs of Pam's
three children. "They are lovely children," she says. "I'm very fond
of them. They call me grandma."[18]

Another Fry visitor, Grace Bollert, now ninety-five years old and
confined to a wheelchair, told of the close attachments she still
maintains with the Native girls she visited in the school.

> I brought them here [her home for fifty years] to visit Florence [her
> sister]. They loved Flori—told her all their secrets. . . . Every girl
> complained their mothers were not strict enough! They wished
> they had been like me! . . . One girl wanted to get married but she
> didn't have any clothes. I sent her a pink suit and she wore that. . . .
> Two of the girls still write me letters. Sometimes they show up at
> the door. One came with her husband a few months ago. They
> wanted to take me out to dinner![19]

These long-term relationships did not always signify that the
girls stayed clear of further conflict with the law. But their letters,
saved by Fry volunteers, reveal a strong desire to uphold the values
they knew were held by their Fry "mothers."

Fry women felt it was difficult for the Native girls to stay out of
trouble if they remained in the city. The neighbourhoods where they
were received without prejudice were those parts of the city where
destitution and addiction too often composed the standards of acceptance. The volunteers were well aware of the difficulties
encountered on a daily basis by the girls trying to assimilate into
middle class neighbourhoods. One Fry woman recounted what she
considered to be police harassment of two girls she had placed in
jobs, one in a west side extended care facility and the other in a
Shaughnessy home. Whenever these girls were out walking in the

evening they were picked up by police who recognized them and believed they had run away from the training school.

One of these girls lived for a time in the Fry volunteer's home and, perhaps in an attempt to find a new role model, she tried to emulate her guardian's actions and also her manner of speaking.

> She even took her pocket money and bought herself some white gloves . . . like mine . . . and she would put on her hat and gloves to go to the grocery store and come home to wash out her gloves and pin them on the line. One day at breakfast, over our coffee, she said, "Do you know, I really don't think it's much fun being a lady."[20]

This story was related with much amusement among Fry women who didn't think it was much fun "being a lady" either, and was one of the reasons they became so involved with their volunteer work! They had no false expectations, however, of their success in all cases. For many girls from the Cassiar and Willingdon schools, the transition from a familiar, if uncertain, pattern of survival was often too difficult to make. The girl whose observations are quoted above had another run-in with a police officer that, according to her Fry sponsor, resulted in bruises on her legs. In the company of her boyfriend, she pulled his knife in panic. Although defended by a Fry member, a lawyer who donated her services and succeeded in getting her probation, the girl disappeared without a trace shortly afterward.

It was, perhaps, an unlikely relationship that developed between the respectable, upstanding, middle-aged and middle-class women of the Fry Society, who went home to orderly houses and well-tended gardens, and the Native girls, under eighteen years old but already labelled delinquent for their ability to survive on the street. However, the strength of these long-term friendships seemed to thrive on these differences. Judith Babb said of her relationship with her girl,

> . . . she could trust me and knew I was sympathetic. Pam always knew she could come back here. She travelled all over in her wanderings but she knew I would always let her stay and help her. She never asked me for money but sometimes shelter.[21]

Unlike Judith Babb who has lived in her modest home in West Vancouver for forty-eight years, Pam was always on the road weaving back and forth across the country. Babb remained for Pam the one constant in her life, the woman who accepted her without reproach and who could always be counted on when she needed a friend.

> I didn't preach at her. I expected her to be good. I didn't come down on her but I was not enthusiastic about her escapades. I gave her empathy as you would to a friend. They [the girls] didn't

trust people. Their families treated them badly. Fry members were
steady. They could trust them.[22]

Babb's long-term residence in one place was typical of the Fry
women who maintained relationships with the girls they visited in
the school. The girls hung on to the address and phone number of
the one who would always be there. Like the trees or the moun-
tains, the Fry women and their homes were familiar landmarks in
an alien landscape.

The friendships that developed between the Fry women and the
girls in the school were based on a mutual understanding and respect. The volunteers understood the girls needed most of all to be
accepted. They saw them as being confused and insecure but not
"bad." If they were "immoral" it was due to a lack of instruction or
absence of role models. The Fry women, on the other hand, seemed
sure of themselves. Their values (and often their faith) stood solid
as a rock and nothing in their experience had shaken their convictions. They were not self-righteous but they were confident. The
girls sensed this and drew strength from their relationships with the
Fry women. In turn, the girls protected the women from the "sordid" details of their own lives and endeavoured to live up to the
expectations that they knew, implicitly, were held by their hosts, but
never explicitly demanded.

> The girls who stayed in my house were always respectful. They
> told me once, "We're always very careful not to shock you."[23]

As the Native girls matured into women, the contrast between
their lives and the Fry women's, as revealed in their letters, makes it
even clearer that female friendship often bridged any differences of
ethnicity or social class. In comparison to the safety of life on the
west side of Vancouver, the Native women, whether in their northern homes or in urban ghettos, faced life and death situations on a
constant basis. They miscarried as a result of beatings by their husbands, and lost babies to childhood diseases. Their relatives suffered
violent accidents, or disappeared, and it was a continual battle to resist
alcohol and to dissuade their friends from seeking refuge in the bottle.
The Native women raised other people's children and left their own in
the care of their kinfolk from time to time. But all these events
served only as a backdrop to an exchange that focused on gratitude
for the friendship or small gifts received, on new resolutions to
make better choices in the future, on the strength that the one
woman took from the other's encouragement.[24]

The Elizabeth Fry Society of British Columbia could not reform
all the social prejudices and inequities that might serve as obstacles
to a girl's resolve to stay on the the right side of the law. The Fry

did attempt to ensure that the correctional institution reflected an enlightened and humanitarian approach to the treatment of those committed to its care. Fry women counted the rehabilitation of the Girls' Training School and their own efforts with the girls as successful if they did not graduate to Oakalla. At a personal level both the girls and the Fry women were enjoined in what was often a lifelong friendship.

The Fry women recognized, however, that they had not homes enough for all the girls who needed security and nurturing to divert them from delinquent behaviour. Not content with having reformed the reform school, the Society, in the 1960s, turned its efforts to establishing a more familial environment—the group home—that might provide preventive and after-care for girls.

5. FROM HOUSE TO HOME

We do not weigh our work against dollars and cents, however . . . as a point of interest . . . our [group] home will eventually save the taxpayers' money. My Society's concern is the welfare of the girls. They are the future mothers to be — bringing young children into the world, into our community. We must see that this future generation is given every opportunity to become law-abiding citizens.

EFSBC brief to City Council regarding purchase of
[house] to establish a group home, October 1964.[1]

On the brink of what would become the turbulent sixties, members of the EFSBC began to reflect on the meaning of their work, to examine their successes, and to question their limitations. The Society had the respect of the administrators in the women's prison and the girls' training school, and the trust of the inmates they visited. But Fry volunteers had become accustomed to playing a reformist role. Their increasing familiarity with the treatment of inmates helped focus attention on the shortcomings of the system and suggested possible remedies that might be promoted by the Society. In particular, Fry members were disturbed by the patterns of delinquency and criminality that followed inevitably in the absence of any substantial after-care for girls following their discharge from Willingdon.

Through their work in the provincial industrial and training schools, the EFSBC volunteers formed close relationships with "their girls." The Fry women learned first-hand about the circumstances of the girls' lives that had led them into conflict with the law. The Fry volunteers were well aware of the difficulties the girls faced, particularly in the crucial first days following their release from custody. Although several of the Fry women acted as sponsors and took girls into their homes, this was usually a response to an immediate crisis and one that relied on the compatibility and goodwill of the parties involved. More often the girls returned to the same destructive environments which sanctioned the behaviour that led to their detention. The volunteers' willingness to remain in contact with the girls after they left Willingdon was an attempt to maintain a vital line of communication or supply some refuge in an emergency; but the girls easily slipped away from this well-meaning but inadequate safety net. These insights troubled Fry women who sensed the need to provide a secure and stable home as an alternative to a girl's returning to an uncertain, often uncaring, situation after her detention.

It was apparent to the Elizabeth Fry Society that without a supportive home, a sentence in the training school was not adequate to deter either delinquency or recidivism—subsequent incarceration. Fry volunteers identified the necessity for after-care as a logical extension of the treatment of juvenile offenders. In the minds of the Fry workers, this need might be satisfied if a girls' residence or hostel could be established. With this goal in mind, the EFSBC began to take careful note of the plans and procedures of the Working Boys' Home Committee formed in 1954 to establish a residence for boys.

The Working Boys' Home Committee had been formed by representatives of the Community Chest and Council of Greater Vancouver Family and Child Welfare Division, in response to a brief presented to the Social Planning Committee, five years earlier, by the B.C. Parole and Probation Officers Association. The first report of this committee confirmed the necessity for specialized resources according to the differing needs of adolescents, and identified the benefits of a group living situation as an alternative to foster care for boys whose own home situations had broken down. Preventive care was a sufficiently new treatment philosophy to be rejected at its first hearing in 1954. However, in response to the recurring need for residential facilities beyond home care, a new committee was formed in 1957, including at least one member from the Elizabeth Fry Society, which was to re-examine the recommendations of the previous report. The committee's proposal to proceed with a group living home for boys "who in the opinion of the court or social agency might develop social behaviour that would necessitate a custodial institution," was accompanied by a request for financial support from the Community Chest.[2]

In 1958, the opening of the group home for boys encouraged the EFSBC to set up its own committee to investigate the possibilities of establishing a similar residence in the lower mainland for girls. Although not immediately apparent, the formation of this committee precipitated significant changes for the EFSBC, not only as the Society expanded its role in the field of correctional services, but also in terms of the entire structure and organization of the Society.

The Society's hostel committee[3] began its work in October and, in the already established tradition of the EFSBC, set out to make a conclusive study, both theoretical and practical, of hostels, residences, and group living homes in social service work. Although primarily interested in after-care, the Society wanted to gather information on all kinds of housing options for girls and women at various stages of their adjustment to community living. This meant surveying the available literature on the subject; consulting social workers, child welfare agencies, and government departments; and investigating, first-hand, similar resources currently in operation. Over the next two years, members of the hostel committee read everything they could find about setting up a home for girls and women needing support and supervision but not institutional restraint.

Although attempts to find alternatives to incarceration appeared as innovative initiatives in the 1960s, community-based corrections really began in the nineteenth century. Philanthropic societies in London, England, established residences for children caught begging or stealing, and Quakers in Boston opened transitional houses for women released from prison. Often these seemingly humanitarian efforts were a means of securing indentured servants when the individuals, especially if they were female, were eventually released into private homes as domestic workers. In Canada, the trend towards finding alternatives to prison had been growing since the 1950s with increased use of probation, parole, work release, and halfway houses. By the 1960s, experimental pre-release residences in urban centres popularized the concept of community-based corrections and the need for reintegration programs for offenders. The EFSBC learned, however, that while there was increasing interest in group-living homes, governmental agencies were cautious about taking the initiative.[4]

The Fry volunteers also found that they were venturing into new territory with their interest in a girls' home. Group homes for boys were more common than for girls. Not only did the need appear greater for boys, but there was also a great reluctance by many "experts" in the field to undertake a girls' home because of the view that "girls were more difficult to work with than the boys."[5] It was precisely these attitudes that convinced the Fry women that they must look out for the girls' welfare.

Although the EFSBC had been satisfied for many years that there was an urgent need both for preventive and after-care for girls, this was confirmed in discussions with social workers and other personnel interested in the welfare of juveniles. The supervisor of Willingdon Training School, (Miss) Winifred M. Urquhart, encouraged the Fry's efforts to establish a hostel for girls discharged from Willingdon and promised her cooperation in screening the girls to ensure their suitability, or as she put it, "not too mixed up."[6] Juvenile Court Judge Winnifred Murphy, who would later serve on the board of directors of the EFSBC, considered there was definitely a need for a girls' home and thought there were times when she would prefer to place a girl in such a home rather than Willingdon. However, she cautioned the Fry about mixing pre- and post-Willingdon girls. Judge Murphy offered to ascertain the legal requirements of setting up a home. Judge W.N.S. Dixon, of the Juvenile and Family Court, also identified the need for a boarding home for girls where they might start anew, away from bad influences, and where they might receive some affection. Judge Dixon, like Derek Thompson, Family Welfare Services, alerted the Fry to the pitfalls that lay ahead in the form of costs, the locating of accommodations, the responsibilities of staffing, and the objections of neighbours. Gordon Stevens, Inspector of Gaols and Provincial Probation Officer, felt that the home could serve a need for the housing of delinquent girls, those before the courts and after Willingdon. Stevens supported the hiring of "a good woman" to run the home but advised that her husband should go out to work and not be attracted or attractive to the girls. The chief probation officer expressed interest in the hostel and recommended that the EFSBC set it up on a solid business footing.[7] These consultations raised many issues about the clientele of the proposed residence and its supervision. The Society also considered the possibility of combining living accommodations with office space, which was becoming increasingly necessary to coordinate all the diverse activities of the EFSBC.

The investigations of existing residences brought Fry members face to face with the practical reality of running a home. Alma House, Vancouver's receiving home, housed girls (ideally six, but more if necessary) ages twelve to seventeen years, who had been through the courts and/or the children's aid and were en route to foster homes. The home was staffed by a matron and her assistant, a cook, and a cleaning lady. The costs, which included food, clothing, and a weekly allowance of $1.50 for the oldest children, amounted to $210 per month for each resident and were paid by government. The YWCA's Baynes' House provided accommodation with meals for twelve to fourteen girls, ages fifteen to eighteen years, who were completing training courses or were working. Three or four girls shared each room in this hostel and their parents paid $15 a week. Occasionally girls were placed by the social services department. The Central City Mission's Youth Hostel, administered by a board of directors and funded through voluntary contributions, offered accommodation for six to eight boys of all ages who were either employed or in school. If the boy had any means of support, he was expected to pay $50 a month. Each resident was expected to work two hours a week around the home, in the garden, or inside the house. The boys came to the hostel from various sources such as the provincial training schools, city mission, children's aid, rec-

ommendations by the police, and from foster homes. Some of the
boys were supervised by social workers, but the couple who ran the
hostel preferred the boys to be accountable to them and their peers.
The recently established Working Boys' Home relied on approximately $6,600 per annum from the Community Chest. This house
had been bought and furnished by the Lions Club and provided
beds for eight boys, ages fourteen to eighteen. Most of the residents
were in school but some worked part-time. A married couple, with
two sons, were houseparents and were aided by voluntary committees who attended to the house maintenance.

The Catherine Booth Home run by the Salvation Army was
maintained by a staff of three and a housekeeper, who reported to
the Fry women that this home was equipped to take eight to ten
women.[8] Women received at this home came from Oakalla, the police court, or were brought by the police. Most were former inmates
and some were newcomers to the city who found themselves in
trouble and with nowhere to turn. Alcoholics, drug addicts, and
abused women all sought refuge at the Catherine Booth Home, but
clearly it was not adequate to meet the demands for temporary
housing for women in trouble. The rates were $1.25 per day for
three meals and a bed although no one was refused for lack of
money. The house revenue fell far short of covering expenses.

After many months of research, which included consultations
with the city licensing bureau to confirm the regulations and standards that must be followed for the operation of a boarding home,
members of the hostel committee presented their findings to the Fry
membership. One conclusion was certain: in the early sixties, the
options for girls in difficulty who needed an alternative to a custodial institution or a foster home, particularly to ease their
adjustment after their release from the training school, were almost
non-existent. The EFSBC was more convinced than ever that its goal
must be to provide "a home as close to a normal home as possible"
for these girls.[9] Nothing in the Fry women's research had overturned their convictions that the family model afforded the most
appropriate environment for the youngsters to receive the love and
security that would engender personal confidence and consideration
of others.

In these early stages, the intention of the Fry women was to
guide the girls' home from an idea to a reality but they were not
altogether certain how this was to be achieved. The financial responsibilities of such an enterprise appeared at first overwhelming and
the Society did not foresee that it would be able to rent a house, let
alone buy one. The EFSBC had always relied on an annual budget of
only a few hundred dollars drawn from membership fees and the
generosity of the Fry's wealthier patrons. The Fry women's first

hope was that a house would be donated and that funds to pay a matron would come from the general financial support provided by the agencies sponsoring the girls. Children who were wards of agencies had their medical and dental expenses, clothing, and room and board paid by the agency. The EFSBC could apply for social assistance on behalf of the non-wards. However, there would be capital costs to be born by the Society. In 1961, the EFSBC proceeded cautiously with an appeal to the public for donations to support this endeavour for the first two years of its operation.

The EFSBC customarily preferred to continue its work with little publicity. Although the Society was interested in educating the public to the benefits of penal reform, it was well aware that issues of innovative correctional treatment were likely to engender criticism and suspicion rather than sympathy. Personal lectures and the occasional newspaper coverage of the events the Fry sponsored at Willingdon or Oakalla usually drew a positive level of interest, but the Fry was careful to avoid introducing contentious issues to public discussion. Controversy was not always helpful to its cause. Too often the truth of the issues was buried by newspapers in search of a flashy headline. The decision, then, to alert the public to their plans to establish a group home for so-called delinquent girls was undertaken with great care so as to ensure understanding and not indignation.

The EFSBC began by advertising in church magazines and the city newspapers about its need for a suitable house, with or without willing houseparents. The Society issued news releases that promoted EFSBC activities and its current campaign. City newspapers responded with sincere and appealing editorials that had the Society's telephones ringing for days. Fry members were stunned by the response. All manner of people offered their houses in various parts of Vancouver and outlying districts. In addition, Fry women received calls from social workers and community people wanting to congratulate them on this undertaking. There was even a call from a distressed teenage girl who looked to the Elizabeth Fry Society to solve the problems of her current living arrangements.

While the Fry was heartened by this evidence of public support, an outright donation of a house to the Society, and an interested party to operate it, did not materialize. Nevertheless, the Fry members believed that it was time to begin in a small way and were considering a couple who had expressed interest in taking girls into their home. The hostel committee felt that two girls could be accommodated on a month-to-month basis on a budget of about $200. This arrangement was far from ideal and fraught with potential difficulties, not the least of which was the inability of the EFSBC to be fully responsible for the quality of the care. Before arrangements

could be finalized, a surprise offer came from a Vancouver business-
man, lawyer, and philanthropist, Arthur Fouks, who volunteered to
help organize a fundraising campaign for the Fry's proposed home.
For the first time, the EFSBC began to consider the possibility of
renting a house and taking charge of its management.

In fact, the Society had always favoured this arrangement but
there was no precedent in its twenty-year history for such an elaborate initiative. The work of the EFSBC had been sustained by its
volunteers who had donated their time and caring. It had appealed
to its traditional networks—church auxiliaries and other women's
organizations—for moral and, occasionally, financial support, but
had never focused, heretofore, on large-scale fundraising drives or
considered its role to be concerned with money management. At the
end of 1960, EFSBC president Thelma Ayling had gone so far as to
express her wish for the following year, and reported in a Vancouver newspaper, that if some twenty-four businessmen would each
contribute $100 a year, the hostel could be started.[10] Thus the
EFSBC's decision to accept Arthur Fouks' proposition that the Society raise a substantial amount of money signified alterations in the
scope and responsibilities of the Society.

Fouks did not personally launch a fundraising campaign for the
Fry, but directed the Society's executive on a course that, in time,
yielded profitable results. Their voluntary consultant, Fouks, sent
the Fry women to key people in the city who were familiar with
raising money for charitable foundations. The idea of the hostel entered a new realm of possibility once Fry members accepted that
they might amass the capital needed to ensure its operation along
the lines they had envisioned.

Early in 1962 the EFSBC was beginning to see the effects of its
careful groundwork over the previous months. Voluntary donations
had boosted the balance in the hostel account to $1,400 and, more
significantly, the EFSBC had the promise of government backing at
such time as the Society was able to establish the hostel's operation.
However, Fry women were taken aback by the withdrawal of support by one whose opinion was respected by the Society. The
superintendent at the Willingdon School, Winifred Urquhart, conveyed to EFSBC president Margery Ottman that in her view there
was no longer a need for a hostel for girls from Willingdon in light
of a new centre for after-care opened by the government in Terrace
in the northern part of the province.[11] The EFSBC recognized that
the government's commitment to their hostel might be in jeopardy
and subsequent queries to Wesley Black of the provincial welfare
department confirmed that, in his opinion, another hostel was unnecessary. Having received four requests for accommodation for
girls in the first eight weeks of the year, the Society remained un-

convinced that the need was indeed being adequately met with existing services. Nevertheless, with the financial backing of the government now in doubt, the Fry's hostel committee was forced to reconsider its decision at this time.

The closing of Baynes House in October prompted a brief from the EFSBC to Black in the provincial welfare department, drawing attention to the loss of one of the few girls' homes in the city, reminding him of the need for accommodations for girls leaving the provincial training school, and affirming the Society's continued interest in making some provision for them. The EFSBC was advised by Mary King, Superintendent of Child Welfare in B.C., that there might be a greater need for a hostel for preventive care as an alternative to Willingdon and suggested the Society examine this field further.[12] This was an interesting idea for the Fry women, who had the Willingdon girls as their first, but not their only, concern. The Fry's interest in measures that might divert girls from eventual conflict with the law was longstanding, and the Society had been recently involved in the preparation of submissions to special committees on juvenile delinquency at both the provincial and federal level. The EFSBC was not averse to changing its focus but wished to hear from other agencies about the areas that might best be served by its efforts.

In March 1963, EFSBC president Margery Ottman and members of the hostel committee obtained a meeting with the heads of a number of agencies to properly reassess the need for a girls' hostel. This meeting took place in the board room at Oakalla and was chaired by Hugh Christie (warden, Oakalla Prison Farm) with Alice Carol (Provincial Mental Health), Winifred Urquhart (Willingdon), Mr. Pinkerton and Father Reitter (Children's Aid Society), Gordon Stevens (probation officer), Bessie Maybee (Oakalla Women's Division), Mary King (Child Welfare), Evelyn Roberts (Catholic Children's Aid) and Mrs. Ralph Gilmore (Provincial Council of Women) in attendance. With the benefit of their first-hand experience, these representatives were able to discuss the current status of rehabilitation services and, in particular, the role that a hostel might play in fulfilling these needs. The advantages of a hostel to the individual girl, the social worker, and the community were considered and also the problems that might occur. While all of the agencies recognized that girls leaving Willingdon could benefit from a hostel, the participants at this meeting were very concerned that many of the girls were sent to the provincial training school because there was no alternative. With this consensus, the EFSBC was satisfied that there was an immediate need for a hostel to aid in the prevention of delinquency. This meeting also clarified to the Society the ideal form of the hostel—a group home—that would be run by houseparents and be conveniently located near to transportation,

schools, and employment for the girls. All agreed that the agency
sponsoring each girl would supply a social worker, medical care,
and generally supervise her stay.[13]

With a renewed commitment and, it might be added, a new
regard by other provincial agencies that would prove to be a source
of support and encouragement, the EFSBC prepared to launch a full-
scale appeal to the public for funds. The Society was now convinced
that in order to live up to the expectations generated by the recent
hostel meeting, it must assume full responsibility for the endeavour.
The EFSBC resolved to rent or purchase its own house, hire a housemother to take charge, and make a real home for pre-delinquent
girls. In effect, the Fry women decided to act with the courage of
their own convictions. While members of the Fry had never doubted
the need for a girls' home and had a strong sense that a domestic
environment would furnish a significant source of rehabilitation, it
had taken them some time to realize that in addition to proposing
this treatment they could provide it.

The EFSBC took as much care in the orchestration of its
fundraising as it did with every other aspect of its work. The Fry
asked one of its patrons, Rosemary (Mrs. Charles N.) Woodward,
well-known in the community both for her own civic-minded endeavours and those of the family-owned Woodward's stores, to act
as a sponsor for the campaign that set its goal at $25,000. A "mas-
terful campaign letter" was composed by Grace Shaw, EFSBC
volunteer, and Simma Holt, journalist for the *Vancouver Sun*. This
letter appealed to the public to forward its contributions and outlined the reasons for the group home:

> It is a plan to establish a home for teenage girls who are very close
> to being in serious trouble with the law. Such a home, provided at
> a crucial turning point in their lives, can keep them from the
> tragic path of petty crime, prostitution, drug addiction, and a long,
> useless life in prison. They are not bad girls yet. They are just
> lonely, scared kids with little or no money . . . no family . . . no one
> with time, interest, or love for them. It is at this time in their lives
> that they need the warmth and friendship of a home.[14]

This appeal was sent to thousands of individuals, church organizations, voluntary agencies, companies, and businesses. City newspapers,
radio stations, Rosemary Woodward and the Fry women who spoke
to numerous clubs, societies, and sororities at the university served
to publicize the history of the Fry's work in rehabilitation and its
hopes to enter the new field of preventive care with a group home
for pre-delinquent girls.

In the spring of 1964, the enormous amount of energy ex-
pended by Woodward and the Fry volunteers began to show results.

The campaign exceeded its goal of $25,000 and the EFSBC was not only on the brink of establishing innovative preventive care in the form of a group home, but also of reforming its own organization to meet the challenge of its increased responsibilities. Over the past several months the EFSBC had made some important decisions about its future involvement as a provider of correctional services. It remained for the Society to formalize the process of expansion to include professional staff. The many agencies and government departments now in close contact with the Fry had indicated that they would be uneasy about assigning girls to the home until the Society had a social worker.

The hiring of a professional worker would mean a radical change for the EFSBC, steeped as it was in the voluntary tradition. Yet, despite some apprehension of being displaced by professional expertise, Fry women recognized that their organization must be equal to the task it had set for itself. Not only was it time to consider hiring an administrator to act as a social worker for the group home, the Fry also needed an office to coordinate the work of the Society that, in addition to planning and raising funds for the group home, continued to be involved at Oakalla and Willingdon. The EFSBC thus resolved to begin a search for an executive director, who would also serve as a social worker for the group home, and to establish an office.

In June, the EFSBC prepared to meet again with the heads of the various social agencies to outline operational policy regarding the proposed group home. Mary King, from the provincial child welfare, chaired this meeting, which in addition to representatives from the Fry and the agencies from the previous meeting, included the welfare licensing inspector, a social worker, and an administrator from the social welfare department in Burnaby. After much discussion, the EFSBC was able to establish some tentative guidelines and procedures. The Society expected to accommodate six to eight girls between fourteen and eighteen years of age in a group home, which would be run by house parents under the direction of the EFSBC and its anticipated social worker/executive director. This executive director would be responsible for the girls' treatment. EFSBC volunteers would provide entertainment, recreation, and aid in finding jobs for the girls. An admissions committee should be established to consider girls from the department of welfare, the children's aid, Willingdon School and the detention court. Any girl would be considered who could not live in her own home and who had the capacity to benefit from the group experience. Although it was expected that many of the girls would be somewhat psychologically distraught, it was not anticipated that the home would be handling extreme cases.[15] The EFSBC did foresee, however, that the services of a child psychiatrist would be necessary.

A per capita, per diem cost that would take into account salaries, services, living expenses, carrying charges, and upkeep would
have to be worked out by the Society and passed on as service fees
to be paid by the referring agency, e.g., the government, Children's
Aid Services, or the Society itself. Dental and medical services would
be the responsibility of the municipality in which the home was
situated. Personal items, including clothing, would be handled directly by the referring agency.[16]

At this meeting the Fry women had been warned of the necessity of preparing neighbours who customarily opposed group homes
and were advised of the delays likely to be encountered in establishing a group home in Vancouver. With a clearer idea of what lay
ahead, the EFSBC was now very anxious to choose a location as
soon as possible and was convinced that because of the energy and
money that would be invested in setting up the group home, their
house must be purchased and not leased. Early in July, the EFSBC
appointed a house-hunting committee to begin the search in earnest.

Although this voluntary society had many innovative programs
to its credit and had succeeded in mobilizing respectable amounts
of financial and popular support, the EFSBC's organizational structure had remained essentially the same since the formation of the
Society in 1940. The old format, whereby the executive took its direction from the membership, was cumbersome in the 1960s in
view of the scope of decisions that had to be made on a daily basis.
(See Chart 1, page 169.)

Constitutional changes and the appointment of a board of directors were part of a process of organizational change that would not
be completed until 1966, but the first tangible sign that the meta-
morphosis of the Society was underway was evident when the
EFSBC acquired an office in the Rogers Building at 470 Granville
Street.[17] Unwilling to cast off the legacy of volunteerism, Fry members had sought donated space equipped with a borrowed
typewriter. This space was available to the Society until the end of
the year but by then an office had become essential. Fry women
also reasoned that the EFSBC office should be located in a part of
town that was accessible to women in need of the Society's services,
or wanting to drop in for a chat. The EFSBC subsequently rented an
office in the Ford Building at 193 East Hastings Street at Main for
$30 a month.[18] Eventually the EFSBC would need to replace the vol-
untary secretarial help with paid employees. An accountant was
already necessary to help with the budget and to keep track of the
donations and disbursements from the hostel account.[19]

The major change in the life of the EFSBC came in 1964 near
the end of August when the members of the house-hunting commit-

tee reported to the EFSBC executive that they had indeed found a house suitable for the long awaited group home. The committee obtained approval to make an interim offer on the large, older house in a residential neighbourhood on the west side of Vancouver. The EFSBC felt this to be a suitable location for the girls' home because of its convenience to schools and public transportation. It felt also that with the house being in an area where many of the homes were subdivided into duplexes and rental suites, both the city and neighbours would be receptive to a group home. The offer stated a purchase price of $17,600 with the EFSBC assuming a mortgage of $12,000, and was subject to approval by city hall of the use of the property for "a ladies' boarding house."[20]

The Fry's application to the city planning department to establish a group home for teenage girls was submitted in early September. Despite repeated phone calls to the planning office, the EFSBC still had no word on the status of their permit a month later. City Hall blamed the delay on an influenza epidemic that afflicted its personnel, but with the closing date (October 21) of the interim offer approaching very fast, the EFSBC was anxious not to have their house a casualty of a virus. In order to speed things up, and on the advice of the zoning planner, the Society called a meeting of the neighbours to inform them of the proposed changes in the use of the property. Only three people attended and one of them was very hostile to the Fry's presentation. The city then contacted the neighbours by mail and gave them ten days to appeal. Hearing that there were several dissenters, EFSBC volunteers went door-to-door to explain personally the group home project and try to allay the residents' fears. The Fry women experienced a rude reception and felt downhearted that the years of effort that had gone into this project hinged on the protest of homeowners who did not want to extend the benefits of their neighbourhood to homeless girls. As a last resort the EFSBC prepared a brief that the president, Margery Ottman, delivered to the Vancouver City Council on October 20.[21]

Ottman carefully outlined the work of the EFSBC over the last twenty-five years and explained that the nature of its work with women and girls in correctional institutions precluded a lot of publicity that would have perhaps made the Society well known to the city councillors. The brief outlined the work of the 170 EFSBC individual members and 72 affiliated associations (group and business memberships) and stressed its dependence on voluntary hours and funding provided by interested citizens. Ottman went on to discuss the group home project and its rationale, as well as the approval already indicated by the community's financial donations, the government's promise of operating grants, and social service agencies' willingness to send girls to the home. As indicated in the opening lines of this chapter, the EFSBC felt it necessary to convince the city council of the economical benefits of preventive care in the form of savings to the taxpayer by way of addressing the concerns raised by residents in the area that the home would increase their taxes. Nevertheless, the Fry's chief concern was for the rehabilitation of individuals and not the weighing of the costs of keeping them in prison or training schools versus a group home. The final comments submitted with the brief were directed to an assessment of the objections of the neighbours to the proposed home and pointed out the number of families who made no protest.[22]

After this hearing, the EFSBC was elated by the news that it would be awarded the permit. However, when committee members tried to collect it the next day, they were told that the planning office had overturned the decision. With their option on the house due to expire at 5:00 PM, the Fry women would not be deterred. Their persistence was rewarded when the permit was finally issued at 4:50 PM with the condition that there would be a fifteen-day extension for the residents to register further objections. With only minutes to spare, the EFSBC made their down payment and prepared to close the deal that they hoped would launch the Fry's first group home.

A few days later the EFSBC combined its semi-annual meeting with a tea given by the female inmates at Oakalla prison, but the Fry women were wary of victory celebrations. In fact, outside the prison walls a growing resistance to the group home was stirring the homeowners to renew their protest of the Fry's proposed residence in their neighbourhood.[23] Within a week the EFSBC was notified of an impending appeal of the city's decision to permit the group home. But before the residents could present their case, which was scheduled for November 18, the owner of the house, impatient with the prolonged completion of the sale, bowed to this pressure from his neighbours and withdrew his home from the market.[24]

The Fry women accepted these events as a temporary setback but were by no means discouraged. They had already begun to regard this group home as only the first of several that would eventually include halfway houses for girls released from Willingdon and Oakalla. The EFSBC had always derived much of its strength from the patience and foresight of its volunteers, which also accounted for the Society's thorough approach to change and reform. While some of the women expressed frustration with the process that had scuttled their recent attempt to establish the group home, out of this experience came a renewed confidence in the project and a commitment to educate the public more thoroughly regarding the great need for increased community resources. The EFSBC prepared to inform the public about rehabilitation issues and to resume house-hunting.

Both of these aims culminated in March 1965. Simma Holt's address to the annual EFSBC meeting was given much attention in the *Vancouver Sun* and *Province* newspapers. Although the publicity that surrounded Holt's attack on the methods of "professional" rehabilitation, the "failure of the welfare department," and her plea that more recognition be accorded "the people without degrees [that] can serve effectively" predictably drew a mixed response, no one could deny that people were being invited to reassess correctional philosophy and treatment.[25] Responding to letters published in the *Vancouver Sun* that protested Holt's ideas, EFSBC president Margery Ottman and vice president Lynn Clark pointed out that "she made us sad, she made us mad, she made us glad, but most importantly she made us think."[26] The EFSBC clearly hoped for a more positive public response to alternative treatment methods, especially as the Society had recently found another house to purchase and was once again embroiled in the residents' hostility to the Fry's home for girls.

After inspecting numerous houses in Vancouver and Burnaby, the house-hunting committee had settled on one on West 11th Avenue that did not appear to need extensive renovations. An interim offer was signed in early March and the Fry could only wait the long eight weeks that were necessary to give residents appropriate notice before a permit could be issued. The first experience had taught the Fry women to expect some resistance from the neighbours, but they were alarmed by the devious nature of the opposition to their current efforts. In addition to legitimate protests, a fake "official" letter, anonymous phone calls, and a whispering campaign were directed against the Fry's plan to establish the home for girls. A counterfeit letter written on official city council stationery was sent to residents and alleged that the West 11th location had been designated as a treatment centre for drug addicts. Phone calls perpetuated this false information that the Fry home would be a narcotics treatment centre and urged the residents to register their disapproval.[27] The city planners conceded that this false evidence served to fan the fire of the opposition out of proportion and gave the EFSBC additional opportunities to make their case before the appeal board.

As in the previous attempt, the testimony of an impressive array of representatives from community and social welfare departments, children's aid, women's organizations, the Vancouver Police Department, and even an independent real estate appraiser did not silence the neighbours' protests. The EFSBC's good intentions were not helped by the words of Alderman Hal Wilson who warned the city council that "as soon as word gets around that the girls are there, it will attract boys like bees to a honey pot."[28] A spokesperson for the sixteen petitioners against the group home claimed that "such a home would change the character of the district and adversely affect tenants and

In 1965, the Elizabeth Fry Society of
British Columbia opened Duncan House,
its first group living home, for adolescent
girls. The EFSBC hoped the group living
home would provide the community with
a preventive measure that would forestall
delinquency and subsequent incarceration
of juvenile girls. The purchase of the
house by the EFSBC initially provoked
outrage and hostility from fearful
neighbouring homeowners in Vancouver's
west side. But after the home opened, its
occupants were welcomed into the
community.

property values." It would not be the last time that the EFSBC heard
residents say, "The home may be good, but we don't want it in this
area." Despite the Society's evidence that group homes tended to
increase and not depreciate property values because the homes and
grounds were well-maintained, the homeowners continued to register their dissent with the city's decision.

In an effort to confront the real fears of the neighbours in the
vicinity, members of the EFSBC met with them to outline the management of the home and discuss their hopes to provide the girls
with a healthy home environment in a friendly community. The
neighbours remained adamant that the house should not harbour
any "delinquent" girls and the Society promised the residents that
there would be no girls in the home who had been to Willingdon
School. This policy, which remained in effect until 1972 when circumstances had changed sufficiently to encourage the EFSBC to
reconsider this restriction,[29] evidently appeased the opposition in
1965 and allowed the permit to be issued and the sale of the house
to be completed. The EFSBC was fortunate that the owner of this
house, who became a supporter of the Fry's endeavours, was willing
to wait until the lengthy negotiations were completed.

With the heat of the battle for their development permit behind
them, the Fry women began to face the cooler reality of the work
needed to convert the house into a home. A renovations committee
was formed and its members toured other group homes for ideas.
The architect, Peter Kaffka (who had designed the graduate
students' building at UBC) donated his services to draw up the
plans that would make the house more convenient and comfortable
for the boarders and houseparents, in addition to satisfying the
city's fire regulations. Because the EFSBC wanted to have the home
ready for occupancy as soon as possible, the Society concentrated
its efforts on the interior restorations. The Society contracted
Kennett Construction who not only submitted the lowest bid but
could begin work immediately. These renovations included a bath-

room for the houseparents, an updated kitchen, additional plumbing on the second floor, new wiring throughout, installation of linoleum, additional electric outlets, a smoke door on the main floor, a fire alarm system, a fire escape, refinishing of wood floors and painting.[30] The Mount Pleasant Lions Club later volunteered to paint and repair the exterior of the house.

At the same time the renovations commenced, a house committee was formed and charged with furnishing and equipping the house, finding houseparents, and establishing admissions procedures—in short, preparing for the operation of the home. The members of this committee were fully occupied with the details of readying the home for its occupants and juggling the finances. There were really no precedents for the Society's undertaking and the volunteers had to formulate both philosophical rationales and practical solutions for the tasks at hand. In terms of decorating the home, the decision to use mainly new and durable items stirred the consciences of many of the volunteers who traditionally believed that donations were preferable to purchases. But the receipt of furnishings, often mismatched castoffs in need of repair, had caused committee members to evaluate the importance of the interior design of the home for both its treatment value and its ability to withstand constant use. It required no small amount of tact on the part of the EFSBC women, who spoke regularly to community organizations asking for their support, to reject old bedding, lamps, and other well intentioned but unsuitable donations. The house committee realized the therapeutic value of a bright, cheery environment, and deemed it important that every detail of the home should convey the message to the child that the agency considered her to be a worthwhile individual.[31]

This philosophy translated into many hours of comparison shopping by Fry volunteers. Jordan's had offered all carpeting at cost and Woodward's department store was particularly responsive to the EFSBC's request for wholesale prices. The store's president, Mr. Glanville, assigned one of his vice-presidents to assist the Fry women in every way. One hardy shopper likened these buying sprees at Woodward's to a marathon run, an observation that gained credence when, "several breathless trips later we discovered Mr. Moore [the vice-president] had been a track and field star in his youth!"[32] The furnishings selected by the EFSBC volunteers were solid wooden reproductions of styles that had stood the test of time. The intention was to create a sense of stability in the home, and undoubtedly the women's own tastes were reflected in their choices, but they also aimed at ensuring good value for the money. The volunteers regarded their responsibility to keep within the allotted budgets as important as their interest in the prevention of delinquency.

While the EFSBC had the capital to make a down payment on

In line with the EFSBC's desire to create a familial environment for girls, Doris and Ken McPherson were hired as the houseparents of the group living home. They are pictured (without teacups) visiting EFSBC volunteers Edna Horsman and Maida Duncan. The quality of the home furnishings and its cheery decor was intended to reassure the girls in residence that they were worthwhile individuals.

the house and complete the renovations, the Society had to show clear title to the home before it would qualify for government grants. One-third of the capital cost would then be recoverable from the Deputy Provincial Secretary and the EFSBC decided to apply for a mortgage to finance the other two-thirds. These payments would eventually be included in the per diem rate charged to the Department of Child Welfare. The EFSBC was thus the first society in Canada to receive a loan under the special mortgage loans on buildings used for charitable purposes from the Central Mortgage and Housing Corporation. This loan had to be passed by an order-in-council in Ottawa.[33]

With the completion of the house renovations expected by the fall of 1965, the house committee prepared to hire houseparents. From the outset the EFSBC had understood how important personnel would be to their project, and the goal to have the home resemble, as nearly as possible, ideal family living meant that preference would be given to a married couple. The job of housemother was not an easy one. She would need to be a good cook, an efficient housekeeper, and possess attractive personal qualities such as tact, understanding, kindness, firmness, responsibility, tolerance, and above all, a sense of humour.[34] The Society believed it had found such a person when it engaged Doris (Mrs. Ken) McPherson, with a salary designated to her of $250 per month plus room and board, a car allowance, and fringe benefits.[35] The house now refurbished in every way to accommodate nine children, and with Mrs. McPherson and her husband installed as houseparents, the EFSBC prepared to receive the first admission in October.

In addition to giving a girl an opportunity to be accepted and cared for by sympathetic guardians, the EFSBC hoped the group home would provide the community with a preventive measure that would encourage public confidence and governmental support. The women in the EFSBC felt also that with the establishing of the group home they were increasing their own knowledge and experience to the benefit of their Society. Volunteers wrote in a house committee report, "In other words, know-how and enthusiasm will keep the Society vital."[36] But the key to government grants and the participation of other agencies that was essential to the existence and survival of the group home rested on the EFSBC's appointment of an executive director who would also serve as the Society's social worker.

The Society had advertised for an executive director with a master of social work degree who would advise the EFSBC Board, supervise and develop programs, supervise the operation of the group home, coordinate planning, and carry a caseload of those who sought the help of the EFSBC from the training school, and provincial and federal prisons. In March 1965, the Society hired Ethel (Mrs. Don) Allardice, B.A., B.S.W., M.S.W., to begin her work in June.[37] With this appointment, the EFSBC began the transformation of its organizational structure, gained credibility as a social welfare agency, and looked ahead to a new era in its work with women in conflict with the law.

Allardice proved helpful in the planning stages of the group home had and supplied the necessary expertise in the search for houseparents. Her qualifications and experience would be indispensable to the EFSBC in all its future undertakings. But, undoubtedly, one of Allardice's most significant duties foreseen by the volunteers who hired her was to preserve an equilibrium between the voluntary and the professional functions of the Society. The decision to hire a social worker was guided by a group of women who believed that the Society had to meet the changing expectations in the field of corrections if it wanted to continue its interests in penal reform and rehabilitation of women. However, these women had no intention of seeing volunteer work devalued, and selected someone who would not have difficulty upholding the voluntary tradition of the EFSBC. Ethel Allardice, the first executive director of the EFSBC, was, quite fittingly, the daughter of Fraudena

Girls settled in to their new bedrooms and decorated their rooms with their favourite things, teddy bears, and photos of their pop stars, the Beatles.

Eaton, one of the founders of the EFSBC; indeed, it had been Eaton who had suggested the Society take the name of Elizabeth Fry. Active in the Local Council of Women, and with twenty years' experience as a volunteer worker in various community organizations before she received her degree in social work, Allar dice had been engaged to maintain a continuity with the past, not sever it.

After her first year with the EFSBC, Allardice addressed the membership and told them: "I am proud of the past history of the Elizabeth Fry Society; I am excited by this very fast-moving present; and confident and challenged by the future."[38] If any Fry volunteers harboured misgivings about the changes in the organizational structure of the EFSBC during the early 1960s that seemed to take the Society so far from its historical beginnings, Allardice's words in her first annual report should have assuaged their fears.

6. THE LIZZIE FRYS
AND THE VOLUNTARY TRADITION

Legal improvements do not occur easily — often they come by violent revolution. But many times the most lasting and beneficial changes finally occur quietly after a long period of effort because "caring people" were persistent, patient, and persuasive. When such people group together to become a cohesive unit, their strength is monumental. If this strength is backed by knowledge and sensitivity, a sense of personal responsibility and initiative, the group can create and maintain an improved situation for those in difficulty. The story of such an association of volunteers is the history of the Elizabeth Fry Society of British Columbia.

EFSBC volunteer Ruth Conlin, "Review of the EFSBC 1970"[1]

In the mid-sixties, the decisions to extend the EFSBC's responsibilities and expertise to meet the increasing need in the community for preventive care ultimately ensured both the credibility of women's voluntary work in the field of corrections and the viability of the Society. However, at the time, these outcomes were not so readily apparent to all Fry members. Although the Society had proceeded cautiously towards the establishment of the group home, the employment of an executive director, and the increasingly complex funding arrangements, the membership was divided in its support for these new directions. Few doubted the need for the Society to instigate preventive care, but many were skeptical about the necessity of hiring a professional social worker. After all, the EFSBC had functioned solely as a voluntary society for twenty-five years and some women felt their customary role would be threatened. Nor could the old-guard Fry members fathom the scale of the Society's financial commitments that would increasingly rely on outside funding, perhaps jeopardizing the autonomy of the EFSBC. Organizational changes to the Society required some re-adjustment both philosophically and practically on the part of the volunteers.

Time would prove the choice of Ethel Allardice as the executive director to have been an effective strategy in maintaining the volun-

Elizabeth Fry Society members (from left) Mrs. T.L. Hackett, Executive Director Ethel Allardice, Grace Black, and Mrs. P.G. Conlin enjoy an informal meeting to discuss fundraising in 1968.

tary character of the Society while contributing to its renewal and expansion. Allardice's years of experience as a volunteer in social service work, her educational specialization in community organizations, and, of course, being the daughter of Fraudena Eaton, renowned clubwoman and founder of the EFSBC, made Allardice an important link to the past traditions of the Fry. She was sensitive both to the history and benefits of voluntary organizations and once remarked that she regarded the volunteers as her bosses.[2] Allardice's work in the field of corrections during her twelve years with the EFSBC, from 1965 to 1978, won her personal citations from Correctional Service Canada as a "strong proponent for progressive policies and programs for female offenders," and enhanced the reputation of the EFSBC. She was also commended for having contributed significantly to the Society's constructive relationship with Correctional Service.

Within a year of Allardice's appointment to the EFSBC, most of the members were persuaded of her value to the Society and enjoyed a good working relationship with her. But several of the old-guard volunteers, who could not fully accept the new EFSBC policies, continued to resent this dependence on a professional worker, complained, "I can't work with social workers" and "what do social workers do anyway?"[3] In turn, the condescending attitudes of some social workers in the field, who regarded volunteers as amateurs likely to prove more of a hindrance than a help, did not alleviate the tensions between the two groups. The prospect of hiring a second social worker in the fall of 1966 to take over the responsibilities of the group home, thus freeing Allardice to supervise the work of the volunteers with the inmates at Oakalla, was to some members evidence of their inevitable subordination and displacement by professional workers. But this was not the only issue to divide the membership that year.

Unrest and uncertainty over the EFSBC's new directions first caused some members to be critical of the decisions made by the house committee, which had been formed to establish the group home. Still uneasy with this financial liability and doubtful about the Society's source of income, several members, particularly those on the finance committee, regarded the house committee's spending with great alarm. Charges were made that this was an ad hoc committee that was functioning without proper authority. Some women on the executive now queried the judgement of this committee regarding the renovations and furnishing of the home. The dissension that accompanied the need for greater spending is suggested by house chairman Lynn Clark's remarks to the finance and house committees in 1965. Clark attempted to place the current squabbles within the larger context of the Society's responsibilities.

> Instead of pulling back every time progress is made we must grow with the project so that we may meet the challenge of greater responsibility and fuller commitment to the community head on. In this way we can create issues and discuss them and reach conclusions about them on the basis of reason, on a basic underlying philosophy, and not on personalities and pettiness.[4]

Because the Society really was breaking new ground, the women on the house committee struggled to find philosophical justification for what seemed to them both practical and correct choices. Questions of whether to paint wooden surfaces in the house, to buy "good" or "better" bedspreads for the girls' rooms, to provide the houseparents petty cash or a charge card for daily expenses worried the consciences of these women.[5] These were not minor issues but reflected the tradition of the EFSBC volunteers to be accountable for their decisions. However, in the face of doubt and uncertainty in one camp, and resolute efficiency in the other, and without any precedents to balance the extremes, a power struggle, of sorts, was predictable.

Throughout 1966, the differences became more difficult to resolve between the old guard, who were understandably reluctant to exchange the familiar ways for the unknown, and the progressives, who were confident that change would, in fact, ensure continuity. Matters came to a head in the fall after a visit to Vancouver from Phyllis Haslam, the executive director of the Elizabeth Fry Society in Toronto. At the suggestion of a board member formerly associated with the Toronto Fry Society, the executive of the EFSBC had invited Haslam to assess the organization of the Society and make some suggestions for its reformation in view of the difficulties it was currently experiencing. She came at her own expense and spent some time meeting with the EFSBC president, the executive director, members, committees, and the agencies that interacted with the Society. At the end of her stay, Haslam discussed her conclusions with the

executive and pointed out that the organizational structure of the
Society was no longer suitable for its increased responsibilities.[6]

In effect, Haslam had confirmed what was all too apparent to
many members. The Society had outgrown but not replaced its original organizational structure and it had become impossible for the
executive to function effectively. (See Organizational Chart 1, page
169.) EFSBC officers had only the specific powers that had been
delegated to them by the members. In other words, the executive
could transact routine business but could not, without the approval
of the membership, make the kinds of decisions that were now necessary to ensure the daily operation of the group home. What was
needed was to invest in the executive the powers normally given to
a board of directors for the smoother management of a society's
business.[7] (See Organizational Chart 2, page 170.)

This sequence of events was the last straw for the old guard
who regarded Haslam's visit and subsequent evaluation of the
EFSBC as being entirely unauthorized by the membership and therefore a contravention of the bylaws. In the opinion of two
long-standing members, who had served in the previous executive,
this action was one more example of the disregard of the members'
rights by "a few individual executive members," and they submitted
their resignations in protest.[8]

With the Society perilously close to disarray, a general meeting
was called to present the legal opinion of the EFSBC's solicitors —
Bull, Housser & Tupper—on the need for constitutional changes,
and to obtain the approval of the membership to begin this process.
The majority of the women in attendance agreed to the necessary
overhaul of the powers of the Society's executive officers in view of
their new responsibilities. After months of revision in November 1967,
an extraordinary general meeting of the EFSBC considered the new constitution and bylaws to set up a board of directors to manage the
business and affairs of the society. In later years, remembering this
period of her presidency, Maida Duncan, who had favoured the new
directions and policies of the EFSBC, wrote, "The majority of members accepted these changes and the way was then clear for the vigour
of the Society to express itself in services to the community, unim-
peded by tangled lines of authority within its own organization."[9]

In the wake of these events, there were a few more resignations
of members unwilling to accompany the Society into this new era.
In retrospect, these former volunteers feel no bitterness and concede
that the changes "were for the best," but still recall their horror at
the mounting expenses and what was, in their eyes, "unnecessary
spending."[10] The EFSBC treasurer during the fundraising for the
group home was one of the women who left the Society in the mid-
sixties because she was convinced that "it had finished being a

volunteer organization and had become professional. There was a new group of people taking over . . . and some ill-feeling over the changes taking place. My husband became an invalid [needing my care] and it was better to leave it [the Society] to new people."[11]

The 1960s was a decade in which many previous assumptions were challenged, and whether it was an issue of social justice or social status, new attitudes caused upheaval at all levels of social organization. Moreover, the perception of the old guard in the EFSBC that volunteers would not have a place in the new order was not totally without foundation. The rising status of professional workers and the concomitant devaluation of volunteerism in social service work was, indeed, at the root of the conflict in the Society. The emphasis in corrections on the model of treatment and rehabilitation, which the EFSBC had supported since the Society's inception, demanded educated practitioners. However, these new professionals, still trying to consolidate their positions in government departments, did not want to compete with untrained personnel. The ideas of the new women's movement that sought greater recognition of women's work in the form of paid employment provided another source of the attack on volunteerism. Throughout North America in the 1960s, women's voluntary work in the field of social welfare seemed doomed to be discredited in the crossfire of a revolution in women's roles that was both technical and ideological. Some of the Fry women expected, therefore, that the advent of the professional worker would subordinate the volunteer, effectively violating the egalitarianism that had characterized the EFSBC.[12]

Although a professional hierarchy often upset the equilibrium of voluntary organizations, this was not the pattern of change that evolved in the EFSBC. Instead, what developed was an unusual partnership of the Society's professional and voluntary personnel. Undoubtedly, the personalities of Ethel Allardice, executive director, and Maida Duncan, president, played a role in this alliance, but the survival of the EFSBC as a voluntary agency can be attributed to the Society's ideology.[13] A strong system of internal beliefs built around the organization's mission and goals preserved the EFSBC's character and, over the years, served as a source of its stability. The mission, or ethos, of the EFSBC rested on dual convictions: that the welfare of women in conflict with the law, although a minor concern in the criminal justice system, should not be neglected; and that it was up to women, as it had been historically, to ensure, perhaps even to define, the just treatment of girls and women while in custody and after-care.

In fact, the ideology that had sustained the EFSBC into the mid-sixties was not undermined by the organizational changes or, in the final analysis, by the hiring of a professional worker. The special qualities of the Fry women, described in the words of Ruth Conlin

The EFSBC ensured that the girls in the group home were assisted by a social worker and received any medical or psychiatric care that was necessary. EFSBC volunteers took the girls on outings and provided various entertainments to stimulate their interest and enjoyment. Here, a volunteer teaches the girls some popular folksongs.

at the beginning of this chapter, ensured that the volunteer remained the vital force at the heart of the Society. Although the reform of the EFSBC had been resisted by old-guard members who found the process too revolutionary, those who remained were won over by the persistence, patience, and persuasiveness — qualities that had always accounted for the Society's success — of the progressive-minded volunteers.

But what accounted for women's continued interest and involvement in voluntary work with the EFSBC? Since the Second World War, the increased acceptability and opportunity for both paid employment and political involvement for married middle-class women surely augured the declining attraction of voluntary work.[14] Interest in prison reform, the treatment of inmates, and the prevention of delinquency were not issues that most people thought about or felt compelled to pursue. Who were the women in the EFSBC and why did they want to spend several afternoons a week in the women's unit at Oakalla, the Willingdon School for Girls, or the Society's office at Main and Hastings?

Appreciatively called the "Lizzie Frys" by the inmates they visited in prison and the girls' school, the EFSBC volunteers were, to casual observers, unremarkable women. The majority were married, middle-aged, and middle-class. In the early history of the Society, these broad characteristics, which signified some economic security and relative independence from child-caring responsibilities, were practically the pre-requisites for women's volunteer work. UBC students of social work and some campus sorority women composed a minority of Fry volunteers, but for them voluntary work was part of an educational program or an organizational service requirement, and they were not necessarily committed to permanent membership in the EFSBC. Generally, women who joined the Society remained members for at least five and, often, up to twenty years or more. It was likely that Fry women had been active in other voluntary work before becoming interested in the EFSBC, but frequently they found their Fry work all-absorbing and chose to drop previous attachments rather than lessen their involvement with the Society.[15]

Conventional wisdom might suggest that religious beliefs or at least altruistic convictions provided Fry women with some common motivation. In fact, until the late 1960s, the EFSBC meetings customarily began with prayer "for guidance." Most members were Protestant, although a few were Catholic or Jewish. However, the Fry women by no means felt that their interest in the Society and its work stemmed from religious zeal and were adamant that members not preach or proselytize while engaged in their Fry work. Generally, Fry volunteers are concerned for the plight of girls and women in a hostile environment both inside and outside of prison; one long-time volunteer declared, "We are all sisters under the skin—one woman's problems are another's."[16] This explanation of allegiance with other women contained no measure of sentiment. It simply affirmed that a female association to ensure that women in conflict with the law received equal treatment as the men (although perhaps different) was deemed necessary by the founders of the EFSBC and continues to attract women fifty years later.

The older women who have been Fry volunteers for many years hold fundamental convictions about putting to work their own strengths, abilities, and experiences for some "useful cause" and "to give back something"; many joined the EFSBC because they "always had an interest in social work," or "the law," or "in teaching girls." One woman found her home economics training useful in planning the group home environment; another, who had worked as a public health nurse among prostitutes in a city in England, found that experience helpful in her visits to the women in Oakalla and their skid road hotels. Other women regarded their work for the Society in terms of their civic responsibilities. One volunteer was adamant that "the volunteer, as a representative of the community, must go into penal institutions because there is too much potential for abuse behind locked doors." Another explained that she felt an obligation as a member of society who was supposedly being protected by the punishment of lawbreakers "to do something for women who were deprived of their freedom and, therefore, their dignity."[17]

Apart from these individual justifications, many Fry women grew up in a home in which one or both of the parents were involved in voluntary community work. They were predisposed, perhaps, to undertake voluntary work because of the example set for them by their parents. Some women recalled their father's philanthropic role in the community but they associated this impulse with his church or business obligations. When it was the mother who was involved, she was often remembered as being an advocate for women's rights and responsibilities outside the home, although in most instances she was herself bound by domestic duties. For Maida Duncan, an active volunteer for the EFSBC since the late 1950s, the pattern was established by her mother, who had helped start a kindergarten for immigrant children in Winnipeg. Maida's mother was a great admirer of women's rights advocate and author Nellie McClung. Maida remembered her mother going to McClung's public lectures and reading her books. From an early age, Maida was involved in her mother's projects and she, herself, became interested in voluntary work after she married and moved to Vancouver. Like other Fry women active in the Fry from the early sixties, Maida was raised in a family environment that actively encouraged volunteerism and regarded it as a female tradition.

For many women who wanted to extend their interests outside the home while maintaining their full-time responsibilities of childcare and homemaking, voluntary work appeared preferable to formal employment. EFSBC volunteers found that the variety of responsibilities and the flexibility of hours enabled their voluntary work to complement their domestic duties. But not all volunteers had their domestic roles defined by the needs of their children; sometimes it was an ailing parent or husband who kept a woman in the home as the prime caregiver. Moreover, husbands and other family members who disapproved of married women seeking paid employment would not object to their involvement in community work. Although Fry women were frequently confronted with the query, "Why aren't you helping more worthy women?" the altruistic nature of volunteer work usually allowed them to pursue their individual interests alongside their family responsibilities, with less criticism.

Undoubtedly, the EFSBC volunteers felt, as one woman expressed, that their work "was a chance to accomplish something quite separate from the usual ties you have as a wife and mother." Although some men, especially if retired, became involved with their wives' volunteer responsibilities, many women regarded their work in the EFSBC as their own world and scarcely discussed their experiences at home. In addition to their commitment to the EFSBC, the volunteers shared an ironic humour that their work—which, as has been discussed in the previous pages, included such diverse and consuming activities as preparing briefs for the government, shopping for bargains for the group home, finding employment for a girl released from Willingdon, or visiting inmates in Oakalla—was seldom regarded as a full-time occupation. One volunteer remembered, "There used to be a joke around the Fry. When your husband came home at night and asked 'What did you do today?' you answered, 'Oh nothing, I was just fooling around!'" Fry women were well aware that work done in their so-called free time, for which no monetary recognition was received, was imperfectly understood by friends and family.

While Fry volunteers would laugh among themselves about how their work was often underestimated, they were not tolerant of outright attempts to trivialize their efforts. Rose Rally recalled her encounter with a police officer in the 1970s.

> I had an appointment to see the police sergeant in charge of Vancouver Court (the old one) about the new courtworker program. He didn't get up when I introduced myself. Instead, he leaned back in his chair and suggested that ladies with time on their hands should play cards or go shopping, and not bother people with real jobs. Grinding my teeth, I told him that I had sent my four children to school, turned my back on messy rooms and a sink full of dirty dishes, had a number of other errands to do, and a little one to pick up at 11:30. My time was a precious commodity and he would bloody well respect it. We looked at each other for the count of ten. Finally he got up, found two cups of coffee, placed one on either side of the desk and gestured me to sit down.[18]

When the responsibilities of homemaking subsided for middle-aged women, they often chose volunteer work rather than paid employment even after it became more acceptable for married middle-class women to seek paid work outside the home. The majority of volunteers in the EFSBC had a university education and/or practical training and had been employed prior to marriage and childbearing. Their need to update skills, the inconvenient hours demanded in occupations such as nursing, an unwillingness to surrender their relative autonomy in the management of their time, and their interest and commitment to their voluntary work kept married women from re-entering the work force.[19] Moreover, women felt that years spent raising their children and managing their households had made them wise and accountable. These qualities were rarely accredited by employers, whereas voluntary organizations recognized and needed workers with these attributes. Fry members liked the variety of opportunities they encountered in the EFSBC. As summed up by a Fry worker who gained experience in all aspects of the Society's work, "The interesting thing about doing volunteer work is you get into all sorts of things you wouldn't get into in paid work, as volunteerism allows you a wider scope."[20]

Some women did, in fact, take on voluntary work in addition to their paid jobs. As one woman put it, "You did your job because you needed the money; you did Fry work because you were interested."[21] The increasing number of members employed in the work force after 1963 was recognized when the EFSBC general meeting in September was scheduled for the early evening instead of the customary time in the morning. Not infrequently, voluntary work provided women with experience that benefitted them in finding employment. In several instances, Fry volunteers were subsequently hired to fill staff positions.

For a few women, membership in the EFSBC or in other women's organizations was a first step in their personal commitment to work for social change. Female political candidates and appointees traditionally emerged from women's club networks. Many of the women in the public eye during the founding years of the Society—Helen Douglas Smith, Laura Jamieson, Tilly Ralston, Helen Gregory MacGill, and Fraudena Eaton—had been active in several women's organizations. More recently, Barbara McDougall, formerly an EFSBC volunteer from 1967 to 1973, was elected as a Progressive Conservative member to the House of Commons and served as a cabinet minister responsible for employment, immigration, and the status of women. As a Fry volunteer, McDougall had been responsible for writing the EFSBC's brief, "Criminal Law and Women Offenders," for the Royal Commission on the Status of Women. The guest speaker at the EFSBC's fiftieth anniversary dinner, the Honourable Barbara McDougall connected her experiences as a Fry visitor to Oakalla with her resolve to ensure that governments address the problems faced by many women in conflict with the law.[22] Another famous PC woman, Flora Macdonald, had been the president of the Elizabeth Fry Society in Kingston in 1969.[23] Undoubtedly, women's club membership helped foster a constituency for women's political ambitions, but more important, those political ambitions often were nurtured by their volunteer work.

Along with the sometimes philanthropic, but usually very practical, reasons for women's interest in the Elizabeth Fry Society, female friendships were an important motivation for women's voluntary work in the Society. Generally, women joined the Fry at the encouragement of a friend who was already a member. Once involved with the EFSBC, women often found themselves affected by the expectations of other members. One woman, Maida Duncan, much respected and loved, inspired others with her commitment and contributions over the past thirty years. Reflecting on why they continued to take up new tasks for the Society, several women stated, "Of course, it was really because of Maida... she lived and breathed the Fry and we would do anything for her."[24] In 1986, Maida Duncan was awarded a medal by the federal government in recognition of her volunteer service to the community. The EFSBC also chose to honour this renowned volunteer when it named its first group home "Duncan House."

A membership that increased by personal recommendations and thrived on mutual admiration served several purposes. Not only was a homogeneity among the membership maintained but also a continuity of purpose. Moreover, by inviting women whose characters and talents were known, an informal control or screening process was exercised. One long-time volunteer suggested that the EFSBC did not like to publicly recruit new members for fear of attracting persons unsuited to the sometimes sensitive work of the Society, notably prison visiting. Marie Legg, an EFSBC member since the late 1960s who served as president in 1968-69 and was a former visitor to Oakalla, observed, "You literally cloned yourself to get a volunteer... it was a great responsibility going into prison and Willingdon... you could do damage without realizing it."[25] There were also limitations to this approach, as noted by a volunteer who visited inmates in Oakalla in the 1960s. Zoe Carter, a member of the EFSBC's independent counselling team, felt there was a need for younger visitors, who might have more in common with some of the women in prison. Yet she admitted that the prison visitor had to be mature enough to withstand the manipulative tactics of many of the inmates, particularly the addicts.[26] Volunteer Grace Black confirmed, "You had to be very disciplined... there was no room for error. One mistake could close down the whole organization."[27]

Although visiting the inmates at Oakalla is only one of the ways that Fry volunteers aid women in conflict with the law, most members of the public, if they know anything about the Society's namesake, associate the Lizzie Frys with this aspect of their work and are curious about it. For the majority, a prison is a dreaded place, replete with horror stories, where none would willingly venture. While few people can imagine a society without prisons, most realize the limitations of incarceration and comfort themselves with the belief that those "doing time" have only themselves to blame. Generally, attempts to inject any humanity into the prison facilities or routine are regarded as profligate spending of public funds on the unworthiest of individuals. In fact, the inhabitants of prisons are barely acknowledged as persons at all. They are called prisoners,

inmates, convicts, criminals, cons, hookers, thieves, addicts, alcoholics, and above all, guilty. Stereotypes of a different kind have hidden
the faces of the EFSBC prison visitors. Over the years, the Fry
women have demonstrated to a thoughtless public that the inmates
were, after all, people. The Lizzie Frys, too, were people, neither
saintly paragons nor self-sacrificing do-gooders; each woman had to
reconcile her intentions with the stern reality of entering the prison.

The emotions and experiences of the Fry women, who on
Wednesday evenings or Friday afternoons might disappear from
their kitchens or gardens to mingle with "the girls in blue," seldom
have been recounted.[28] Amongst themselves they joke about their
encounters to ease the tension and relieve the despair, but Fry
women seek above all to preserve the dignity of the women in prison
and they do not repeat their stories for entertainment. Although their
motivations for becoming Fry members and volunteering to visit the
women in Oakalla were varied, EFSBC women all held the same misgivings each time they approached the prison gate. And they
welcomed the fresh air when they went back outside!

In an institution notorious for its visual regularity, perhaps it is
not odd that the dominant impressions retained by visitors to the
women's prison at Oakalla are its sounds and smells. In retrospect,
the volunteers are less sure about the details of the appearance of
the rooms, what colours and whether there were pictures . . . "proba-
bly the Queen's portrait in the visitor's waiting room . . . " but the
noise of doors being locked behind them and the odour of "clean"
has forever been etched in their memories.

> We went in the rotten old door, with the rotten old gate that
> would clang, clang, clang behind us . . . and then the smell of
> clean, forced clean, of wax and all the cleaning fluids in the world,
> mixed with some smell of dinner from the kitchen . . . that "clean"
> was too much![29]

While most volunteers experienced some initial nervousness at
being in the prison, a few found their discomfort overshadowed the
purpose of their visit as the inmates sensed their uneasiness and
would not open up to them. But for those who adjusted to the
unfamiliar surroundings and established a fairly comfortable rapport with the women inside, these meetings became a routine.
Although the Lizzie Frys were counselled not to interrogate the inmates about the reasons for their being in Oakalla, these women
were not shy about delving for the motives of their visitors. Unused
to the attentions of anyone who did not expect something in return,
the inmates would initially quiz the volunteers about why they
came. Zoe Carter, who was a member of the EFSBC individual coun-

selling group that went regularly into Oakalla from the mid-1960s, recalled how perplexed the women were by the interest of the Fry volunteers.

> I told them that we were interested in them and wanted to do what we could to help them stay out of jail. I offered to help them find a job or training so that they might get their children back when they were released. They couldn't believe we would do it without pay.[30]

Carter observed that many of the women they visited had been abused by both women and men all their lives and it took a while for them to accept the caring that the Lizzie Frys offered. However, the Fry visitors believed that the fact that they were not salaried professionals eventually ensured a good rapport with the women in prison. EFSBC's executive director, Ethel Allardice, recognized the success that a voluntary corps could have and initiated counselling groups. With Allardice available as back-up in the event of the need for professional expertise, individual volunteers met with several of the inmates for discussions. The volunteers found they were able to establish trusting relationships with the inmates that the social workers in their official capacity could not always maintain.

Apart from the counselling groups and the entertainment committees, the basic function of the EFSBC Oakalla volunteers was to offer friendship to the inmates and to bring the outside community into the prison.

> We met them in groups for tea or coffee . . . it was always interesting . . . we always had an embroidered tablecloth, carefully ironed and starched by the women. They always wore clean uniforms . . . we were their guests coming to see them. It was rather more so than if you called in at my house! The rooms we went into were as tidy as could be . . . ashtrays cleaned out. (I know the staff wouldn't allow it to be dirty, but we were their guests . . . a touch of normalcy.) How many of those women in their own rooms they lived in had the opportunity to have starched cloths on their table? Betcha not many! Everyone became a little more normally human in those sessions.[31]

The inmates offered their Lizzie Frys tea in the manner they imagined their guests were accustomed. The Fry women, in turn, engaged the prison women in activities—sewing and craftwork using clay, batik, macramé, and beadwork—to offer some relief from their habitual pastimes. The unspoken agreement was to effect normalcy— and each group projected what that might mean to the other in this very abnormal setting.

The Fry women organized dances (sock hops), sing-songs, volleyball and ping-pong in the gym. But mostly they shared conversations with the inmates and endeavoured to satisfy their requests. The wants and needs of the women in prison ranged from felt-tip pens to copies of the Criminal Code of Canada. From November 1973 to November 1974, Fry visitors helped female inmates obtain passes to look for work after their release, brought them articles of clothing, found places for the women to stay after their release, wrote for news of the prisoner's family members, looked for someone to put up bail, relayed phone messages, provided information about a pre-sentence report, paid the rent outstanding and forwarded the personal effects of a woman going to the Kingston Penitentiary, and advised women about the terms of their sentences and the processes of appeal and parole.[32]

Not all volunteers were suited to prison visiting. Grace Black laughingly concluded this aspect of Fry work "wasn't my thing because I was too easily taken in . . . they could make me believe anything." Some EFSBC members were simply overwhelmed by the personal histories of the inmates or the magnitude of the task at hand and preferred to work "behind the scenes." One volunteer stopped visiting Oakalla when her own children matched the ages of the youthful drug users or "flower children" caught up in the drug culture of the sixties. She felt she would "lose the balance for making judgements."[33]

Self-knowledge was essential to the well-being of the Fry volunteer and her ability to continue as an effective prison visitor. The older Fry women remember a volunteer whose personal preoccupations and search for her own identity left her confused about her role in the EFSBC and her relationship with the Oakalla women. Eventually she became absorbed by her efforts to find out what it was like to live their lives and abandoned her family to move in with a woman discharged from prison. This was a unique occurrence among Fry volunteers but they understood the temptations.

> It was easy to get carried away . . . you wanted to help them so much you could put yourself in a terrible position. . . . You had to harden yourself . . . they could be so manipulative . . . unless you've worked with addicts you can't understand.[34]

The volunteer had to be able to maintain her objectivity in the face of her sympathy for the women in prison. The fact that the Fry women lived very different lives from the girls and women they visited was a strength. As one volunteer wrote, "I think the girls are hungry to relate to someone who is different from themselves. Their own points of view they know only too well, if you like. Learning happens when you get this diversity of view point."[35]

Apart from a secure personal image and a mature outlook, the qualities that made a good prison visitor were evident in the ability of the volunteer to conform to prison protocol while seeking its reform. Above all, she had to remember that she visited the prison as a member of the Elizabeth Fry Society and not as an autonomous citizen. Sometimes the struggle to balance these conflicting impulses called for hard choices. One Fry volunteer, who decided independently to supply legal counsel to a young woman injured, apparently, as a result of police brutality, caused a temporary hiatus in the Fry's visiting program.[36] The EFSBC was placed on the defensive by this individual's action, which appeared to carry the approbation of the Society, therefore exceeding its mandate. The Society had to clarify its purposes in going into Oakalla to prison social workers who regarded the personal involvement of volunteers in the legal problems of inmates as being inappropriate. Fry members generally viewed this experience as an isolated misunderstanding of the Fry volunteers' responsibilities but it heightened their awareness of the thin line on which they walked.

Following the installation of the executive director, the process of screening prison visitors was formalized with more extensive interviewing of prospective candidates, and each woman spent a pre-requisite period as an EFSBC member before she was permitted to go into Oakalla. Ironically, it was after the Fry's implementation of this more rigorous selection process, and the prison's tightening of bureaucratic procedures in the late 1970s, that a volunteer found herself compromised by a prisoner's devious ingenuity. After accompanying a woman on a day pass to a family birthday dinner, the volunteer returned her charge to Oakalla. A subsequent search uncovered that the inmate was in possession of a contraband drug. Although the EFSBC volunteer was required to file a report accounting for every minute that the inmate was in her custody, her adherence to established procedures and the longstanding reputation of the Society saved the volunteer from any culpability.

However, this incident within a context of increasing drug use and violence among women prisoners drew attention to the vulnerability of the Fry volunteers, who were not assured of any special treatment by the RCMP. Oakalla had tightened security and the Fry visitors had to have their cars checked for drugs when they went out to visit. They asked the RCMP what would happen to them if drugs were found taped to their cars. They were told that "the police would be very considerate of the Elizabeth Fry, no question, but *they* would be *in there* and not visiting!"[37]

By the late sixties, the EFSBC had advised its volunteers against taking women on leave from Oakalla into their own homes because of the risks to the household if the police suspected the inmate was hiding narcotics. By the eighties, there were new government regulations in response to an increasingly fearful public. Fry women were no longer permitted to accompany inmates on outdoor excursions. Although the Lizzie Frys had never felt personally threatened, in retrospect, Beth Weese, a petite Fry volunteer who often escorted Oakalla women to look for jobs in the 1970s, is somewhat astounded at her confidence on those occasions.

> I look back on it and I think it really was courageous. It didn't bother me then but I would frequently have gals twice the size of me and I guess anything could have happened! But I trusted them and never had any problems. . . .[38]

Mutual trust was, in fact, the basis of the most enduring relationships between Fry volunteers and women in conflict with the law. However, trust was undermined when, as was increasingly the case in Oakalla, the inmate had a drug dependency. The Fry women admit ruefully, "the drugs ruined everything." The success rate for rehabilitating addicts involved in criminal activities was very discouraging. Initially hopeful that the methadone clinics would provide addicts with an alternative to illegal dealings to support their habit, Fry members became quickly disillusioned. They realized that addicts going in for treatment were being beseiged by drug pushers of all kinds. However, Fry volunteers continued to offer their support to even the most hardened addict in the hopes that their friendship might make the difference.

Volunteers like Barbara Eacrett, who has been teaching crafts to the female inmates for twenty years because she "wouldn't like to let them down," and Zoe Carter, who "tried to show them I cared" with her weekly counselling sessions, believed they made a difference.[39] It was difficult to go into Oakalla each week if there was any doubt or cynicism. Frequently, in an effort to maintain some sort of lifeline, the Society and its volunteers maintained connections with the women from Oakalla after their release. After 1968, the EFSBC was increasingly involved in the supervision of parole and sometimes distributed the welfare cheques of their clients from the Society's office. Carter explained that it was impossible for volunteers to go all over the city (although she used to check regularly on one woman who lived with her baby in a room in a skid road hotel). The parolees were encouraged to come in to the Fry office because:

> . . . for many addicts it was seen as part of their rehabilitation to get down to the Fry office. Some would stay in bed all day too scared to get the bus, or would get to the office and be too scared to get in the elevator. They are people who are not part of the general population. They find it difficult to cope day to day . . . they need a lot of support . . . their families gave up on them, but

you can't blame them . . . you have to work with them one-on-one for
years . . . you hate to think there is someone you cannot get to.[40]

Carter and other Fry women also assisted women on an informal and friendly basis after their discharge from Oakalla. At an
EFSBC volunteer workshop in 1972, a former inmate in attendance
spoke of the importance of this relationship. She said the relationships that are formed inside with the volunteer should continue in
the street, "because you are the people we respect."[41] Whether it was
to prepare for a wedding, or to encourage them to stick with a
tough job or a challenging course, Fry women continued to help the
women they had befriended in prison. Sometimes they were dinner
guests in the volunteer's home; sometimes the guest provided a
fresh-caught salmon. Regrettably, relationships were sometimes re-
established due to the woman's return to Oakalla, or their discovery
by an EFSBC visitor on a tour of the federal prison for women in
Kingston. Even more unfortunate were the friendships that ended
abruptly when a woman was found dead from a drug overdose or a
beating inflicted by her pimp and drug dealer.

Their loyalty and commitment made it difficult for EFSBC volunteers to retire from active service unless they became disheartened.
In the late seventies, Carter made this decision after she had moved
some distance away, both in the sense of her relocating to another
part of the lower mainland and her experiencing a change in her
attitude towards what was being accomplished in corrections. She
felt, "I had accomplished all I could. I was still interested in rehabilitation but my attitude had hardened toward the constant, hard-core
criminal behaviour." Carter recognized her disillusionment when,
one night, she refused a collect call from a former inmate. Although
this person, an alcoholic whose numerous children had all been
taken from her, called from time to time over the years, and Carter
had always accepted the charges, talked to her, and sometimes sent her
money, she believed at that instance, "I wasn't doing her any good."[42]

Helplessness and frustration were common dilemmas for Fry
women. Maida Duncan remembered a time when "frustration was too
mild a word" to describe how she felt as she witnessed how bureaucracy could thwart the intentions of a drug addict to kick her habit.

> I worked closely with one girl and I felt if she could be supported
> after her release she would be willing to go on a methadone pro-
> gram. She was very talented and artistic and able to get work. I
> used to drive her to work every day and to the methadone clinic —
> but old friends found her and got her to buy drugs. Her boyfriend
> was out on bail and she got drugs from him. After he was sen-
> tenced for seven years, she phoned me and said she wanted off
> drugs and needed my help. Her mother then talked to me on the

phone and I could hear crying and screaming in the background and I said if they could get her dressed I would take her to the hospital. I tried to get her in to the addiction clinic but the doctor was away for the weekend . . . there was no one to help me. Also they said I had to have proof she was on heroin before they would give her methadone. When I picked her up at home her mother and sister had her dressed and had done her hair and she looked lovely. I took her to emergency at the General Hospital but they wouldn't accept her! I couldn't believe it but she told me they wouldn't take her when she had come herself, earlier. They said she couldn't be in that bad shape because she looked too good. I told them her mother had made an effort to fix her up. I eventually had to drop her at the corner of Main and Hastings . . . it was one of the most awful things I ever had to do. There was no help for her any other way . . . I knew what she was going to do . . . but I left her there. There was no way she could get methadone that day. But I felt that was a real turning point in her life, if she would have been taken in and given some treatment, I had great hopes in it working for her. But she had to show [the clinic] urine samples for three days to show that she was an addict. They wouldn't give her methadone in case she wasn't. That meant she had to get her drugs illegally downtown and to leave her there for three days . . . well, she was gone.[43]

But far from forcing volunteers into retirement, these experiences usually helped them to define the future directions of the EFSBC. Duncan's experience and other similar stories strengthened Fry women's resolve to establish a residence for women who came out of Oakalla, or who faced a crisis and needed immediate care. Duncan believed, "If we had had a residence that day for supportive help, we would not have had to let that girl go. She was eventually picked up and served a long term in Kingston. One year she sent me a Christmas card which said, 'Sorry I've disappointed you.' But I felt *we* had let *her* down."[44]

A residence, or halfway house, for women released from Oakalla, could not stir the same public enthusiasm as a group home for girls. But the EFSBC had never confined itself to popular causes. In 1969 the Lizzie Frys prepared to work hard to satisfy this urgent need for women and continued to develop programs in the relatively new field of after-care.

The Elizabeth Fry Society of British Columbia emerged from the organizational upheaval of the mid-1960s with its mission intact and its goals reaffirmed. As anticipated by its progressive faction, the partnership of voluntary and professional EFSBC workers expanded the realm of what was possible for a prisoners' aid society to achieve. Although by the 1970s and 1980s the EFSBC was becoming an increasingly sophisticated social service agency, its members showed no sign of relinquishing the voluntary tradition.

> *It has never been . . . either desirable or practical to isolate people in conflict with the law from the world of which they will always be a part. The influences they encounter from correctional staff, probation and parole officers, agencies such as the Elizabeth Fry Society, and the community at large overlap so materially that it is impossible to judge where one begins and the other ends. The opportunities for liaison between the prison community and the whole community are enormous.*
>
> Summary of EFSBC Achievements and Objectives, 1970[1]

Since the first years of the Society's formation, the Fry women had looked to reforming the institutions of corrections to make them more conducive to the rehabilitation of offenders. But the EFSBC's work with female inmates reinforced an awareness that incarceration was, at best, a last resort. Although the EFSBC could neither support the militant position for decarceration that was held by prison abolitionists, nor agree with radical feminists who argued that economic and sexual autonomy for women would eliminate the need for women's prisons, the Society did believe that women in conflict with the law needed more positive interventions than imprisonment.[2] The 1970s and 1980s thus proved to be decades in which the EFSBC sought to reduce the extent to which the criminal justice system continued to eclipse the community.[3] In other words, the Society increasingly looked for ways that the proven or potential offender might benefit from social services within the community. In practical terms, in addition to providing more group homes for teenagers, the Society's initiatives would include a women's residence for released inmates, and programs to help women cope with some of the specific problems that had led to their conflict with the law. Also in these decades, the EFSBC would provide support for a more extensive provincial and national network of Elizabeth Fry Societies that would link penal reformers in all parts of the country. As suggested above by the words cited from the 1970 EFSBC "Report on Achievements and Objectives," Fry women believed the opportu-

The success of the first group living home led to a succession of Fry homes. Cambridge House was established in Burnaby in 1967.

The EFSBC operated Orenda House, in Burnaby, from 1969.

nities for bridging the communities inside and outside the prison walls were enormous.

By April 1968, the Society had strengthened its commitment to preventive care with the purchase of a second group home for adolescent girls and, before the year's end, was planning for yet a third. A year later an old farmhouse that was part of a well-known berry farm in Burnaby was bought and refurbished to become the Fry's fourth home. The process of fundraising, locating, renovating and licensing these properties, not to mention pacifying hostile neighbours, differed little from the Society's experience setting up Duncan House, the EFSBC's first group home in Vancouver (see chapter five). New federal legislation that provided special mortgage loans for charitable purposes from the Central Mortgage and Housing Corporation eased the strain on the Society's financial resources in the purchase of subsequent homes. CMHC funded one hundred percent of the cost, and in the case of older homes, provided a residential rehabilitation assistance program in the form of grants up to $500 per bed. The EFSBC was the first in Canada to apply for one of these mortgages and led the way for similar ventures by other agencies. Houses bought under these terms were limited to a certain use and could not be sold to any other than a non-profit society without the approval of CMHC. That provision actually enabled the EFSBC, in 1977, to take over an existing mortgage of a group home built by the Action Line Children's Village Society in Burnaby and assume the responsibility for the operation of the Burnaby Receiving Home—the fifth group home operated by the Fry Society. Inman House (the name referred to the street where it was located) provided emergency twenty-four hour residential care for adolescents for up to six weeks.[4]

Prior to the availability of the special CMHC loans, the EFSBC directed considerable energy towards fundraising in order to purchase its group homes. Although the provincial government promised capital grants for one-third of the total cost of the first four group homes, the EFSBC had to show clear title to each property before these monies would be awarded. The business of raising and managing donations to the Society, therefore, occupied much of the volunteers' time. The EFSBC appealed to the government to modify its regulations in light of the Society's goals to provide preventive care. With British Columbia's juvenile crime rate the highest per capita in Canada (figures for 1961 showed B.C. had 605 juvenile delinquents per 100,000 population, well over the national rate of 392 per 100,000),[5] the Fry's efforts eventually drew the notice of legislators. The EFSBC won the attention of the Honourable Grace McCarthy, Social Credit MLA, who, in the manner of her female predecessors in the legislature, worked on the Society's behalf to

EFSBC's Inman House, or the Burnaby Receiving Home, was established in 1977.

The Vancouver Receiving Home has been operated by the EFSBC since 1978.

ensure the government's support, streamline provincial funding, and expedite bureaucratic procedures.

The lower mainland community that had responded so favourably to the EFSBC's fundraising efforts, contributing $30,000 in 1965 and $31,000 in 1968, continued to take a financial interest in the Fry's group homes. In 1969 over $13,000 in proceeds from the Siwash Auction (Society for the Welfare of Arts, Sciences, and Health) was donated to the EFSBC. In the previous year, the Vancouver Foundation had pledged ten percent of the total cost, which was the amount the Society had to raise, and the Vancouver Junior League paid for furnishings for the third group home.[6] A national women's organization, with chapters in many Canadian cities, the Junior League helped to establish social services, promote educational issues, and support penal reform.[7]

In May 1969, the EFSBC became a member agency of the United Community Services. Funding from this source could not be used to operate group homes but could provide for additional staff, social workers, and office space. As a recipient of United Appeal donations, the Society was able to move into a system of planned program budgeting. Although some Fry women were concerned that the EFSBC might lose a measure of its autonomy, most were convinced that membership in the United Community Services (United Way) would establish the reputation of the Society as a recognized part of the social work services of the community.[8]

Clearly, the Fry had succeeded in more than providing young girls from emotionally inadequate homes with a caring familial environment. In winning the support of people in public office and in service organizations, the Society had brought government and members of the community to a realization of their responsibilities and an expression of their commitment to preventive treatment for girls who might be headed for trouble. Thus the EFSBC had come nearer to another of its major objectives, that of changing attitudes towards crime and punishment, in this case, juvenile delinquency.

Willingness of the public to contribute dollars to the Fry's homes for girls did not necessarily translate into unreserved acceptance when it came time for the Society to purchase a house. Homeowners were seldom enthusiastic at the prospect of a group home for troubled teenagers being located on their block. Individuals might agree, in principle, to ideas for more innovative and humanitarian treatment of delinquency, but most people argued in favour of the status quo when they felt uncertain of the impact of these changes on their own lives. Thus the pioneering efforts of individuals or social agencies to integrate correctional programs, whether preventive or after-care, into the community were likely to arouse fear and opposition. The EFSBC encountered these reactions from neighbours each time it established a new group home. Members of the Society attempted to dispel hysteria and alarm with personal interaction and information sessions with neighbourhood groups. After the home was occupied by houseparents and children, the EFSBC invited neighbours to an open house to further assuage any doubts about its respectability or its threat to the community. Seldom were there any complaints from residents after a home was in operation, an indication that ignorance had been displaced by knowledge, fear had been replaced by trust, and opposition had been converted to support. According to Mamie Maloney's editorial in the *Vancouver Sun* in September 1967, residents who, two years earlier, had petitioned to stop the first EFSBC home from being located in their neighbourhood, now called the houseparents to see if the girls were available to baby-sit.[9] Of course acceptance by the community was a vital part of the positive socialization that was being offered to the juveniles. But from the Fry's perspective, it was equally beneficial to have increased the public's tolerance and understanding of these needy children.

Fry women were heartened by the greater concern for juveniles reflected in the MacLeod Report on Juvenile Delinquency in 1966.[10] In addition to other reforms to the juvenile court, the MacLeod committee recommended the abandonment of the old labels of "incorrigible" and "unmanageable" that allowed children to be placed in junior prisons or training schools. According to the report, children apprehended in this regard should be recognized for what they were: youngsters in need of protection, discipline, or supervision.[11] The aim of this review of juvenile court procedures and the Juvenile Delinquents Act was to curb the use of "quasi-criminal legislation" to deal with anti-social behaviour that was, essentially, a matter of social welfare. Certainly the EFSBC had been thinking along these lines for a number of years. The motivation for the EFSBC's group homes had been to provide counselling and psychiatric treatment, in addition to a nurturing environment, in the hope of averting adolescents from future legal conflicts.

The membership was content but never complacent concerning the EFSBC's expanded role as a social service agency. In fact, new responsibilities for the Society always seemed to reveal increased opportunities to assist women in conflict with the law. In the late 1960s, as each group home had filled to capacity and the Society was forced to turn away applicants, Fry members had set about planning the next facility. But the success of the group homes also encouraged some women to return to an idea that had been around the Fry since the 1940s. A number of Fry volunteers reactivated the old dream of establishing a hostel, in this later era often termed a halfway house, where women might reside after they left Oakalla. From their first contact with female inmates, Fry women had seen the necessity for after-care to ease the re-entry of discharged prisoners and to reinforce their intentions to stay away from their former haunts and habits. Although the Society originally considered establishing a hostel for women in the early 1960s, the EFSBC had been convinced of the pre-eminent need for homes that might divert young girls from delinquency. The idea of a women's hostel had thus been set aside when the Society decided to pursue preventive care for girls.

In retrospect, the group homes had proved to be a good choice for the EFSBC, which needed to secure a track record and win popular support in its initial years as an expanding social service agency. Not that the Fry women sought popular issues when it came to penal reform, but the fact that the Fry had gained credibility with both the prison and the outside communities and also with the provincial government, which paid per diem costs for the girls placed in the homes, enabled the EFSBC to pursue a women's residence—a project far less appealing to the public.

The EFSBC's concern for the women at Oakalla had not waned despite the energy that was directed throughout the sixties to the building of the group homes. A stalwart group of volunteers worked closely with the Fry's executive director, Ethel Allardice, to provide group and individual counselling to female offenders. The chief matron of the women's unit at Oakalla, Bessie Maybee, and the Fry volunteers shared a mutual regard for each other's dedication to the best interests of the inmates. Out of this respect had grown the Fry volunteers' increased responsibilities that included taking inmates out on day passes to look for jobs.

Although the EFSBC brought speakers to Oakalla to talk to inmates about their future, the Fry women were anxious to take more substantial steps to alleviate the problems faced by women after their discharge. EFSBC work in Oakalla had alerted volunteers to the immediate plight of women after their release from prison. The Fry women who had ventured into the skid road boarding houses to retrieve clothing for the inmates had glimpsed the grim reality of their lives on the outside. The volunteers had also seen the "boyfriends" and "husbands," alias pimps and drug pushers, who waited at the prison gate to ferry the discharged women back to "work" on the city streets.[12] Fry women sometimes forestalled these reunions by transporting the released inmate to the bus depot and paying her fare to her home town. But without a support system to help withstand the recurrence of physical abuse, drug dependency, or alcohol addiction, the women tended to drift back to the city where the cycle of events leading to Oakalla was often repeated. (See Table 5, page 164.)

The idea of a hostel had been around almost from the beginning of the EFSBC when the volunteers realized that many women released from prison had no alternative but to go back to their former haunts. Later in 1953, Fry volunteers seeking rooms for women on probation experienced the rejection that undoubtedly faced former inmates. Landladies in "respectable" boarding houses, afraid of trouble from "problem girls" who might be addicts and attract undesirable associates into their rooms, were unwilling to have probationers on their premises.[13] Unable to obtain any significant response to a public plea for accommodation for these women, the EFSBC again considered the idea of a hostel.

An additional incentive was derived from another source. In 1959, the Toronto Elizabeth Fry Society had established a hostel along the lines of a halfway house for women released from prison.

While it was evident to volunteers who were familiar with the Oakalla women that a hostel or residence was a matter of great urgency and should be a part of the EFSBC program, as with any new initiative they had to convince the EFSBC Board. Early in 1968 eleven volunteers formed a committee to determine "how the E. Fry Society could aid women from prison and women in conflict with the law who require accommodation."[14] Volunteers were already providing rooms in their homes to former inmates in need of immediate shelter, but both the Society and the RCMP foresaw the risk to Fry members and their families in the event that their guest was suspected of any drug dealing.[15] Also, a plan to have the YWCA coordinate referrals with available beds in hostels around the city had not proved successful.[16]

In wanting to establish a residence, the Fry women were concerned implicitly with the inmates' dependencies on drug and alcohol. In the years of working with women at Oakalla, it had become apparent to the Fry that much of female crime was rooted in substance abuse—a perception that is reflected in the data on female offenders. (See Tables 1-3, pages 162 and 163.) For many women, drugs and alcohol constituted both the problem and the solution in the cycle of despair and entrapment that characterized their lives. Too frequently women (often Native women) were apprehended while under the influence of alcohol, charged with vagrancy because they could give neither a permanent address nor show any means of support, and sentenced to Oakalla. (See Table 8, page 166.) As described by Maida Duncan in the previous chapter, in their attempts to aid former inmates wanting to kick their drug addictions, volunteers had experienced first-hand the frustration of trying to effect intervention without adequate support. Prison visitors had seen the devastating effects of alcohol and drug dependencies on women's lives and had long been advocates of a treatment centre as well as the need, in some cases, to sentence a person for treatment. A large part, though not the whole, of the EFSBC's motivation for wanting a women's residence was to provide refuge and treatment for women seeking rehabilitation of this kind.

Coincident with the first meetings held by the residence committee was the passing of new legislation in B.C. to amend the procedures of arrest and detainment of individuals picked up on alcohol offences.[17] In this Bill 101, a new section dealing with chronic alcoholics provided magistrates with greater powers to commit an intoxicated person to a psychiatric institution for observation and treatment. The Fry women had several reservations. Although they had always been dissatisfied with the quick release and lack of medical treatment of a person picked up in an intoxicated state, they recognized the potential violation of civil liberties if individuals were detained for any length of time without charge.[18] The EFSBC regarded rehabilitation as preferable either to confinement in prison or a mental hospital. Nevertheless, the spirit of this new legislation paralleled the view held by the Fry women that there must be alternatives to incarceration for chronic alcoholism.

The fact remained that there were few such alternatives for women. The Salvation Army's Miracle Valley retreat, near Mission, B.C., for twenty-five to thirty men, had had a waiting list since 1963. A similar facility for women was not available. A federal institution in Matsqui opened in 1966 that promised to be a model treatment centre for criminal offenders (both men and women) serving two-year sentences who were addicted to drugs. However, neither Matsqui's relatively pleasant physical setting nor prison security were able to guarantee results; this program was abandoned within ten years and Matsqui became a medium security institution for men. In the residence committee's discussions with the Vancouver Social Service Department, Teen Challenge (a drug treatment centre run by an inter-denominational church group), the Alcoholism Foundation of B.C., the Narcotic Foundation, the matron of Oakalla Women's Unit, the Department of Social Planning and Development, and the Indian Post-Release Centre,[19] there was a consensus that for any rehabilitation program to be effective, an individual needed to live in a residence as part of her sentence or as a condition of parole. Even then, it was understood that only those individuals who positively committed themselves to the program would have a good chance for success.[20] It appeared evident to the residence committee that the lack of any residential care or programs for women leaving prison would likely prolong their stay behind bars.

The committee also became aware of other inequities that constrained women's opportunities to serve part of their sentences outside prison. Although the EFSBC was increasingly involved in supervising female parolees and probationers, the residence committee noted that men were more frequently paroled than women. Some of the reasons for this were discovered in the course of investigating the facilities currently operating in the city. Members of the EFSBC visited the Salvation Army's Catherine Booth Home, the Sancta Maria House run by the Catholic Church, the East Enders Society and the inter-denominational St. Leonard's House[21] and found little accommodation for women.[22] Not only were there few beds available, there were neither programs nor treatment opportunities. Again, it seemed clear to the Fry committee that, with fewer after-care services for women than men, there was less incentive for the parole board to release women. A post-release residence with surroundings conducive to rehabilitation would certainly ensure women a greater opportunity for parole.[23]

The residence committee knew that many women leaving prison had few options other than to return to their familiar but unsuitable rooms in neighbourhoods associated with their old pastimes. From 1966 the Society aided the City Social Service in the weekly distribution of welfare cheques to single female clients (former inmates, usually suffering from low self-esteem and drinking problems) living in the skid road area of the city.[24] Fry women reasoned that a residence would surely provide an immediate alternative to old patterns of relocation in skid road. Supporters of a women's residence sought to establish a supportive environment in which a discharged woman could reflect on her life and establish long- and short-term goals.

After a year of research, which had confirmed in the minds of the members of the committee that a residence for women was a necessary and overdue project for the Society, the committee presented its findings to the EFSBC board. Proud of their work and full of conviction about their recommendations, the volunteers were stunned by the cautious reception of the members of the board.[25] The committee was told there were too many unanswered questions, particularly about controlling the mix of ages, experiences, and different problems of the residents. In short, the board needed more information and greater clarification, but committee members feared the hesitation was unjustified. Some of the Fry women felt angry that this project had been rejected at this time and believed that the board was perhaps too eager to follow the line of least resistance and continue "to concentrate on the kids."[26]

This was not the first time that the residence committee members had encountered attempts to dissuade them from their purpose. In their discussions with the Department of Social Planning for Vancouver, Joan Greenwood, Betsy Bennett, and Maida Duncan had been advised unequivocally against expanding the Fry's services in this direction. In fact, they were told that it was extremely difficult to change the lives of older women and, in view of the Society's success with the group homes, it would be wise to continue working with young girls and "not to expand too far or too fast."[27] The Fry women had responded to this advice the same as they did to the board's lukewarm reception; they reflected on the evidence that had been gathered and resumed their efforts with an even greater determination to overcome the obstacles.

If anything, resistance tended to strengthen the commitment of the Fry volunteers to their ideas for reform. They were not blind to reason but realized it was not their aim to uphold the status quo, especially when the chief impediment to change was its degree of difficulty. Mindful of the Society's purpose to promote constructive attitudes, procedures and rehabilitative programs, and to assist female offenders, the hostel committee resolved to satisfy the board's misgivings with further planning. Six months later, the committee's additional research proved more convincing to the board. The EFSBC was now ready to contemplate a residence for young female adults referred by Probation and Parole Services, Children's Aid Society, YWCA, Social Welfare, judges, lawyers, institutions, or those who might seek it out for themselves.[28]

By February 1970, Marie Legg, formerly president of EFSBC from 1968 to 1969 and a diligent proponent of a women's residence, was able to report that a realtor who had promised (in his words) "to keep an eye out for a home for the dollies," had located a house for the Fry to consider. (The Fry's efforts to win respect for their clients' needs seemingly began with their consultations with male real estate agents.) In striving to reduce the anticipated barriers to setting up this residence, Legg and the other committee members had focused on properties in an industrial district where there would be no householders to complain about its establishment. The plan was to rent a house for two to three years on an experimental basis and to review its success before making a commitment to purchase. The Fry was introduced to a willing landlord, who owned an old house "with possibilities" near 2nd Avenue and Ontario Street. The fact that it needed a new roof, new floors, and plumbing had not deterred the current occupants, about two dozen squatters. The Society felt mildly guilty about evicting these unofficial tenants until it learned the house had been an armed camp. The guns and ammunition that had been left behind filled a half-ton truck!

After major repairs and renovations were completed, the EFSBC prepared to welcome its first occupants. Despite somewhat uncertain funding arrangements at the outset, the EFSBC had agreed to rent this house for $300 per month for the first year and $265 for the second and third. The financial responsibilities for operating the residence required a great deal of support from the community and the provincial government. In this venture the EFSBC's reputation for high performance and balanced books served as collateral. The Junior League donated $10,800 to pay the houseparents' salary, rent, heat, light, and telephone for nearly nine months. After much effort on the part of EFSBC members and the executive director, the provincial government initially agreed to pay $600 per month. But the government's commitment in the form of permanent funding arrangements had not been formally established and the operation of the residence was not secure. The Vancouver and Donner Foundations offered to help the Society with monthly subsidies until the provincial government approved a further $500 which would keep the residence open.[29] (Volunteers had used every method of persuasion to move government officials. For example, well-connected volunteers whose social circles intersected with those of the attorney general remembered, "we were not above unrelenting badgering.")[30]

By 1971 the residence received support also from the National Parole and Probation Service.[31] As in its endeavours with the group homes, the EFSBC had taken an important initiative towards community-based corrections for women but its first task had been to influence government policy and redirect government spending.

After three and a half years, the Society evaluated the needs of its clients and reviewed the prospects of continuing the residential program. The ninety young women who had stayed in the home during this period ranged in age from fifteen to twenty-five years with the average age being twenty-two. They were women currently before the courts, sentenced to a correctional institution, just released from an institution, on probation, or parole.[32] Thirty-five were heroin addicts, twenty-five were alcoholics, eighteen were soft drug users, and eleven had been arrested for fraud and theft. The average length of stay was about three months.[33] While it was unrealistic to expect that all the women would remain immediately free of further personal or legal conflict after living in the residence, there was evidence that the occupants found more than material comforts in the home-like milieu.[34] As in an ideal home, women could and did return, taking strength from the acceptance they found there.[35] A warm, competent housemother, Pauline Fell, and her husband, a retired RCMP officer, had greatly contributed to what one resident described as "a real homey family atmosphere."[36]

Fell's contribution in making this residence a home to many women who had never experienced a safe, ordered, loving environment cannot be overstated. She inspired all who knew and worked with her in the residence, be they staff, volunteers, or the "girls" who lived with her in the Fry home. Marilynne Brager, residence supervisor for two years while Fell was housemother, wrote, "I admired the way she dealt with her responsibilities and consider her one of the best in the field. Our relationship was close and with the adventures we went through, we learned and grew and shared."[37] Volunteer Beth Weese, who had first donated her services to the EFSBC as a member of the Junior League and stayed as a Fry volunteer, also grew fond of Pauline Fell. Weese remembered, "She was a saint . . . she gave everyone a lift and I really enjoyed my visits with her. Pauline was one of the reasons I continued with the Fry and the women's residence."[38] The Society often received letters addressed to "Mrs. Fry," "Mrs. Fell," "to whom it may concern" and even "Dear Sir" from numerous women, past and current residents, detailing the importance of their relationship with Fell and the significance of their time spent in the Fry residence. Although the crimes of these women varied, their personal histories reflecting intense family problems were remarkably similar. Therefore it was not surprising that their testimonials, some written when the future of the residence was in doubt, often focused on Pauline Fell's maternal role.

> We couldn't ask for a more beautiful, warm, understanding mother than the one we have here in *our house*. If you could only have time to see for yourself you'd understand why we are all fighting to save this house for all the girls who are here, for the ones who have been here, and for the ones who may come.

> This is the only home I've ever had and I, as well as the rest of the girls who live here, really need this house.

> I could move out on my own but I'd rather be here with her [Fell] and help other drug addicts that come to our house in any way I can.

> She has been so good and kind and understanding. She helped me to have the confidence to be secure and find strength within myself. She helped me to learn to be independent and capable of functioning in the real world. I am working now and I have *my own apartment!*[39]

Even after Fell left her position at the Fry residence, "girls" who came to regard her as the mother they never had, kept in touch with her. Fell's compassionate acceptance of the women in her care is evident in a little booklet of poems and recipes, *From the Heart and Kitchen of a Vancouver Housemother*, that she compiled hoping to raise money for "the needs of other people. . . . to buy anything from a can-opener, a real treasure to a man living in a lonely room, to a radio for a burnt-out musician or a maternity outfit for a girl."[40] In a poem entitled "My Girls," Fell wrote:

> They limp — they do not walk
>   As straight as some, who have not hurts
> From grim days they have known,
>   Who have not felt the cold
> And unkind hand of fear and hate,

And cannot understand how it would be
For those so scared and small,
Who could not understand
Their world at all.

In fact, her "girls" were adult women in the eyes of the law, but Fell often reflected on their vulnerability, as in the following poem:

'Tho she is twenty-one or two
And sometimes thirty-four
She sleeps with light that burns all night
And music that does blare.
The silent darkness she can't fight
She hugs her teddy-bear.
Her eyes do burn with unshed tears
She dreads tomorrow's dawn.
This child from jail, so full of fears
Where has her mommy gone, oh world?
Where has her mommy gone?

Reminiscent of a popular folk tune sung by the flower children of the sixties to protest the threat of war and death, which hovered over that generation of young Americans, Fell's poem "Where have all the teaspoons gone?" registered a more bitter protestation.

Where have all the teaspoons gone?
Long time I'm asking
They're long gone every one
Where can they all have gone.
Where have all the young girls gone?
Long time they're missing
They're junkies every one
They're young but they are gone.
Where have all the narcos gone?
So many passing
To find the young girls gone
The girls and spoons are one.
Where have all the flowers gone?
So soon they're wilting
At sick beds everyone
At graves they rest upon
When will they ever learn?
When will they ever learn?

In addition to Pauline Fell, who, like any parent, performed so much more than the duties of a housekeeper, a social and a psychiatric worker were involved in individual counselling and weekly group therapy sessions at the residence. But the home was only licensed for seven women, and two to four referrals a week had to be turned down. In terms of its value as a resource for women offenders engaged in community re-entry programs, the house had proved to be as successful as it was hoped. In view of changes in 1969 under Section 151 of the Prisons and Reformatories Act, whereby female offenders under the age of twenty-two began receiving definite-indeterminate sentences,[41] the residence, along with the EFSBC's pre-release planning and post-release assessment services, was a necessity.[42] The Society was concerned that with the age limit on group homes set at seventeen years, women from seventeen to twenty-two fell between the group homes and Oakalla. The EFSBC was anxious, therefore, to have a larger facility to meet the needs of these women.

In 1973, an alarming increase in the number of young heroin addicts in the city caused the Society to consider segregating beds for the specific use of women experiencing withdrawal. In addition to helping addicts through this difficult period, the EFSBC wanted to be able to support women until they were ready to resume their independence. The new Drug and Alcohol Commission had confirmed extra funding for operating expenses for these purposes. The EFSBC now determined the time was right to purchase a permanent residence.[43] As was expected in light of neighbourhoods' reactions to group homes, this proved to be a trying experience for the Fry Society.

A number of locations were submitted for approval to the City or municipality. In each case the EFSBC encountered opposition. An application on a small apartment building at Granville Street and 12th Avenue was taken right through to the Board of Variance, which ruled in the Society's favour. But the Society reconsidered this property and rejected it as unsuitable Another, for a nursing home in Cloverdale, proceeded through all the necessary steps except the final one. Finally, a house that seemed to fit all the necessary qualifications was found on Balaclava Street in the Kitsilano neighbourhood of Vancouver and the Fry women were hopeful that they would be accepted in this area of rental suites and apartments.

Situated on the corner of a quiet residential street, the old, well-kept, three-storey building was surrounded by a lovely garden and backyard. An interim agreement for sale was signed the first week in September, 1974. However, violent objections from the neighbours forced the Society to appear before yet another Board of Variance. Although the Fry obtained a ruling in their favour, the women representing the Society were uncertain whether the animosity and hysteria that had been directed towards them during the hearings would dissipate. One volunteer remembers this as "a truly dreadful experience with people crying and shaking their fists at us, and

Balaclava House, the
EFSBC residence for
women released from
prison, was purchased in
1974. The residence had
been a goal of EFSBC
volunteers for many years
but they had to overcome
much opposition from
neighbours before it could
open its doors in 1976.

shouting that it would be our fault if their children were murdered."[44] But tempers cooled over the year it took for all licences and permits to be granted, renovations and furnishing completed, and the house occupied. An official opening was held in May 1976 with about 250 people in attendance. After neighbours came and found nothing to be frightened of either in the home or with its occupants, they were finally accepting, even welcoming of the houseparents and the women in their community.[45]

The Fry residence offered the opportunity for women released from prison to adjust to new responsibilities and freedoms in a supervised, supportive, stable environment. Over the years many women have appreciated the caring staff and volunteers who tried to make this time spent in the residence an important first step in a new life. One former resident conveyed her memories of this experience in the following verse printed in the EFSBC newsletter, December 30, 1977.

There is a house so big and white
And once you enter, it is a fight!
The people there are all your friends
Who stand behind you till the end.
The rules are hung in every room—
And if you break them, there is gloom.
But keep in mind, you've got your chance
It's hard to see that at first glance.
As time goes by, we know you'll see
E. Fry is one great place to be.
And when your troubles seem so deep
That all you do is mope and weep,
Go down to talk to Barb or Pru,
or Imogene—yes—Sue will do.
Then Liz—now there's a sight.
She baby-sits us Tuesday night.

Oh yes, dear John—he comes and goes —
When supper's ready, he always knows!
But keep in mind to pull your weight
Or we'll all be swinging on that old gate[46]
So here we are—giving it a try
And all our "thanks" to old E. Fry!

The "old E. Fry" was indeed responsible for ensuring that new and beneficial trends in corrections, available to the more numerous male offenders, were extended to female offenders. However, the EFSBC's initiatives in the sixties and seventies reflected not only a concern for the equal treatment of women but also a shift in correctional philosophy. The high per capita prison population in Canada coupled with the increasing disillusionment with the ability of incarceration to rehabilitate or deter offenders caused penal reformers to search for more innovative programs.[47] Community-based corrections, or preventive and after-care administered by voluntary agencies, and the increased use of probation and parole were attempts to reduce Canada's prison population and solve the problem of recidivism. Prisoners' Aid Societies like the John Howard and Elizabeth Fry, church organizations, philanthropic associations, and humanitarian individuals, were at the forefront in developing practical alternatives to imprisonment.

The impact of this voluntary activity was mirrored in the Report of the Canadian Commission on Corrections in 1969, Hon. Mr. Justice Roger Ouimet, chairman. The Ouimet Commission recommended that governments recognize the need to form partnerships with the voluntary agencies to strengthen community-based corrections. This report went further, challenging the effectiveness of any rehabilitative model of corrections within the prison setting. Clearly a new assessment of the criminal justice system and the fate of the offender was underway. However, this new wave of concern did not reflect a consensus among the general public. Although the Ouimet Commission called for stronger links between corrections and social service agencies, the doubts raised about the ability of the rehabilitative approach to alter attitudes and behaviours of criminal offenders hardened popular attitudes in the seventies. Indeed, the perceived failure of the medical model—the diagnosis and treatment of physical or mental aberration as a means to rehabilitate offenders and reduce recidivism —inevitably swung public opinion back to an ideology of punishment. This sentiment was reinforced in the wake of prison unrest as the turmoil of the sixties reverberated behind prison walls.[48] Although, in this era, the attempts of the EFSBC and similar societies to bridge communities gained the support of the solicitor general and the Canadian Corrections Association, and an

Office of the Elizabeth Fry Society of British Columbia located at 2412 Columbia Street, Vancouver, B.C.

extensive review of the criminal justice system at the legislative level was begun by the Law Reform Commission of Canada, these combined efforts laboured against the prevailing current of popular opinion. Nevertheless, in 1970, the solicitor general heeded Ouimet's recommendation and introduced "fee for service" contracts for halfway houses, parole supervision, and community assessments. In their turn, governments were building bridges to link the work of voluntary agencies and federal corrections in the hopes of finding more economical and successful alternatives to incarceration. The EFSBC was gratified by this greater recognition of community-based services and prepared to increase its connections with the Office of the Solicitor General.

The demands on the EFSBC of these new, formal responsibilities, in addition to those of maintaining and expanding the group homes, women's residence, and programs at Willingdon and Oakalla, necessitated hiring more staff and prompted the search for larger office space. Also, the location of the Fry's office at Main and Hastings, with its proximity to skid road, had proved to be disadvantageous—but not because of any discomfort it afforded the Fry volunteers. Fry women learned to walk in this part of town "eyes straight ahead," picking their way through broken bottles and other debris. They stepped carefully over the daily obstacles posed by sorry, unconscious bodies that blocked the entrance to their offices.[49] The EFSBC was forced to relocate, however, because the courts deemed the address off-limits to parolees trying to stay clear of drug dealers and pimps. In February 1970 the Society moved to premises at 314 West Pender Street, which satisfied the need for a board meeting room, staff offices, and also for a more convenient location for the Fry's clients. Since October 1976, the EFSBC offices have moved three times in search of economical yet adequate space for the varied responsibilities of the Society. Currently located off East Broadway at 2412 Columbia Street, staff and volunteers appreciate larger offices and meeting rooms but regret the loss of street traffic and drop-in visitors that was customary in their downtown locations.

The Society was not only concerned with finding ways to bridge the prison and the outside community in the1970s but also to increase communications between the EFSBC and other Elizabeth Fry Societies that had been established independently in eastern Canada. It appeared that a national organization might provide a strong voice to speak for matters concerning the female offender, especially with regard to the housing of women in the federal penitentiary in Kingston.

Fry delegates from societies in Vancouver, Kingston, Toronto, and Ottawa attending the Corrections Congress held in Vancouver in 1969 met to discuss a proposal for a national association of Elizabeth Fry Societies.[50] The meeting raised many questions regarding the purposes, geographical representation and funding. However, a decision was reached to strike a committee to explore the possibilities and implications of establishing a national body.

Within two years the Canadian Association of Elizabeth Fry Societies (CAEFS) was born and the EFSBC was asked to select the first president, secretary, and one delegate.[51] Lois Horan, an EFSBC member, contributed a great deal of time and effort to draw up the first CAEFS constitution.[52] The Association would be administered by a board of directors and staff including an executive director and be funded by private donations and grants from the Ministry of the Solicitor General. By 1978, the year of CAEFS' incorporation, there were thirteen member societies; ten years later, nineteen societies represented all ten provinces. In its first twenty years, CAEFS has been actively involved in law reform, information exchange, and joint action with other national women's organizations and criminal justice associations, public education, and the provision of bursaries to encourage education in the field of justice.[53]

The EFSBC has always been concerned to maintain local autonomy, particularly with regard to funding matters, but this has not kept the Society from taking its share of responsibilities in the national association. Daphne Paterson, instrumental in laying the foundations for the Canadian Association since 1969 and president of the EFSBC in 1970 to 1971, was the first president of CAEFS in 1971.[54] The third president of CAEFS in 1976 was Grace Black, who in 1976 hired CAEFS' first executive director and increased communications between CAEFS and member societies; she also came from the EFSBC. In 1988, CAEFS awarded honourary memberships to both these women along with Maida Duncan, long-time EFSBC member and former treasurer of CAEFS; Joan Sprague, past president of EFSBC, founding member, and first chair of the CAEFS bursary committee, vice-president CAEFS; and Ethel Allardice, first executive director of EFSBC and founding member CAEFS.[55] The honourary memberships are awarded to persons who have not only worked for

CAEFS but who have done significant work in their home societies and for women in the criminal justice system. All of the women mentioned were volunteers except for Allardice, who was cited in a way that celebrated the Fry's partnership between its professional and voluntary workers. Allardice was honoured for "her exceptional talent for developing the potential abilities of those around her."[56]

In addition to launching the national association, the EFSBC, under the guidance of Ethel Allardice, had nurtured several new societies elsewhere in British Columbia. By 1973, branch societies were established in Kelowna (Okanagan Branch) and Kamloops. In 1979, five years after the opening of the women's unit at Prince George Regional Correctional Centre, interested volunteers began an Elizabeth Fry Society in Prince George in the form of an advisory committee, which became a branch society in 1981. The hard work of the Fry volunteers in Prince George gained funding from the Vancouver Law Foundation that enabled them to hire a half-time courtworker to provide services at the Provincial Court. A fledgling society was also established in Ashcroft. The EFSBC offered counsel and guidance to these new societies and supported their efforts to extend the availability of Fry programs and services to clients throughout the province.

In 1985 delegates from these societies met in Kamloops to discuss the idea of a provincial association of Elizabeth Fry Societies.[57] A number of themes relating to the purposes of a provincial body emerged from this session. These Fry women were eager to share information about programs, sources of funding, personnel policies, and administrative problems. They saw the potential of a provincial organization to provide unity, credibility, and a more powerful voice for correctional change.[58] By March 26, 1987, this group had formally established itself as a committee of Elizabeth Fry Societies in British Columbia with its purpose "to enhance the services of individual societies through the provision of strategy development, networking, and program development activities."[59]

The EFSBC found other bridging opportunities in the seventies as the Society recognized the strengths of the partnership between volunteers and professional Fry workers. In the spring of 1969, the EFSBC formed a court study group to determine how the Society might instruct and assist women and their families about basic court procedures.[60] Often asked by inmates, parolees, and probationers, after the fact, to explain the court proceedings that had decided their fates, Fry volunteers perceived there was a definite need for the Society to extend its services into the courtroom. EFSBC executive director Ethel Allardice pointed out the particular needs of the first offenders and the young and inexperienced to be informed of their rights and legal terminology. In the next year, members of the study

group visited different courts in the lower mainland and invited officials within the criminal justice system to address group meetings.
The members concluded that the Society should train courtworkers
who would then be able to coordinate and supervise volunteers.

In 1971, the EFSBC was able to obtain funds from the federal
government's Local Initiatives Program (LIP grants) to develop the
Fry's courtwork program. Full-time volunteer Carol St. Pierre and
staff member Jocelyn Stratton met with probation officers, prosecu-
tors, and judges in municipalities in the Greater Vancouver area,
visited courts in session, and established the aims and objectives of
the program. By 1973 the EFSBC courtwork program offered services in Vancouver, Haney, Surrey, Burnaby, and Richmond, with
further requests from Langley and Victoria. Funding had been provided initially by LIP grants but once the program was underway it
had to find other sources. The provincial government provided a
small grant but the generosity of the Vancouver Foundation, the
Legal Services Commission, and the Vancouver Law Foundation
sustained the program in the early years of its operation. The pressure on the Society to extend courtwork services in Delta,
Coquitlam, Cloverdale, and White Rock (and eventually elsewhere
in the province) incurred greater expenses to meet the demand for
more staff and office equipment. The EFSBC relied increasingly on
the Legal Services Commission and allotments from the United Way
to maintain this essential service for those without benefit of legal
counsel.[61] In 1977, a grant from the Leon and Thea Koerner Foundation allowed the Society to purchase essential library resource
materials needed by courtworkers.[62]

The duties of the volunteer in the courtwork program were varied and interesting. Her primary role was to explain and interpret
charges, court procedure, and legal terms to the accused; she was
also able to assist the accused to obtain counsel by processing Legal
Aid applications or referring her to another social assistance agency.
The Fry volunteer provided encouragement and moral support,
much appreciated by a first offender. In special circumstances the
courtworker might speak to bail, remand, and sentence.

After barely a year in court, Fry courtworkers detected some
disturbing patterns of criminal activity in women who had no previous record of any offence. The numbers of girls and women charged
with shoplifting not only exceeded the men but also constituted a
large proportion of female crime. In 1970, 2,500 women in Vancouver were convicted of shoplifting.[63] Moreover, discounting a number
of "professional criminals" who stole "for a living" or to support a
drug habit, the majority of women apprehended for shoplifting were
in every other way respectable, law-abiding citizens.[64] In their discussions with these women, usually first offenders, it was evident to

the Fry courtworker that shoplifting was but a symptom of deeper psychological distress. It appeared to the Fry courtworkers that this was an area that required further investigation by the EFSBC in the interests of providing this group of women with some meaningful interventions.

With the aid of an LIP grant, the Society hired Michael Townesend to research the subject of shoplifting. (The EFSBC had previously commissioned this librarian/researcher to assess the library facilities at Oakalla for the purposes of upgrading them.) Townesend's report revealed that women outnumbered the men arrested for shoplifting at the ratio of twenty to one. Those women were not differentiated by any particular age, social class, or educational background. But they were nearly all first offenders, with average intelligence, and not intoxicated at the time of the crime. Of significance to the Fry workers was the report's conclusions about the motivations of shoplifters, which showed that in middle-aged and elderly women, depression was as much a factor as actual need. In the young, it appeared that shoplifting was a manifestation of conflict with authority, frustration, and/or influence of the peer group.

The Society also noted that criminologists attested to the beneficial effects (reduced recidivism) when shoplifters received clinical treatment for their psychological problems. The EFSBC concluded that it would be in the best interests of both the individual and the community to develop a treatment program for shoplifters. Group therapy might provide effective and economical rehabilitation to women who had demonstrated the need for counselling intervention and the desire to cooperate.

In 1972, the EFSBC began group counselling for women who shoplift. This program originated as a demonstration project sponsored jointly by the EFSBC and Forensic Psychiatric Services (Ministry of Health). Subsequently, the Society obtained funds from the Donner Foundation, an international philanthropic organization with Canadian headquarters in Toronto, before B.C. Corrections assumed responsibility for primary funding in1978.

The groups were specifically designated for middle-aged, depressed, "amateur" shoplifters. Referrals were made by judges, probation officers, courtworkers, lawyers, security officers, and the women themselves. Sometimes the groups served as alternatives to imprisonment and often were acknowledged by the courts as a condition of sentencing. The Fry "shoplifting clinics" met on a weekly basis for a period of approximately six months. They were led by an experienced, professionally-trained Fry worker aided by Fry volunteers and psychology or social work students.

Over 160 women participated in these sessions in the first five years of the counselling program. An evaluative study of the group treatment program undertaken for the EFSBC in 1976 by Mary Russell, assistant professor in UBC's School of Social Work, confirmed that the program had succeeded in relieving the psychological distress of its clients that had caused their anti-social actions. Moreover, the therapy appeared responsible for changing women's outlook and their life situations which ultimately kept them from repeating the offense.[65]

The EFSBC could not hope for more from their programs than to alleviate the conditions that precipitated crime and, therefore, to ensure that women did not have to serve time in jail. The court referral program, like the group homes and the adult residence, fulfilled these goals and more. By the 1980s, the Society provided increased opportunities for spanning the distance between incarceration and independence; these opportunities came to be recognized by all participants in the criminal justice system. The EFSBC's focus on supportive preventive- and after-care meant that both the community and the offender had to take greater responsibility for rehabilitation. The partnership formed in the mid-sixties between the volunteer and the professional Fry workers began this bridging process, which made possible more effective liaisons within corrections and increased the alternatives for women in conflict with the law.

8. THE HONEST BROKER RETURNS TO PRISON

It is the role of Elizabeth Fry Societies and their Canadian Association to raise federal female offenders high on the list of priorities as never before. . . . now we have a responsibility to be an active participant on [regional consultative] committees. John Braithwaite, deputy commissioner, CSC, at the meetings in October referred to Elizabeth Fry Society's role as an "honest broker." The danger lies in being co-opted by the interests of either the province or the federal government. We must not lose sight of what is best for each individual in federal care that might be discussed by these regional committees. We must think of individual program planning innovatively, practically, and realistically.

Barbara Kilbourn, president,
Canadian Association of Elizabeth Fry Societies, 1979[1]

By the mid-1970s, the Elizabeth Fry Society of British Columbia had widened the meaning of penal reform and prisoners' aid to encompass a range of community services that could scarcely have been envisioned by the founders of the Society over thirty years previously. But in the midst of this expansion there were urgent reminders of the need to maintain humane standards of incarceration where this extreme form of deprivation was deemed necessary. Although group homes for juveniles and the adult women's residence might provide preventive and after-care, and even spark interest in community-based alternatives to prison sentences, one of the primary concerns of the EFSBC was still to improve prison conditions for female offenders.

In general, the special needs of women in custody, a small minority of the overall prison population, had never been adequately addressed by the corrections system.[2] In British Columbia, there was little evidence of expansion and renewal of programs and services in the women's unit at Oakalla Women's Correctional Centre, where overcrowding and disciplinary problems added to the pressure on the prison population. Nor had the problems of housing federal offenders in the Kingston Prison for Women (P4W as it is familiarly termed) been resolved to the satisfaction of the EFSBC.

However, under the watchful eye of the EFSBC there had been some recent additions to the correctional facilities in British Columbia that allowed for a greater degree of flexibility in housing sentenced women. In 1960, the opening of Twin Maples Correctional Centre provided a minimum-security institution for female offenders who were likely to benefit from the opportunity to work or acquire further education. From 1967, this unit received women with alcoholic problems—many sent directly from court for an indeterminate period not exceeding twelve months. After one month in the institution, a resident could apply for a temporary absence during the day that allowed her to work in the community, receive on-the-job training, or further her education.

The physical structure of this centre resembled a rural motel complex, modular in design. Located on 320 acres approximately sixteen kilometres east of Maple Ridge, Twin Maples attempted to establish a total living environment in an open, farm setting. In time, Twin Maples also accommodated children up to the age of two, a feature the EFSBC regarded as significant for mothers not wishing to be separated from their infants. Believing these natural surroundings more conducive to rehabilitation, especially for Native women and chronic alcoholics, the EFSBC had welcomed the opening of Twin Maples and established visiting and recreational programs similar to those at Oakalla.

In 1977 and 1978 respectively, the B.C. Corrections Branch had also opened community-based correctional centres known as Lynda Williams House in Vancouver and Graham House in Victoria, where female offenders who did not have drug problems might serve part or all (if short-term) of their sentences.[3] The residential model established by the EFSBC perhaps served to convince B.C. Corrections of the value of this type of facility. The Fry residence was now available to women out on bail or granted a temporary absence, on probation, or experiencing a crisis situation; it filled the need for a post-release support network. The community-based correctional centre was essentially an alternative to jail.

Increasing violence within the prisons, along with disturbing trends in female criminality from 1964 to 1974 that indicated greater numbers of women were being both charged and convicted, prompted new attention towards housing female offenders at provincial and federal levels.[4] From the 1970s into the 1990s the EFSBC, in its association with sister societies across the country, sought to raise the question of housing female offenders to a position of greater priority within corrections. As providers of services and recipients of government funds, it might be expected that the EFSBC, along with CAEFS, would be compliant participants in the advisory process. But as

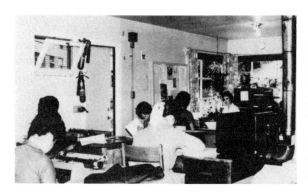

In 1960, the Twin Maples Correctional Centre near Maple Ridge provided a minimum security institution for female offenders. After one month, a woman could apply for daily leave to allow her to receive job training or further her education. This photo shows women studying and working at their school assignments.

suggested above by the president of CAEFS, if the Society was to sustain its reputation of being an "honest broker," Fry women would have to take a firm stand against forces for change that did not necessarily represent the best interests of female prisoners.

Since 1939, it had been the practice of the EFSBC to educate public opinion and promote legal and penal reforms. In the early years of the Society's history, sometimes under the umbrella of the Provincial Council of Women, the EFSBC would send unbidden briefs and resolutions on legal matters affecting women and children to provincial and federal governments. As the Society gained status in the province, it was increasingly invited to contribute to the reform process and expected to speak for women who were or might be in conflict with the law. The EFSBC's Social Action Committee, which studied and responded to Royal Commission hearings and government bills, performed much of the groundwork that gave the Society its direction. Prior to 1970, this committee had considered the conclusions of the Royal Commissions on the Penal System—the Archambault Report in 1938 and the Fauteux Report in 1956—and made presentations to the Report on Criminal Law Relating to Sexual Psychopaths, 1958; the Report on the Female Offender, 1968; the Ouimet Report of the Canadian Committee of Corrections, 1969; and the Ledain Report on Drug Use, 1969.[5] But in the 1970s, the EFSBC laboured at its most arduous tasks to date as it returned to the very issues that had first brought women interested in penal reform in British Columbia to found the Elizabeth Fry Society—the conditions of women's incarceration.

The EFSBC acknowledged that the purpose of imprisonment was to protect society from dangerous offenders and to condemn criminal behaviour. However, the Society believed that for those persons sentenced to penal institutions, which the EFSBC found acceptable only if alternative methods of sentencing were not possible, the loss of freedom was the penalty for crime, and further unwarranted deprivations were not to be tolerated. Prison conditions, therefore, must include discipline, meaningful work and recreation, academic and vocational training, entertainment, and socialization that would aid the offender in coping with her incarceration and provide avenues for her to experiment with changing her lifestyle.[6] For its part, the EFSBC, through its prison visiting programs, sought to provide personal support for female inmates, to be an advocate of their rights, and to establish a liaison between the prison and the community.

To these ends, the EFSBC preserved a steady but diminishing presence in Oakalla during the mid-1970s when the Society experienced difficulties in maintaining strong numbers of volunteers to visit the prison.[7] Despite discreet advertisements for volunteers in local community newspapers, a screening process, and a revamping of the volunteer training program, the EFSBC was unable to attract individuals suitably committed to prison visiting. From March to June 1976, the EFSBC lost fifteen Oakalla volunteers, with only seven remaining in the group going out to the prison on Wednesdays and three or four on Fridays.[8]

The Society struggled to devise reliable recruitment practices at the same time it encountered a waning enthusiasm for the Fry's presence from the prison staff. On several occasions, recreational activities planned by the Fry women were cancelled at the last minute by staff attempting to discipline the inmates. This caused much frustration to both inmates and Fry women. Without encouragement from the prison staff, and faced with a very difficult atmosphere within Oakalla, new volunteers easily lost heart after their first visit. Even the old standbys began to question what they were doing and what they were accomplishing. Volunteers lamented the loss of the cooperative climate that had predominated before the retirement of matron Bessie Maybee in 1972.[9]

In fact, the EFSBC regarded many of the recent administrative policies at the women's unit both regressive and questionable, particularly the increasing use of male guards and the replacement of Maybee with a male director. Historically, the Society had always promoted the hiring of women to deal with female offenders, whether probationers, parolees, or inmates. Certainly nineteenth century reformers such as Elizabeth Fry had emphasized the need for female custodians as a first objective in penal reform for women.[10] For these early prison reformers the presence of men, either inmates or jailers, was regarded as both a real and potential threat to incarcerated women. Although respective of individual issues of equal rights and averse to practices of discrimination, the EFSBC held to the belief that only women should be hired as staff or inspectors in the living units and sleeping rooms of the women's jail.[11] Allegations of sexual misconduct between male staff and female inmates aired in October 1977 by Vancouver radio hotliner

Jack Webster, reinforced this conviction.[12]

Prior to Webster's revelation, the EFSBC had been concerned for some time not only about various rumours of this type that circulated about the prison, but also about specific incidents that seemed to thrive in a climate of inept management and low staff morale. Escapes, assaults on staff and other inmates, and self-inflicted mutilations—slashings and suicides —occur as part of the horror of life behind bars. But in the early 1970s, a proliferation of these events indicated that the Oakalla women's unit was approaching a crisis situation.[13] These incidents included twenty-three escapes in a ten-month period from September 1973 to June 1974, a needless death when an inmate suffered a seizure and drowned in her bath in February 1974, a suicide in August 1975 by an inmate who was considered to be malingering after medical treatment, and a scalding in January 1976 of one inmate who was held for an hour in hot water by others seeking revenge while male guards were being distracted by female inmates out of earshot of the girl's screams.

A witness to the effects of the scalding incident—Vi Roden, a Fry volunteer and chairman of the Oakalla Committee—was dissatisfied with the staff's response to her request that the inmate receive medical treatment for her burns and reported her concerns to the EFSBC. The Society wrote to the attorney general and the head of B.C. Corrections demanding an investigation of both the attack and the conditions, generally, at Oakalla.[14] It was several months before the EFSBC received a response in June 1976 from the assistant executive director of Institutional Services of British Columbia, W. (Bill) R. Jack, assuring the Society that an investigation had occurred and a number of procedural changes were in the works. The Society suspected that there had been an attempt by prison administrators "to smooth things over" and resolved to "keep an eye on things and, if not satisfied, to keep going back to the attorney general's department."[15] A subsequent meeting of various corrections officials, including the head of the Oakalla women's unit, the Oakalla classifications officer, and the EFSBC executive director was held at Oakalla to discuss the Fry's continuing concerns. This group advanced the idea of establishing a community advisory board to the institution and also a community representative sitting at warden's court.[16]

Following this meeting, the EFSBC was more satisfied that hourly checks of prison rooms and washrooms, the hiring of more staff, and improved staff training might avert further violent incidents at Oakalla. However, the issue of the continued employment of male staff was still contentious. In April 1977, the female inmates threatened a sit-down strike due to a problem with male guards, but the strike was averted when the guards were removed.[17] Rumours of improper conduct and suspected liaisons did not subside.

During the following months, tensions increased within the women's prison. The few Fry volunteers still visiting Oakalla noted a tightening of security and were discouraged when arrangements made for softball and volleyball games with the inmates were frequently suspended without notification due to staff shortages.[18] The female inmates seemed to think it was the EFSBC that let them down. On the other hand, the Fry women expressed frustration with rules that changed at the prison "according to who was on duty" and described the staff at the prison as being in an "apathetic state of limbo."[19] With their recent knowledge and experience of the problems in Oakalla, Webster's allegations aired in the fall of 1977 were, therefore, neither surprising nor totally unwelcome to the EFSBC women. The Society was eager for a more open inquiry into the conditions at Oakalla.

Always eager for a sensational story, the press was unrelenting in its exposure of various alleged improprieties within the women's prison until the Royal Canadian Mounted Police were called in to investigate matters. The EFSBC wanted a government inquiry into the conditions in Oakalla. It was relieved when, subsequent to the RCMP's report to the attorney general of British Columbia, a Royal Commission was appointed in December 1977 to "make inquiry into and concerning all aspects of the management and operation of programs and facilities related to the disposition and incarceration of female offenders whether under sentence or on remand in British Columbia. . . . "[20] The sole commissioner appointed was the Honourable Madam Justice Patricia M. Proudfoot who, a few months earlier had become the first woman to be appointed Justice of the Supreme Court of British Columbia.[21]

The commission first visited all of the institutions housing female offenders in the province and interviewed both staff and inmates. Formal hearings commenced early in February and before they concluded on March 31, 1978, forty briefs had been submitted including two (one plus a supplement) from the EFSBC, 103 documents filed, and 87 witnesses made a total of 115 appearances.[22] The findings and many recommendations of the report, completed by the end of April, left no doubt about the woeful state of mismanagement within the women's prisons and of the inadequacy of the programs available to female offenders.

The commission heard evidence relating to sixteen allegations of sexual misconduct between male staff and female inmates at Oakalla and of welfare fraud. It had been the publicity surrounding these allegations—the extortion of sex for privileges, the fraudulent receipt of welfare cheques, and even a gold-smuggling operation engineered jointly with a staff member and an inmate—that had led to the appointment of the commission.[23] Neither the RCMP investigators nor the commission hearings could provide factual support for the specific allegations of criminal offences. Nevertheless, the allegations were revealing of the internal problems and discontent within the institution. It was clear, too, that many of the actions of individuals working in the women's prison showed a lack of judgement and disregard of the rules and regulations governing correctional institutions.

Of course it was part of Proudfoot's mandate to locate both the general and the specific source of the problems within B.C. corrections and Oakalla at this time. However, the commission could scarcely be expected to resolve the philosophical dilemmas which, in fact, underscored corrections throughout the country in this period. The age-old debates about the causes of crime and the effects of punishment, the methods of rehabilitating offenders, and the alternatives to incarceration had been left to the criminologists in the 1970s. Unfortunately, social scientists were no closer to finding satisfactory solutions than the humanitarian reformers had been thirty years previously. In fact, Robert Martinson's controversial article entitled, "What works? Questions and Answers About Prison Reform," with its conclusions that "nothing works," set a tone of disillusionment that reinforced uncertain attitudes and the reluctance of governments to give precedence to the reform of correctional institutions.[24] Nevertheless, along with its discussion of the local and specific causes of the crisis in Oakalla, the Proudfoot Report did demonstrate the effects of the philosophical dilemma, public apathy, and political irresponsibility at the institutional level.

The testimony of the B.C. Commissioner of Corrections, Dr. John W. Ekstedt, in his brief to the Royal Commission on the Incarceration of Female Offenders, expressed how the lack of consensus in correctional philosophy reverberated throughout the system in the 1970s. He stated, "The problems faced by the correctional system across Canada and in this province are very great and have reached crisis proportions in some institutional programs. Hostage-takings and riots are the most extreme evidences of the malaise which is currently affecting many correctional programs in Canada."[25] Ekstedt cited three contributing factors which made the administration of correctional programs difficult and paradoxical in the 1970s: the lack of clear definition of the social or political expectations related to the provision of correctional services; the prohibitive cost of correctional reform; and the problems of coordination within the administration of justice.[26] While this analysis would prove insightful to historians reflecting on the crisis of corrections' philosophy during this period, the Honourable Madam Justice Patricia M. Proudfoot found the commissioner of corrections contributing to the problem and not the solution with his admission that "we don't really know what we are doing . . . as a collective enterprise we suffer from a loss of direction in a number of areas."[27] Proudfoot reasoned that any journey into "this interesting socio-philosophic area" [the debate about institutional treatment] was not the mandate of the head of the B.C. Corrections Branch and had inhibited the leadership essential to the orderly and effective administration of prisons.[28] Ekstedt resigned prior to the commission's recommendation that he be relieved of his duties.[29]

In this climate of uncertainty, stylistic alterations in the form of bureaucratic reorganizations were more prevalent in corrections than substantive changes. This was evident in the B.C. Corrections Branch with a massive restructuring begun in 1973-74 that was intended to decentralize authority. Proudfoot suggested some of the problems within the administration of the Oakalla women's unit—including "a zigzag method of reporting caus[ing] no end of delays"[30]—stemmed from too many levels of bureaucracy. Similarly, a "permissive" attitude toward discipline, whether regarding the behaviour of inmates or staff, was evidently responsible for some of the laxity and demoralization in Oakalla.

Proudfoot took much the same approach to the dilemma of corrections philosophy as did the EFSBC. Rather than getting bogged down in the debate about incarceration, she logically addressed the problems at hand and suggested some practical solutions. With the implication that Oakalla fit this description, the report offered a clear statement of what institutions must not be.

> Institutions should not, if possible, contribute to a further erosion of the inmate's personality; they should not contribute to a deterioration of behaviour and lifestyle. Boredom and lack of challenge were two problems that appeared to us to pervade the day-to-day life of women inmates.... This sort of atmosphere, perhaps a type of defeatism, can work its way into an institution and weigh heavily on staff and inmates.[31]

The majority of the Proudfoot Report's fifty-seven recommendations, therefore, attempted to reverse and overcome the defeatist atmosphere prevalent in Oakalla by redirecting administrative procedures. These recommendations ranged from the wearing of uniforms by all staff (there were complaints that since the inmates were no longer compelled to wear their blue prison garb, it was difficult to tell the staff from the inmates) to the training, selection, and the reporting of staff, and, in particular, the use of male staff "in any area where human decency and privacy are not affected."[32] The report also specified the need for certifying work training and educational programs; introducing life skills training and counselling; and increasing monies for schooling, supplies, and library books.[33]

The EFSBC particularly applauded these latter recommendations. One of the first projects of the EFSBC had been to install some vocational training and to establish the library at Oakalla. But by the early 1970s both these services were badly in need of renewal. The EFSBC had employed a researcher to assess the library facilities at Oakalla for the purposes of upgrading them. Although Fry volunteers continually made an effort to satisfy individual requests—for example, they provided the Doukhobor women in prison with reading material in Russian—additional funds were necessary to improve the library for general use. Similarly, the EFSBC was eager to prepare female inmates to cope better with their lives on the outside. The Fry recognized that the educational needs of many of the women in prison were very basic. Most offenders seemingly lacked the practical skills to survive in "straight" or "normal" circumstances. The EFSBC believed that a "life skills" program—which provided information on budgeting, dealing with government bureaucracies, child care, nutrition, filling out welfare and unemployment forms, and preparation for job interviews—would help to build the inmates' self-esteem and confidence.

The commission also attempted to address the question of what constituted proper incarceration of female offenders. Again the report focused on administrative reforms, many of which were in accord with the EFSBC's convictions and had been put forward in the Society's brief to the commission.[34] Proudfoot noted that "women's corrections have often been viewed as a poor cousin of the much larger and more visible area of male corrections" but that "there are different problems ... less flexibility ... and policies that generally may make sense to the men's unit at Oakalla, may have little relevance to the women's unit."[35] The commission also observed that there were inequalities, both real and perceived, that stemmed from the attempt to operate Oakalla women's unit as a wing of the men's. Women had testified to the commission, "In the matter of supplies and food, the men took what they needed, and the women took what was left."[36] Proudfoot's conclusion echoed that of her predecessors on women's penal reform: "If the women's unit is to be treated as truly equal ... it must be treated as an entity separate and apart from the larger men's unit."[37] She concurred with the EFSBC and recommended the autonomy of the women's unit from the men's.[38]

The EFSBC was satisfied that the commission had uncovered many of the causes of the discontent and inefficiency that existed at Oakalla. (The majority of the report was concerned with Oakalla although the other institutions for women were also investigated. Twin Maples Minimum Security Unit for Women had had its share of administrative problems while it operated under the direct auspices of the Alouette River Unit for Males. On November 1, 1977, Twin Maples gained independent status and it was hoped that, in time, many of the difficulties would be eradicated.) The Society felt it had made an important contribution with its own brief that provided an extensive assessment of the prison's deficiencies and proposed reforms. Indeed, the credibility of the EFSBC had been earned by its many years in Oakalla working with the staff and inmates.

However, the fact that serious problems developed in Oakalla during a period in the EFSBC's history when prison visitors failed to materialize in sustaining numbers, deserves some comment. The apathy towards offenders and the disillusionment with methods and results of corrections that characterized popular and even professional opinion were evidently demonstrable even at the grass roots level, within the voluntary sector. In addition, the atmosphere within Oakalla deterred even the most experienced and dedicated volunteers. In this period, a long-time visitor to Oakalla, Zoe Carter, retired from the EFSBC not only because she moved out of the city but also because she lost faith that she could make a difference.[39] It seems conclusive, however, that the very conditions that discouraged volunteers made their presence even more imperative.

With the declining visibility of the E. Fry volunteer, unhealthy pockets of abuse and discontent developed within Oakalla that troubled Fry women. With their numbers weakened and a more tenuous working relationship with the prison staff—a result of personnel changes, staff shortages, and reorganization—the Fry women "heard things" but could not pursue these rumours to their source. For example, volunteers had heard complaints from inmates about improper body searches and their isolation in the "hole," the area used to confine "security or disciplinary problems."[40] One inmate described her experience:

> I spent three days in an outside room with a window but the sink had been plugged for six months or more and was full of putrid, black, infested water. It literally stank up the whole cell like something was dead.[41]

Fearing repercussions, neither staff nor inmates confided openly with the volunteers while tensions escalated within the prison. For its part, the EFSBC was anxious not to be viewed by the staff as exacerbating an already volatile situation. An outspoken critic belonging to the Prisoners' Rights Group, Clare Culhane, had been barred in March 1978 from visiting Oakalla.[42] Women of the EFSBC believed they must maintain their access to the prison if they were to be of any assistance to the female inmates over the long term. The EFSBC chose not to "go public" with its criticisms of the institution but to work for reforms through established channels. Thus the Society was ready and able to assume the role of "honest broker" and provide the Royal Commission with recommendations that would preserve human dignity and humane treatment for female inmates in B.C.

Many of what the EFSBC regarded as the key recommendations of the Proudfoot Report were implemented. A Citizens Advisory Board was set up by Ted Harrison, B.C. Corrections District Director, and the EFSBC became an active participant. The autonomy of the women's unit was highlighted with the renaming of the provincial women's prison to Lakeside Regional Correctional Centre, an appelation designed, no doubt, to invoke more tranquil expectations than had been customary at Oakalla in recent years. Moreover, the B.C. Royal Commission took a significant stand on current and future policies regarding the separation of remand prisoners, the unsuitability of co-correctional facilities, and the undesirability of transporting female federal offenders out of the province. These were all issues under discussion elsewhere in Canada at provincial and federal levels.

Both Proudfoot's Report and the EFSBC's supplementary brief, "Structural Changes Suggested to Integrate Federal Inmates into the Provincial Corrections System," confronted the perennial problem of the centralized housing of federal women (women sentenced for more than two years into federal custody). The EFSBC had long been critical of the practice of transferring federal female prisoners from their home regions to the Prison for Women in Kingston, Ontario. Fry women believed the distance prevented friends and family from visiting inmates during their prison term, and that their separation from community support systems, which were necessary to plan post-release programs, constituted further deprivation. Indeed, the continued operation of the P4W, regarded by many as an antiquated facility, was a fundamental issue for penal reformers concerned about the equal treatment of female offenders.

Compared with men, significantly fewer women were convicted of criminal offences, although the ratio had decreased from seventy-seven to one in 1969 to forty-eight to one in 1977.[43] The Proudfoot Report argued that with this disparity in numbers, dual corrections systems for women at the provincial and federal levels made little sense either from an economic or a social point of view. Proudfoot suggested that this policy was "perhaps another example of the erroneous assumption that what works for male offenders should work for female offenders."[44]

It would seem that the fate of female federal offenders did rest on historical procedures that were designed to cope with a larger male prison population and the belief that the *equal* treatment of women meant *separate but the same* treatment as for men. In fact, for many years this had been the rallying cry for penal reformers who saw female inmates denied opportunites because of their smaller numbers. For a variety of reasons, however, identical policies for housing both women and men proved less than equitable. There were federal penitentiaries for the numerous male federal offenders in all the regions or provinces. With only thirty-four female federal offenders in 1935, the year the P4W opened, more than one facility for federal women was deemed unnecessary.[45] This meant that women more than men severed family ties when they were transported from their homes to Kingston, yet the possibility of a different policy for women, such as integrating them into existing provincial institutions, was not considered.

Conservative thinking also determined the design of the women's prison would not differ substantially from the model already in existence for men despite the differences in female criminality — for example, that women committed less violent offences than men. Although by 1925, when the Canadian government began construction of the P4W, the trend in women's prisons in the United States had been towards cottage-type institutions, this one was built on the design of nineteenth century maximum security prisons for men. One hundred barred cells were constructed, each with a wash basin and an open toilet. A twenty-six foot stone wall topped with six strands of barbed wire surrounded the whole structure. Completed nine years later in 1934, the P4W received women who had up to that time been housed in the Kingston Penitentiary across the street.[46]

Penal reformers were undoubtedly dissatisfied with the unprogressive model of the newly constructed institution but were relieved to finally have women removed from the predominantly male penitentiaries. Female prisoners and children had been in the Kingston Penitentiary from 1835, its first year of operation, albeit the inspector reported it had caused "some inconvenience."[47] They occupied a ward that formed part of the north wing. At the time of Confederation, there were sixty female inmates in the men's penitentiary. Similarly, Saint John and Halifax Penitentiaries held some women and, when these institutions were replaced by Dorchester Penitentiary in 1880, women were housed in a small ward in the west wing.[48] Typically, prisons were the last of the public institutions to feel the effects of the social reform movement that in other respects was subsiding by the 1920s. It is not surprising, therefore, that the small number of female inmates were accorded the lowest priority (their different needs still considered "some inconvenience") when it came to considering conditions of incarceration.

Although it had taken almost a century before the decision was made to construct the federal women's prison, and nearly a decade to complete it, the financial and social costs of the P4W had been questioned within five years. In 1938, the Report of the Royal Commission on the Penal System (the Archambault Report) stated:

> There is no justification for the erection and maintenance of a costly penitentiary for women alone, nor is it desirable that they should be confined ... in one central institution far from their place of residence and their friends and relations ... [the prison's] further continuance is unjustified, particularly if arrangements can be made with provincial authorities to provide custody and maintenance in their respective provinces. ...[49]

The recommendations of the Archambault Report regarding the incarceration of women helped formulate the original position of the newly established EFSBC, that the P4W be closed. The Society has not wavered in its convictions. But in 1938 there were no immediate plans to dismantle a building so recently constructed. By 1960 the prison population had risen to capacity, 100 women. The pressing need for enlarged quarters prompted a decision to renovate the old prison rather than devise new policies. An auditorium and fifty bedrooms were built on a prefabricated design within the prison walls at a cost of approximately $200,000. In 1964, three isolation cells in the basement of the prison, still in use for "uncontrollable inmates" although classified as unfit for human habitation, were replaced by a section of the cell block. The next year saw a proposal from the Ministry of Justice to construct a new women's prison at Cornwall, Ontario. But objections concerning the lack of educational and vocational opportunities for inmates and parolees in that community caused the project to be abandoned.[50]

Engrossed in their projects to celebrate their country's centennial in 1967, few Canadians spared much attention for the hearings of a joint Senate and House of Commons committee that was investigating the conditions at the P4W. The previous year the resignations of the superintendent, the psychologist, and the social worker had signalled the level of discontent felt by the staff. Perhaps it was believed that the problems could be better solved by a man because, since 1966 (until the mid-1980s), the position of superintendent was in male hands. In 1968, the solicitor general established a committee to plan a new federal prison for women. The concern of federal officials during this neo-nationalist decade in Quebec was to provide an institution near Ottawa where both French and English facilities could be available. However, the committee was dissolved despite a few initially successful meetings and this plan for a new prison was also dropped.[51]

In 1969, the Report of the Canadian Committee of Corrections (Ouimet Report) repeated the recommendations of the Archambault Report and elaborated on the differences between the criminality of men and women and the implications for correctional planning. The Ouimet Report pointed out that the smaller numbers of female offenders, the types of offences they committed, and the different attitudes of society towards women suggested they be more suitably housed in smaller, well-staffed, modern units. As an alternative to the Kingston Prison for Women, Ouimet advised the federal government to purchase services for federal female prisoners from the larger provinces, and to provide regional services in other areas.

The Report of the Royal Commission on the Status of Women was released in the following year. One of the most potent ideas to come out of the feminist movement responsible for the Royal Commission on the Status of Women was that policies that were designed for men and applied to women did not necessarily represent equal treatment. This was nowhere more evident than in the treatment of the female federal offender in view of Ouimet's findings on the different nature of female criminality. In its findings on criminal law and women offenders, the Status of Women Report argued that historical custom, out-of-date social attitudes towards women, and administrative convenience served to discriminate against women and perpetuate inequalities within the criminal justice system. The Status of Women Report stressed that the lower number of incarcerated women should not be regarded as an obstacle but an opportunity in correctional planning for women.

The Prison for Women was not abandoned in the 1970s. Provincial jails were already overcrowded and the provinces found it as difficult as ever to reconcile issues of federal jurisdiction and provincial responsibility. But there was some movement in the direction of Ouimet's recommendations. In 1974, Exchange of Services Agreements were made between the federal government and nine out of ten provinces, Ontario excepted. These agreements applied to both male and female inmates but signified a greater gain for women who, for the first time, might have an opportunity to remain in their home province. The terms of the agreements allowed women whose home provinces were willing to house them to be voluntarily transferred from the P4W, while the federal ministry paid a per diem rate based on the operating costs of the receiving institution. By 1974, forty-six federal women were in provincial institutions and the numbers crept up each year.[52]

In the 1970s, the idea that incarcerated women had different needs coincided with an unforeseen rise in the female inmate population. It is ironic, perhaps, that the pressure for equality of the sexes coincided with an apparent increase in women's criminal activity; but there was also the likelihood that a lessening tolerance for paternalism on the part of the police and judiciary led to increased charges and longer sentences for female offenders.[53] In 1974, in an effort to document issues and trends in female criminality and plan for the future, the solicitor general appointed a National Advisory Committee on the Female Offender to study the needs of federal female offenders. Chaired by Donna Clark, director of Dixon Hall Settlement House, the committee was composed of five other women: a judge, two members of the National Parole Board and the executive directors of the Elizabeth Fry Societies of British Columbia and Toronto, Ethel Allardice and Phyllis Haslam. This committee was to develop "a comprehensive plan to provide adequate institutional and community services appropriate to her [female offender's] unique program and security needs."[54]

The Clark Report, January 1976, presented an extensive profile of the female federal offender. It recommended the closure of the Prison for Women within three years, suggested two alternative plans for housing the federal offender, and focused on difficulties encountered by women in provincial corrections facilities. Although the closing of the P4W was the central recommendation of the Clark Report, the Canadian Corrections Service took the position that this would not be the primary goal of planning for female offenders. One of the several obstacles to the decentralization of federal services would be the issues of redefining federal and provincial jurisdictions. The Clark Report had suggested two options to deal with women affected by the closure of the P4W. One plan would be to retain the federal government's responsibility for female offenders sentenced to two years or more, with the seriously dangerous women to be housed in several small but secure regionally-based facilities. Those inmates needing a less secure confinement could remain in provincial institutions through existing exchange of services agreements. In the second plan, the provinces would assume the responsibility for the incarceration of all female offenders and could negotiate with other provinces for programs and services as necessary. The federal government's role would be to coordinate financial assistance, research, and staff training.

The Canadian Corrections Service recognized that the recommendations of the Clark Report had far-reaching implications which would need the cooperation of the provinces and the federal government. In 1977 the Parliamentary Subcommittee on the Penitentiary System in Canada established the federal government's position. Chairman Mark MacGuigan had not failed to take into account the conclusions of the many previous inquiries into the subject of housing federal women, or the views of CAEFS representatives who testified before the committee. The MacGuigan Report therefore urged that the

P4W be replaced by smaller regional institutions, or if there were too few inmates to warrant this construction, then alternative community resources must be found.

The provinces had yet to be similarly convinced, concerned as they were about the costs of modifying their facilities and programs for so few long-term offenders. In a separate statement at the end of the Clark Report, a member of the committee, Judge Sandra Oxner, expressed her concerns that uniform standards had to be in place at provincial institutions prior to any provincial takeover. Clearly, the provinces had to have an opportunity to take part in the planning process. Consequently, a National Planning Committee on the Female Offender (NPCFO) was appointed, made up of representatives from each province and the federal government to address the key recommendations of the Clark Report. (Quebec did not send representatives but decided to conduct its own study; neither of the territories were represented.) As a result of the CAEFS response to the Clark Report, the Canadian Association was invited by the NPCFO to present its views regarding alternatives to the P4W. Fry women were gratified to be recognized as a voice for women in conflict with the law and noted in the CAEFS newsletter that this was the first time the solicitor general's department had asked for any advisory opinion from a private agency.

During the deliberations of the NPCFO, the B.C. Royal Commission on the Incarceration of the Female Offender released its report. It recommended that all federal women prisoners be returned to the provinces, that federal and provincial governments join forces to provide facilities and programs, and that the P4W in Kingston be closed. In effect, the Honourable Madam Justice Proudfoot in her report expressed support for the second option of the Clark Report and was in agreement with the EFSBC's long-standing position.

The NPCFO did not find all the provinces in agreement, however, and there had to be unanimity regarding their willingness to accept federal offenders before the P4W could be closed. Moreover, as long as the P4W remained in operation, the federal government was slow to make any real financial commitment to install services and programs for federal women in provincial institutions. Yet as long as provincial institutions failed to meet national standards, the P4W would have to be retained. This "catch 22" situation made women's rights groups uneasy. The Canadian Advisory Council on the Status of Women (CACSW) was initially unconvinced that the P4W should be phased out. In its evaluation of the Clark Report and its submission to the NPCFO, the CACSW supported the retention of the Prison for Women but agreed that programs needed to be improved.[55] The unwillingness of the provinces to integrate female federal offenders into the provincial system, and the apparent desire of the inmates (who were also aware of problems they would face in provincial systems reluctant to accommodate them) to stay in Kingston, had shaped this position of the CACSW in September 1978.[56]

Nevertheless, briefs submitted from the Canadian Advisory Council on the Status of Women, the Canadian Association of Elizabeth Fry Societies (CAEFS), the Kingston Elizabeth Fry Society and the Citizen Advisory Committee at the Prison for Women had all identified similar concerns about the effects of geographic displacement on federal women and of the inadequacy of the current facility. CAEFS deplored the lack of opportunity for federal women to maintain family ties (and this was an additional deprivation for French Canadian and Indian inmates removed from their cultural milieu) or to benefit from a support system that would allow for their gradual release into the home community.

In October 1978, the NPCFO upheld the Clark Report's recommendation of the closure of the Prison for Women and stated that no major expenditures should be made to the prison before replacing it with regional facilities, at least one in the east and one in the west. The NPCFO Report endorsed much of the Clark Report and urged that a task force be appointed with representation from the federal and provincial governments and the private sector, to determine minimum standards for all female offenders in Canada.[57]

Although a consensus appeared to be growing regarding the fate of the P4W, provincial and federal governments were a long way from agreements that would assure its closure. In an attempt to complete the process, the commissioner of corrections had established the Joint Committee to Study the Alternatives for the Housing of Federal Female Offenders in July 1978. This committee was to explore and assess in detail the options available for the housing of federal female offenders and to make specific recommendations to the commissioner by the end of September to coincide with the report of the NPCFO.

Penal reformers were heartened by the formation of the joint committee because its mandate was to base its recommendations on "the special needs of the woman offender along with the facility maintenance and implementation costs." This unique consideration of both the needs and costs of housing for the female offender was not the only significant aspect of the joint committee. The study was to be undertaken by a steering group that included representatives from the Toronto Elizabeth Fry and the Prison for Women Advisory Committee. This was the first time that the solicitor general's office had sought private sector representation in a matter which so directly affected decision making in a critical area.[58] Members of the steering group included chairperson Doug Chinnery, the Director of the Prison for Women; Jack Holder, Regional Coordinator of Education and Training for the Ontario Region of the Canadian Corrections Service; Lynn Good, chairperson of the Prison for Women Citizen Advisory Committee; and Gillian Sandeman, executive director of the Toronto Elizabeth Fry Society.[59]

The EFSBC had been delighted with this recognition of a sister society but was concerned that the overall perspective of the participants was limited by their experiences in central Canada. The Society's fears were realized when rumours of the committee's recommendations reached the EFSBC in October 1978. The unreleased report of the joint committee proposed that the P4W be closed within three years and federal women from western Canada be transferred to the men's facility in Mission, B.C., on a co-correctional basis—male and female offenders in the same institution. While there was no question the Society supported provincial responsibility for all female offenders, the EFSBC was disconcerted on two accounts. First, the plan was contrary to the Proudfoot Report's recent denunciation and rejection of co-corrections for B.C.—a position the Society wholly supported in light of evidence that women did not receive equal benefits in co-correctional institutions. Second, no feasibility or implementation studies regarding the suitability of converting the Mission institution had been done. Unofficially, EFSBC staff had grave doubts about a plan to relocate federal female offenders to Mission, albeit a model institution, but one that had been designed for men.

Anxious to formulate an immediate and informed response to the joint committee's report, the EFSBC assembled a small task force of board members and senior staff. A week was spent visiting Mission, researching the contents of the joint committee report, and preparing an alternate proposal for the development of services for federal women in a facility separate but adjacent to the Mission institution. This did not represent the best solution, perhaps, but the Society wished to send a clear message that the recommendation of the joint committee (Chinnery Report) for a co-corrections facility in B.C. was unacceptable. The EFSBC forwarded their proposal to the solicitor general, with a statement about the need for full local consultation with the provincial commissioner of corrections, and a request that the Society become a part of any western consultation process on this issue. The EFSBC also hastened to secure the support of CAEFS on this matter.

The EFSBC thus found itself in a delicate position as a front ranking advocate for the closure of the P4W, but in opposition to a long-awaited plan for joint service to federal women. The Society in no way wished to thwart the plans to close the P4W or jeopardize B.C.'s long-term goal to provide joint service, but it did not believe that the current solution represented the best interest of female in-

mates. The EFSBC was invited to meet with senior federal corrections officials and members of the joint committee. These meetings
were scheduled to take place during the International Symposium
on the Female Offender held in Vancouver, in January 1979, at
which time the Chinnery Report would be made public by Solicitor
General Jean Jacques Blais. It was a measure of the esteem in which
the EFSBC was held that it received assurances from the commissioner of corrections, D.R. Yeomans, that the proposal would not be
adopted due to the strenuous objections of the Society.[60]

The time was ripe for the EFSBC to participate in the planning
process as an "honest broker." Indeed, the Society found it necessary to take on the responsibility for examining the merits or
limitations of co-corrections and devising a feasible alternative proposal for the housing of female federal offenders in British
Columbia. Athough all parties were undoubtedly eager to reach a
consensus, the politics of the situation demanded the independent
analysis that the EFSBC could offer. For example, B.C. could not be
seen to reverse its stand on co-corrections in light of the attorney
general's acceptance of the Proudfoot Report, which regarded the
co-corrections facility in Prince George as disastrous for female inmates, and advised its termination and no further developments along
this model. Nor could local corrections officials or Mission staff be
expected to put forward a service proposal contrary to the stated policy of the Commission of Corrections. The EFSBC, then, in its
position as a long-established voluntary agency, working closely with
provincial and federal ministries, had the freedom to take the initiative
in seeking the most humane and economically feasible solution.[61]

The Society was given a commitment that sufficient time would
be allowed for full consultation with local, regional, provincial, and
federal representatives; and to study co-correctional facilities in the
United States; and that if a viable alternative proposal to Mission
was developed, it would receive serious consideration. To aid the
Society in its task, the EFSBC was assisted by federal and provincial
corrections staff and received travel expenses. The EFSBC study also
benefited from the wide range of academic research on the female
offender that was presented at the aforementioned international
symposium by academics, administrative personnel, and line staff
workers variously involved in implementing policy that affected the
female offender.[62]

An enormous amount of energy and expertise on the part of Fry
volunteers, professional and support staff contributed to the completion of the EFSBC's *Report on B.C. Federal Women; an Alternative
Proposal* six months later, in June 1979. The report dealt with three
issues: the feasibility of the joint committee's co-correctional proposal; the feasibility of B.C.'s preferred position for the development

of joint federal-provincial services; and a feasible alternate interim placement plan in support of the early closing of the Kingston Prison for Women.

The evidence amassed by the EFSBC on co-corrections included observations of three co-correctional facilities in the U.S. and discussions with managers, staff, and inmates of these institutions. This on-site research was conducted by EFSBC volunteers and the executive director.[63] The EFSBC's conclusion was that even if the many necessary conditions were met regarding programs, management style, treatment options, staff attitudes, living unit conditions, restrictions on movement and physical contact between the sexes, and a balanced ratio of males to females, co-correctional placements remained relatively unsatisfactory for women. At the root of the difficulties with co-correctional facilities lay the social and psychological characteristics shared by the majority of female offenders. Research showed them to be "under-developed social beings" or "persons whose childhood hungers have never translated into social skills, whose attachments are dependent and often destructive."[64] The Fry saw that rather than contributing to a female inmate's social development, the Mission proposal would reinforce her street image and low self-concept. Too often the Fry found that co-corrections was promoted for the benefits that would accrue to the male inmates (who were reportedly more manageable and whose good behaviour was ensured by the promise of social activities with the female inmates), but found no corresponding gains for the women. The EFSBC had other concerns about the impact on the community and on the "very fine male institution" that was in danger of being disrupted and damaged by the new demands of a co-correctional facility.[65]

On the second issue, the B.C. position on the female federal offender had been consolidated by the recommendations of the Proudfoot Report: " . . . That if all federal women prisoners are returned to the province then the federal and provincial governments should join forces to provide these facilities and programs." The return of the B.C. federal women had been a goal of the EFSBC for many years and the Society had made such a recommendation to the Proudfoot Commission. Both B.C.'s concern, and its extensive experience in the provision of services to federal women under an exchange of services agreement, were unique among the provinces. B.C. had been waiting for a commitment from the federal commissioner to begin planning for a joint facility, and during the course of the EFSBC's study the commissioner agreed to participate in discussions regarding a proposal for a joint federal-provincial facility.

The EFSBC study reviewed the observations and assumptions that were the basis of B.C.'s decision to seek unified services for the total B.C. female offender population: the relatively small numbers, the less violent behaviour, and the range of individual needs of women, as well as the need for economically feasible and more efficient management. The EFSBC report also outlined the financial arrangements, planning requirements, and program and treatment standards that would have to accompany agreements for joint services. The EFSBC concluded a joint federal-provincial facility could be located in B.C. on the site of the existing provincial prison for women.[66]

The EFSBC proposed that federal inmates in B.C. utilize the full range of existing minimum security and community placements; and the central facility be developed on the upper Oakalla lands as a major renovation or building project, thus replacing the current Oakalla Women's Unit. This facility would offer a full security range, and could provide for the training and work placements for the long-term inmates.[67] The Society was adamant in its rejection of the Mission option for even an interim period of three to five years. The belief that co-corrections was not in the best interests of women, and a suspicion of "temporary" solutions, led the EFSBC to strive for a plan that could make the early placement of federal women in B.C. economically feasible.[68]

The Fry's alternative proposal to use the Oakalla facility in the short-term had to address the issue of this institution's credibility in light of the recent publicity and exposure during the Proudfoot inquiry. The Society was convinced that a total transformation was taking place at Oakalla following the implementation of Proudfoot's recommendations. It was confident that the renewal of Oakalla would be complete by December 1979, and observed that the perimeter fence was being installed, which would allow for the secure movement of inmates outdoors; as well, trailers were in place for the library, school, administration, and staff lounge. Improvements to the interior decoration, as well as to the morale of inmates and staff, were expected. In addition, the EFSBC's proposal outlined a number of additions to the programs and personnel at Oakalla that would accommodate federal women.[69]

Unfortunately, by June the momentum that appeared to be carrying the provinces and the federal government closer to a joint agreement was halted by the federal election that ended sixteen years of Liberal government. Although the EFSBC's recommendation was accepted by CAEFS at the national meeting in July and in early August, the Pacific Regional Department of CSC examined the feasibility of the Fry proposal; the newly-installed Conservative government scarcely acknowledged the EFSBC's alternative proposal. In September the president and executive director of the EFSBC were invited by the Office of the Solicitor General to accompany Madam Justice Proudfoot to Kingston to tour the Prison for Women. This was evidently an attempt to have the EFSBC reconsider its position

Forty years after its construction, the Women's Unit at Oakalla, or Lakeside, was no longer a commendable institution. With three and four women sharing a room, like this one, women had scarcely space for themselves let alone any personal effects.

on the closure of the P4W. The EFSBC remained more convinced than ever, however, as Vi Roden, president of the EFSBC, and Dru Anderegg, executive director, stated in their letter to the solicitor general, the Honourable Allan Lawrence:

> While we were impressed with the fine spirit and motivation of Prison for Women staff, our visit has underlined for us the urgency of *the need for a federal initiative in the creation of new, integrated regional facilities* serving federal and provincial female population. It is truly shocking to realize that a system that has produced both a Mission and a Kent, in B.C. alone, presents no alternative for women beyond an antiquated institution wherein a substantial portion of inmates on all security levels are literally *caged.* And no alternative to automatic separation of women from dependent infant children, elderly parents, friends, community— while routinely housing male offenders in their region and contracting for services to their wives and children. We find the continuation of this situation quite unacceptable. Differential access by sex to program and work opportunities, alone, seems a questionable interpretation of essential human rights; and the potential for repeating generational cycles of deep social problems, when single mothers and their children are arbitrarily separated without investment in support service, may prove to be a compounding and complex problem for the future.[70]

There still had been no official response to the EFSBC's alternative proposal for federal women prisoners. In October of 1979, the president of CAEFS, Barbara Kilbourn, learned from the commissioner of corrections, D.R. Yeomans, that the feasibility of closing the Kingston Prison for Women was to undergo yet another investigation. Kilbourn indicated that this was unacceptable to CAEFS. She pointed out that the provinces were ready to negotiate the concurrent establishment of regional options and needed federal initiative and not another study. The solicitor general agreed to meet with the CAEFS executive in order to explain his position further.

The solicitor general's comments to CAEFS made it clear that his ministry intended to make its own re-assessment of the future of the P4W. He noted that, historically, ad hoc decisions had been dictated by public pressures and that the several different building programs announced in the recent past had not been based on a reliable statistical forecast of building needs for the future.[71] The CAEFS representatives pointed out that their wanting the closure of the P4W and the creation of regional options for federal women were not merely issues of prison construction. Rather, CAEFS emphasized that, historically, women have been discriminated against, and that federal women prisoners only have one place of incarceration regardless of offence, age, circumstance, needs, or residence. This discrimination was also evident in the expenditures for female offender housing and programs. For example, the average maintenance cost for a male offender in a federal maximum security prison was $81 a day, whereas for a female inmate it was $67.[72]

CAEFS also raised the inconsistency of policies within the ministry regarding the intention to close the Kingston prison. In particular, CAEFS questioned the minister's proposed construction of an $8 million activities centre at the P4W, while at the same time citing the exorbitant per diem requests by some provinces as a cause for reconsideration of the closure of the prison. CAEFS argued that this expenditure could be allocated instead either to improvement of regional options, or at least on the living area in the P4W. In short, Lawrence was by his own admission undecided as to the fate of the P4W. He made it clear to the CAEFS executive that he did not feel bound by the previous government's plans and had no intention of making a decision in the immediate future. Any announcement of closure, Lawrence noted, would place him in the unenviable position of having to negotiate reasonable options with the provinces.[73]

Over the following decade of political change and economic uncertainty, CAEFS and the EFSBC had to come to grips with the realization that a prolonged delay of the decision to close the P4W was, by default, a decision to maintain it. The efforts of the women who had worked hopefully and tirelessly to effect penal reform for female offenders watched the critical time for effective provincial negotiations come and go.

Gains were made for federal women on a piecemeal basis. An agreement was reached in the fall of 1979 between Quebec and Ottawa to transfer all French-speaking inmates from Kingston to Maison Tanguay—a provincial institution near Montreal.[74]

In British Columbia the Elizabeth Fry Society did a great deal of

In January 1991, the Burnaby Correctional Centre for Women replaced the old provincial prison for women at Oakalla. The EFSBC was an active participant in the planning of this institution in the hope that it might provide both a facility and programs that would reflect the needs of female offenders.

work "behind the scenes" to bring about an agreement that would enable federally sentenced women from B.C. to be accommodated in their own province. The Burnaby Agreement incorporated resource standards and provided for ongoing federal involvement and joint federal-provincial responsibility for women transferred under this agreement.[75] The agreement anticipated a new provincial prison that would replace the old women's unit at Oakalla.

Although many critics of the Lower Mainland Regional Correctional Centre (Oakalla) condemned the prison for being harshly outdated, it was rising land values in the 1980s that caused the provincial government to finally move the LMRCC from the prime residential property in Burnaby. Construction began on new provincial facilities, two for men in Maple Ridge and Surrey and one for women in Burnaby, that would accommodate federal female offenders. As representatives on the Users' Committee, the EFSBC maintained an advisory role in the planning and building of this new prison, which opened in November 1990.

The Burnaby Correctional Centre for Women is located south of Marine Way, near the Fraser River in Burnaby. The building is replete with state-of-the-art security systems—cameras, electronic communication, alarm systems, and remote control locks—but it was designed also to provide natural light and a sense of space. Although one inmate observed, "with concrete walls it still looks too much like a prison," in fact, on the outside, the facility bears more resemblance to a community college. Inside, the individual bedrooms cluster in living units arranged around a central rotunda that serves as a meeting place adjoining a library, classrooms, and workshop areas. Because of the electronic surveillance, inmates can move in and out of the building if they are working on the grounds, in the greenhouse, or the dog training programs. There are plans to complete an aboriginal healing lodge to meet the needs of Native women.

The correctional centre was conceived with the exchange of service agreement in mind and can house up to fifty federal women, nearly a third of its total capacity of 142. A number of programs are in place for the federal women and more are in the planning stages. Also on the site is the "open living unit," which houses women considered to be low risks to the community. These inmates are usually working towards their release. Both the "locked" and the "open" units have provisions for visiting family members, husbands, and children who may wish to spend some private time with the inmate. While not ideal in every respect, the new women's correctional centre is regarded by the EFSBC as an environment that may encourage positive changes in offenders' lives. In the opinion of Maida Duncan, the EFSBC member on the user's committee that worked with the architect in designing the building, the prison contains much that had been envisioned by the Society since the 1940s—a well-stocked crafts room, a sewing workshop, a fully equipped gymnasium, a library, educational programs, and access to outdoor exercise and horticulture work. The EFSBC also regarded the new structure as the most hopeful sign that the P4W would soon be able to close its doors forever.

The latest word on the future of the Kingston Prison for Women came from yet another study, *Creating Choices: The Report of the Task Force on Federally Sentenced Women*, released April 1990. Members on the steering committee included women from Elizabeth Fry Societies in all the regions. Bonnie Diamond, executive director of CAEFS, co-chaired the task force with James A. Phelps, Deputy Commissioner, Correctional Service of Canada. Nearly half of the ten members of the working group were Fry women.[76] Representatives from Corrections; the National Parole Board; the Department of Justice; and a variety of women's organizations, including the Status of Women, Aboriginal Women's Caucus, Native Women's Association, and Immigrant and Visible Minority Women ensured a wide perspective would be brought to this examination of federally sentenced women and to develop a plan responsive to their needs.

This report stands as a remarkable document, both for its discussion of a number of "principles for change" that are offered as a foundation "for broader justice and social reform in the future"; and also for its recommendation and detailed plans for the creation of five regional women's facilities across Canada to be operated by the Correctional Service of Canada, and also an "aboriginal healing lodge" for federally-sentenced Native women. In its underlying philosophy and methods of research, the report has been influenced by the feminist critiques of traditional sociological and psychological interpretations of women's criminality, which began in the 1970s. Many of these studies argued that "women in prison have more in common with other women than they do with male inmates, and that programs and services should be designed to meet local needs and circumstances, or planned individually, not on the basis of some 'centralized blueprint.'"[77]

The media reported as "news" the recommendation of this latest task force that the P4W be closed. In response, the women in the EFSBC and CAEFS undoubtedly smiled, shook their heads, and shrugged before they took up their pens and organized their social action committees to continue their efforts to shut down this antiquated structure that embodied a corrections philosophy of a different era. As "honest brokers" the Elizabeth Fry Society of British Columbia along with the national organization, CAEFS, had been influential in reformulating attitudes towards the incarceration of women and they would ultimately succeed in closing the Kingston Prison for Women.

9. STOPPING TO LOOK BACKWARD AND FORWARD

As a Minister, I receive many requests to speak, but of all the invitations that I have received, this is the one that I have anticipated the most. Not only because we are honouring the work that the Elizabeth Fry Society has done over the years, but also for me on a very personal note, because of the impact that the Elizabeth Fry Society has had on me as a woman, and as a woman helping other women. . . . For me, it seems a long way from being a volunteer counsellor at Oakalla to a cabinet minister in Ottawa. And yet, each of us is really just the sum of our life experiences. I know there is still a lot of Oakalla in me — I hope that in the next fifty years the Elizabeth Fry Society of Vancouver continues to do its fine work, not only for women in conflict with the law, and this is still as important today as it was fifty years ago, but also for the thousands of volunteers who, through Elizabeth Fry, will come to know their own potential as women and will continue to make our country a more caring and equal society for all.

The Honourable Barbara McDougall, address to the fiftieth
anniversary meeting of the EFSBC, September 28, 1989[1]

In the fall of 1989, 300 supporters of the Elizabeth Fry Society of British Columbia gathered in uncustomarily opulent surroundings, a banquet room of the Hotel Vancouver, to celebrate the Society's fiftieth anniversary. The commemorative dinner was an event designed to remember the past, affirm the present, and envision the future of the EFSBC. It was an occasion for Fry women to look backward and forward, thereby linking the achievements of the past with the expectations of the future.

The dinner speaker that evening was former Fry volunteer, the Honourable Barbara McDougall, Minister of Employment and Immigration and Minister Responsible for the Status of Women. Although a cabinet minister, the Honourable Barbara McDougall's celebrity status that evening was related to her previous connection with the EFSBC. McDougall was also representative of a variety of political women associated with the EFSBC over the years whose volunteer work represented their initial commitment to social change and whose subsequent political success conferred, in turn, some prestige to women's voluntary work. She shared distinction on this occasion with the Society's other honoured guests that included the first woman to be appointed Judge of the Supreme Court of British Columbia, Madam Justice Patricia Proudfoot, and several women, now senior citizens, who had served as Fry volunteers over twenty years previous. The great great granddaughter of Elizabeth Fry, Elizabeth Fry Ellis, a resident of Port Alberni on Vancouver Island, was also a significant presence and a further reminder of women's historical connections to penal reform.

McDougall's speech offered an analysis of the social and equality issues that face women both in and out of prison. She noted,

> ... that for women who have come in conflict with the law, life is a cycle of gender, racial, and class discrimination ... whose efforts to regain control over their lives can be frustrated by a criminal justice system which seems ill-equipped and unresponsive to their real needs as women, wives, and mothers.[2]

Her comments were well understood by her audience—EFSBC volunteers and staff. But it was not McDougall's intention to arouse feminist indignation; indeed, she knew that for many Fry women, any identification with the women's movement was the farthest thing from their minds. Rather, Fry volunteers would concur with McDougall's own observations:

> For many of us who were working with female inmates and with former female inmates over the years, we didn't see ourselves as part of an important social movement, nor did we attempt to politicize our actions. We were simply filling a need that we perceived to exist in the community.[3]

McDougall's words indicated that neither the mission nor the predominant motivation for the EFSBC's work for penal reform had altered significantly since 1939. It still stemmed not from a feminist consciousness but from a female voluntary tradition. The celebration of this tradition was evident in the motto—"a legacy of caring"—that the EFSBC chose for its fiftieth anniversary.

In the first fifty years, the Society's ethos, or mission, was conveyed and perpetuated in a variety of ways but most obviously in the name and visage of Elizabeth Fry. In using Elizabeth Fry's name, the Society did not just honour a pioneer of the prison reform movement but celebrated a heroine of volunteerism. Like a maternal ancestor, a kindly intelligent portrait of this nineteenth century

Quaker woman overlooked the Society's offices and, for many years, adorned its official stationery.

As indicated in the opening pages of this history, the story of Elizabeth Fry's work in London's Newgate Gaol in the 1800s, and her testimony before the British Parliamentary Committee, was part of every member's initiation and served as a basis for making the Society's purposes meaningful to its members and its supporters. These Fry stories, of women's historic endeavours in aid of women sentenced to prison, linked women in the twentieth century to a tradition of women's prison reform, thereby confirming the mission of the Society.[4]

Stories of women's efforts and victories in the more recent past also circulated within the EFSBC and endorsed women's voluntary work for penal reform. In the early years of the Society, the history of women's work in British Columbia—to revise laws affecting women and children, to establish the Girls' Industrial School, the Juvenile Court, and better facilities for the female inmates in prison—was easily recalled by the still active participants. Moreover, the heroines of the earlier women's movement, for example, Helen Gregory MacGill, served as significant reminders of women's work in social reform in British Columbia. At the annual meeting of the EFSBC following MacGill's death in 1947, Fraudena Eaton paid tribute not only to MacGill's accomplishments in penal reform but to the example she set for other women. As illustrated by the words that opened the second chapter, Eaton recalled her own discouragement in the past and the inspiration provided by her friendship with MacGill, who had told her "in no uncertain words to go on." Eaton remembered MacGill for "her driving force in all matters where she took an interest," and attributed her own commitment and tenacity to "this power that our beloved departed had of forcing others to carry on."[5] Accolades such as this reinforced the determination of Fry members to uphold the voluntary tradition.

The recounting of the Fry stories and of remembered history helped to create the identity of the EFSBC and contributed to a distinctive ethos that fortified successive generations of volunteers. Female role models and the bonds of friendship similarly confirmed women's commitment to service and persistence against opposition and indifference. The knowledge that the women in the Fry Society were continuing a tradition of women's work engendered a female solidarity that also strengthened the EFSBC's sense of mission. In the interests of providing a legacy for women in the future, a written history—this book—was envisioned by Fry volunteers to preserve the collective memory.

The EFSBC's voluntary tradition has been challenged but not abandoned in the course of social changes that ranged from expanded opportunities for women in the work force to new philosophical outlooks in the field of penal reform. Nor has the periodic structural reorganization of the EFSBC, which emphasized divisions of voluntary and professional responsibility, prevented many women from finding volunteer work an attractive and satisfying occupation on its own terms.

In recent decades, however, more women have regarded volunteer work as a bridge, if not a pre-requisite, for the fulfilment of their political or career aspirations. Younger women joined the EFSBC in greater numbers, but their terms as volunteer workers were relatively short-lived in view of their long-term goals to become paid professional social workers in related fields. These predominantly student volunteers have not offered the same degree of stability and commitment to the Society that distinguished the older volunteers in the past. Although, as was the experience of Susan McKechnie, occasionally "a funny thing happened on the way to a career!" After McKechnie graduated from law school in 1983 she volunteered for the EFSBC, expecting to gain insights that would complement her legal training. A combination of events, including the seeming reluctance of law firms in the city to offer articling positions to female graduates, caused McKechnie to re-evaluate her own career options. She decided not to practise law but remained a dedicated Fry volunteer who undertook the responsibilities of membership on the EFSBC Board in 1983, and served as the Society's treasurer and president from 1988 to 1990.[6] McKechnie was one of the younger women to make that "old time" commitment to volunteer work with the EFSBC.

Clearly, a woman's age is significant inasmuch as it may determine the amount of time and also the variety of experience she can offer to the Fry. While any organization looks to youthful members for its renewal and regeneration, women in their middle years have made a particular contribution to the EFSBC. An EFSBC volunteer in the 1970s, Theresa Citterelle, who was hired by the Society as a community access worker at Lakeside in the 1980s, recalled:

> Older women used to be the backbone of the Fry. The younger ones tend to want the experience promised by volunteer work and know that time spent as a Fry volunteer will look good on their resumes, but we need the dedication of the older person. The women in prison often relate better to a mature mother figure.[7]

Citterelle looked back to the future when she suggested that in the 1990s the EFSBC should endeavour to recruit mature women into the organization to ensure these valued qualities of Fry volunteers endure in the years ahead.

As the EFSBC approached its 50th anniversary in the late 1980s, several EFSBC longtime volunteers – all past presidents – formed a committee to collect and organize the Society's records. Impressed by the immense changes to the EFSBC's structure and responsibilities and wanting to pass on the story of its origins and transformations to the next generation of volunteers, (from left) Marie Legg, Maida Duncan, Grace Black and Beth Weese guided the history project to its completion.

Although Citterelle might have noted any number of contributions by the Fry volunteers, the reference to their role as prison visitors was both natural and significant. This aspect of Fry work remains primary to any summation of the history of the EFSBC. In looking backward and forward, the centrality of the experience of prison visiting to the progression of the EFSBC's efforts to effect changes to the Canadian corrections system is unmistakable. Whether or not prisons reform the behaviours of their involuntary inmates cannot be determined from the vantage point of this history; but, as reflected in the words of Barbara McDougall, the impact of the prison on its voluntary visitors and, thereby, the evolution of the EFSBC, is readily apparent. Another former Fry visitor to Oakalla expressed that in her view, "Only by understanding the enormity of the fact of *prison* can the rationale of the Elizabeth Fry be truly understood."[8]

Certainly it was the sordid conditions in which women and children were imprisoned in the early nineteenth century, without regard for their spiritual needs, that aroused the Quaker conscience of the first, most famous prison visitor, Elizabeth Fry. Following her visits to Newgate, Fry felt compelled to organize her ladies' committees to perform practical improvements for the female inmates and to focus public attention on the need to reform a medieval penal system. Also in the nineteenth century, outraged by the moral neglect reflected in policies whereby women were housed under the same roof as male inmates and guarded by men, female reformers in North America sought "separate but equal" institutions in which female custodians were installed to be "their sisters' keepers." These reformers hoped women's prisons would reinstate values of moral purity and uphold ideals of womanhood among the female inmates.[9]

In the early twentieth century, women in British Columbia had been no less moved than previous penal reformers by the degrading and inadequate circumstances in which women were incarcerated. In B.C., women prisoners were confined apart from men but still under the same roof. Their fewer numbers served to render them invisible in the competition with male offenders for the scarce resources of the correctional services. The women in B.C. who would eventually form the Elizabeth Fry Society wanted initially to correct the injustice that perpetuated inequitable and negligent treatment of female inmates. In subsequent years, the "enormity of the fact of prison" moved Fry women to explore concepts of rehabilitation, preventive, and after-care that might serve as alternatives to incarceration.

The EFSBC's initiatives contributed to an evolving philosophy of corrections and were guided by theories and practices derived from the insights of the social sciences. However, for the majority of the Society's first fifty years, Fry women looked to female networks, family, schooling and education—those familiar institutions of women's culture—to provide both the means and the models for the changes they wished to make to correctional treatment for women.

Historically, female networks such as those afforded by women's associations had been the means by which women were able to address political issues and social reform. By uniting women's efforts, organizations like the influential Council of Women and the University Women's Club in B.C. had become effective lobbyists for social change. Nurturing interest in prison reform in the early part of the century, these groups had spawned a women's prison auxiliary that became the Elizabeth Fry Society. In the early years, the EFSBC sought well-connected women to be patrons of the Society. The fledgling prisoners' aid society needed both these individual women and organizations like the Council of Women to give credibility to its intentions. By the 1960s, the EFSBC had shed its formal connections with women's organizations not primarily involved with penal reform.[10] However, the EFSBC did not underestimate the power of organized women and sought this traditional source of female support with the founding of the Canadian Association of Elizabeth Fry Societies (CAEFS), which established a national voice for women interested in penal reform.

Bureaucratic changes within the administration of corrections had invited consolidation of local interests into a national body.[11] However, the founding of CAEFS in 1971[12] was not unrelated to another social movement gaining strength in Canada. Civil rights activists in the United States during the sixties had focused attention on the inequitable treatment of minorities and women. In Canada, a new generation of organized women, female journalists, and politicians breathed fresh life into the Canadian women's movement with their demands for a Royal Commission on the Status of Women.[13] Thus the formation of CAEFS may have satisfied bureaucratic demands but undoubtedly was influenced by social and political considerations brought into focus by the new feminist consciousness that sought a female consensus.

CAEFS increased the visibility of women in a field long dominated by men. Fry women increasingly attended the biennial sessions of the Corrections Congresses, presenting papers and taking this opportunity to hold the meetings of CAEFS to discuss the activities of Fry societies across the country. Not surprisingly, CAEFS increasingly became concerned with the larger issues of women's inequality under the law and the feminist cause of advancing the status of women. Although the EFSBC had its roots in an earlier women's movement, over the years the EFSBC aligned itself more with a female tradition of philanthropic caring than with feminist politics.[14] The Society's goal to aid women in conflict with the law ensures its allegiance with CAEFS despite the EFSBC's more conservative, or perhaps more practical, outlook.

The strength of women's organizations (also minorities and labour unions) lay in their solidarity, or collective action. In the same vein, Fry women believed their interests in the welfare of female inmates were shared by the staff of the correctional institutions; the Society, therefore, strove for harmonious cooperation with correctional personnel and eschewed adversarial tactics in its work to achieve penal reform. The ideal of partnership that underlies the relationship of the volunteer and professional Fry worker also stems from the value Fry women place on collective action within a non-hierarchical framework.

Female networks, with their emphasis on collective responsibility, provided both the structure and the *modus operandi* for women's involvement in penal reform. However, the ideal of collectivity has not superseded the EFSBC's belief in accountability. The EFSBC attributes its longevity as a voluntary association to its ability to maintain both its high standards in services and balanced budgets. The EFSBC has ever been conscientious regarding the management of both its human and fiscal resources. In the face of improper attention to the standards set by the Fry for its services, the Society has not hesitated to remove unsuitable staff and volunteers. Nor has it hesitated to cut its losses, cancel programs, and redirect its energies in more constructive directions. Although adamant that government budgets should reflect a greater priority for correctional services for female offenders, where possible, the EFSBC has pursued alternate sources of funding with diligence, innovation, and patience. These strategies have enabled the Society to survive government cutbacks in 1983 to 1985 and to be in a position to undertake new challenges. Albeit, the mission and commitment of volunteers and staff have ensured their shouldering much of the burden imposed by government restraint policies. Sandy Simpson, EFSBC's executive director from 1982 to 1988, was frustrated by the provincial government in those years when she charged—"it doesn't plan, it just reacts"—but she expressed pride in the ability of the Society to maintain and even expand its level of services.[15]

Much of the hope and inspiration for the Society's work was derived from Fry women's unshaken belief in the affective benefits offered to an individual by a caring home and family. In the 1940s, the Society had attempted to replace the harsh, institutional atmosphere of the provincial industrial school for female juvenile offenders with a more familial, home-like environment. At the Cassiar Street site, neither cosmetic nor management changes were entirely successful in fulfilling these objectives, but the Society was optimistic that its ideas would be incorporated into the building of the new Willingdon School for Girls. The EFSBC regarded the rural features of Twin Maples Correctional Centre and, later, its accommodation of young children with their mothers, as recognition of Native women's needs and the importance of the preservation of familial bonds. The Society had supported the concept of family visiting for men and women's prisons, although this idea was rejected by public opinion made nervous by sensational representations and suggestive repercussions of conjugal activity that appeared in the press.

The first group homes established by the EFSBC rigorously upheld the form and function of family life with houseparents who emphasized family routine and mutual responsibility of individuals within the home. The Fry believed that a loving but disciplined home would provide stability and engender confidence in the children in its care. The ultimate goal of the Fry's homes was to divert troubled and delinquent adolescents from a prison course.

Apparently, the quest for a nurturing environment was shared by many of the girls and women who lived in Fry homes. By their own admittance, the EFSBC's women's residence was often the first real home its occupants had ever experienced. The simple, caring acts of Pauline Fell, the housemother of the women's residence, to make birthday cakes for her "girls" (usually the first they had ever received) would result in tears of joy and gratitude. For these women, Fell fulfilled their fantasies of "mother" and helped ease the sorrow and anger they felt for their lost childhood.[16]

Although the Society remained convinced that the traditional family model held the potential for the most effective socialization, by the 1970s the EFSBC increasingly hired experienced childcare workers to head the Fry homes. Houseparents in the group homes and women's residence were replaced by staff with specialized training who worked shifts. These changes were directed by government policies that attempted to standardize the qualifications of childcare workers and their hours of work.[17] After a worker was murdered in a halfway house in Ottawa, the EFSBC women's residence on Balaclava Street had to formalize procedures to enforce stricter levels of security to comply with revised government regulations.[18]

The residential models operated by the EFSBC over the years have attempted to provide a safe environment for the healthy socialization of its occupants while trying to maintain a home-like and not an institutional environment. To a degree, the changing structure of the group homes paralleled changing definitions of family that decreased the emphasis on the stereotypical roles of men, women, and children within the nuclear family. However, the substitution of trained staff for houseparents indicated a shift away from the remedial towards the more clinical aspects of preventive care. In some respects this was recognition that a child's anti-social behaviour stemmed from complex causes.

The EFSBC's impulse to strengthen and uphold family relationships as a means of preventive and after-care, now widened its focus. The Society established non-residential programs that offered counselling to the families of the children in the Fry's group and receiving homes. It was hoped that by working with the entire family unit, the Fry could establish a broader support structure for families in trouble and ensure a better adjustment after the child's return. Several of the EFSBC group homes extended therapeutic services and intervention with "outreach" programs to families needing assistance in keeping their children in their own homes.[19] Family therapy is expensive and the EFSBC's efforts have been constrained by government cutbacks.

Throughout its first fifty years, the essence of the EFSBC's viability lay in its ability to recognize and respond to the changing needs of the community even if this meant discarding outmoded models and devising new ones. The Fry regretted the closure of Willingdon School for Girls in March 1973 and the conversion of that facility to a juvenile detention centre for male and female youths. However, volunteers eventually resumed educational, recreational, and social programs at Willingdon Youth Detention Centre.[20] Two years later, the Society rescinded its own limitations with regard to the age and gender of the applicants for its group homes to allow for more flexibility.[21] In 1978, the EFSBC's second group home, Cambridge House, became a long-term co-ed residence for five older adolescents (sixteen to eighteen years) who had been through foster and group home programs but were not yet ready to assume complete responsibility for their lives as young adults. The goal of this program was to provide the residents with skills directed toward their independent functioning in the community. In January 1981, the EFSBC's sixth group home, Catherine House, served as the juvenile receiving and assessment home for the Coquitlam area. The Society's seventh group home, Tatlow House in Vancouver, opened in 1982 as a long-term (six months to a year) residential treatment facility for six boys aged twelve to seventeen years who were experiencing difficulties in the home, school, or community. Duncan House, the Fry's first group home, currently offers a cooperative model of residency for adolescents aged sixteen to nineteen years who are in the process of learning to live independently in the community.

Changes in the EFSBC group home admission policies and juvenile programs increased the need for male voluntary and professional workers to provide good role models for the boys. Since the late seventies, men have served the Society both in voluntary and professional capacities.[22] Because many of the girls and women have been victimized by men and have learned manipulative or dependent behaviours to survive these relationships, male staff and voluntary workers have to be both non-threatening and sensitive to women's need to gain confidence and self-esteem.

While the EFSBC has made significant changes in keeping with social expectations and correctional reform—opening more group homes, introducing new treatment programs and employing more specialized staff—the greatest impetus for change in the future, as it has been in the past, will be the demands of the client group. The increasingly severe problems presented by the young people in provincial custody—kids using alcohol and drugs, accustomed to violence, vandalism, prostitution, and perhaps having been exposed to the deadly disease AIDS—will have an impact on child-care services offered in British Columbia. Apart from issues of how to best serve these children and adolescents, the EFSBC is concerned that the rising costs have made it impossible to extend care to other than the most visibly needy.

The need for the Fry's residential programs (and, in fact, their success) was evidence that two parents and their biological offspring did not guarantee loving, caring homes. But in recent years, social workers report an increasing number of "very damaged children"—a description frightening in its implications. Much of this damage has been inflicted by families as much in need of counselling as the children. In 1988, Sandy Simpson revealed:

> ... the kids we get now in the receiving homes are very different ... they are very streetwise. They have been sexually and physically abused ... disclosure is more common today—kids are less hesitant to disclose. We see adolescents who are now abusers. They have been abused. That is one problem. Now, their behaviour towards others is another problem, a new component. We are dealing with a very different population of very damaged children and their families do not want to be part of reconciling or contending with that child. There are teenagers—fifteen and sixteen years old—coming into care for the first time because families do not want to continue the responsibility of dealing with them.[23]

Human and financial resources are easily absorbed by individuals in circumstances that demand immediate intervention. Group homes may fall out of favour with the government because six- and seven-bed facilities are expensive to maintain. The Society has had to include in its budgets the costs of re-training staff to prepare them for their legal responsibilities and to counsel children disclosing histories of abuse. In an effort to curb costs, more permanent placements and long-term counselling may be solutions favoured by the B.C. Ministry of Social Services and Housing. The Ministry may prefer to place two or three children in an existing family or a "parent-counsellor home" and pay the parents for their services. This arrangement resembles a "foster home" in many respects, although the family could expect psychological support from a counsellor/therapist assigned to the children in care.

The Society has serious reservations about this model. Many of the problems that caused the Society, in the 1960s, to establish group homes as an alternative to foster homes still prevail. Primarily the EFSBC is skeptical that foster parents are skilled enough to provide the special kind of care these damaged children require. From its own experiences, the Society is well aware that some communities can be intolerant of group homes or foster care in their neighbourhoods.[24] Moreover, as long as the province sets no standards for child care, and requires no financial audit, the Society fears there is inadequate accountability within the parent-counsellor homes. There is always the risk that individuals may regard foster care as profitable.[25]

Ideally, the EFSBC would like to extend therapy to entire families of children in the Society's care, whether or not the outcome is reconciliation. In 1990 on the north shore, the EFSBC provided comprehensive in-home assessments and counselling services to sixty-five families with children aged six to eighteen years. The Society also offered a crisis intervention program. Two family workers enabled families to live together through a period of teen-parent conflict by teaching short-term conflict resolution strategies and counselling in the areas of mediation, communication, and parenting.

As part of its commitment to provide aid to youth in conflict with the law, the Society tries to preserve the family as the primary institution of socialization. The family is clearly an institution that absorbs and reflects the stress present in the larger community; often children and women are the most visible victims of dysfunctional families. Although the EFSBC cannot correct all the injustice that may be found in Canadian society, the Society's counselling programs teach individuals and families more positive ways to cope with their problems.

The EFSBC has always regarded education to be the best hope for reform but did not restrict this solution to offenders. The founders of the EFSBC kept themselves informed about current innovations and theories in the field of corrections. Volunteer training workshops for prospective Fry members educated women on a variety of issues related to criminal justice and the rehabilitation of offenders. In later years, the EFSBC promoted instruction and research in corrections and penology. In 1964, the EFSBC had called for a Department of Criminology to be founded at a B.C university and was gratified when criminology was finally established at Simon Fraser University in the early seventies. At the suggestion of EFSBC volunteer Grace Black, who concluded her term as president of CAEFS in 1976, the national association raised funds for a bursary, in honour of the contributions of penal reformer Agnes Macphail, to aid research in the field of corrections.

In the interests of public education the EFSBC continually provided organizations with speakers on all aspects of the Society's work and recent trends in reform and rehabilitation. The Society's public relations and social action committees distributed information regarding their work to radio stations and newspapers. The preparation and presentation of briefs to government commissions on numerous aspects of the law related to women and young offenders served to educate public opinion and reshape government policy on matters of social and penal reform.

Throughout the Society's first fifty years, much attention had been focused on education as an agent of change in the lives of the girls and women in conflict with the law. The EFSBC was a persistent advocate of schooling and job training for the girls in the Provincial Industrial School, Willingdon School for Girls, and for the women in the provincial prisons. Shoplifting clinics, courtwork programs, and the teaching of life skills courses were attempts to provide offenders with knowledge that could help them understand

and alter their circumstances. To commemorate Elizabeth Fry's 100th birthday in 1980, the EFSBC inaugurated a bursary to assist eligible persons (currently receiving services from the Society) to upgrade their skills towards a concrete objective. The Society named the bursary the Patricia Ware Development Fund in 1985, to honour the life-time contributions to corrections made by EFSBC volunteer Patricia Ware.[26]

As with the EFSBC's residential services, programs offered by the Society had to be deemed successful if they were to continue. In the view of the executive directors and board members this was the essence of accountability and essential to maintain the Society's credibility. Success in the fields of corrections and social services is not always easy to define. In a report delivered in 1971 by EFSBC social worker J. Laurine Greig, she talked about the difficulty of measuring the success of the group homes:

> ... it very much depends on the goals that are set and what one has to work with at the outset. Some of the girls have quite severe behaviour problems when they come to us; some have not. Some of them have homes from which they continue to derive some encouragement and support. Some of them have no one. Some of them are well motivated to change, some are not. It therefore depends on the individual girl. If she has been a truant and now attends regularly, that is a success. If she applies herself to school when she previously failed, that is success. If she has been promiscuous and now has self-control, that is success ... If she was always before the Juvenile Court for misdemeanors and is no longer, that is success. If she now has a feeling of self-worth, of having a contribution to make, that is success. If she was glue sniffing, experimenting with drugs and is no longer, that is success![27]

Volunteers sometimes wrote of their "successes" in the EFSBC newsletters. In December 1968, Joan Driedger contributed the following "happy story to warm your heart at Christmas."[28]

> Helen is a young Indian girl from a small town in the interior. She came to Vancouver and lived common law, became pregnant and was abruptly deserted. Helen became ill and was unable to work ... an overdose of sleeping pills seemed a way out. Because of the attempted suicide, Helen was sentenced to six months in Oakalla ... but through the cooperation of the Attorney General's Department her sentence was suspended. At this point the Elizabeth Fry Society took over, and one of the members took her into her own home. Helen had her baby and kept it. Many Elizabeth Fry Society volunteers were friends and the professional staff offered intensive services. That was a year and half ago. Two weeks ago Helen was married. Many of her Elizabeth Fry friends received letters and pieces of wedding cake and Helen reports all is going well.

Not all of the young women aided by the Society "married and lived happily ever after," nor was that the Fry's chief measure of success. The EFSBC was more often concerned that women in conflict with the law be equipped to find work to be able to support themselves. This was the objective of the EFSBC-sponsored Frywork, a pre-employment program begun in 1979 and funded by Canada Employment and Immigration Commission, to help women – offenders and others with employment problems – to raise their employment readiness. This program was to provide an opportunity for the participants to identify negative and dependent behaviours that reinforced a low self-image and the inability to meet basic expectations of employers. Frywork aimed at familiarizing women with the many practical issues related to applying for jobs, winning, and keeping them. During the eight-week course the participant was able to spend ten days in a company in the community working at a job in which she expressed interest. Although Frywork was discontinued after five years because the expectations of subsequent employment for the women in the program were not met, the EFSBC continues to search for better ways of preparing female offenders to cope with their lives after their release.

Perhaps the most significant success that can be claimed by the EFSBC has been the Society's record of implementing change in the field of corrections for women. That is, after all, what the founders had envisioned in 1939 after they volunteered to go to prison. The sounds, sights, and smells of prison convinced the women of the Elizabeth Fry Society that more could be done for the female offender than locking her up and denying her existence. In its first fifty years, the EFSBC has been able to achieve its objectives because of the many hours of dedicated volunteer work and the quality of its professional staff and services.

In recent years the EFSBC has been recognized as an integral part of provincial and federal corrections. The Society's legacy of caring has won it individual recognition as a sophisticated agency and has generally enhanced the relationship of the voluntary sector with government. This is apparent in governments' willingness to consult with the EFSBC with regard to the role of the voluntary or private sector in corrections, and in the Society's representation on committees, task forces, and Royal Commissions. From the late 1980s, the EFSBC was a member of the User Committee for the new Burnaby Correctional Centre for Women. The EFSBC had been a logical and active participant in planning the state-of-the-art facility that replaced Oakalla (a.k.a. Lakeside) in the fall of 1990, and the Prison for Women in Kingston, for female offenders from B.C.

With this concern and interest, both in the use of space and the programs to be established at the new provincial prison, the women of the Elizabeth Fry Society of British Columbia have come full circle since 1940. In the 1990s, as in those initial years of the Society, Fry women prepare to renew their commitment to the female inmates housed in the new provincial prison and to meet the continuing challenge of penal reform.

In the intervening years, the Fry's aid to women in conflict with the law extended well beyond prison visiting; indeed, the previous pages attest to the variety of preventive and after-care services initiated by the Society for the benefit of girls and women. But perhaps what is most noteworthy about this assessment of the EFSBC's history is that although much has changed since the nineteenth century, both inside and outside prisons, much has stayed the same. Many issues from the eighteenth and nineteenth centuries continue to the present, for example, the debate over capital punishment, the concern for the successful reform of the offender, and the controversy over the use of prison labour. The characteristics of female inmates also indicate a pattern of continuity. Fewer women than men are sentenced to prison, and the majority of women's crimes are against property rather than persons. Women in prison tend to be poor, unemployed, underskilled, lacking in education, and are often single mothers with one or more children.[29] Consequently, many of the principles that distinguished the work of Elizabeth Fry and her Ladies' Committee continue to direct the activities of the Elizabeth Fry Society of British Columbia in the twentieth century. These principles relate to the need for supportive and remedial services to girls and women in correctional institutions, and the promotion of constructive change in the justice system.

What is more surprising than the continuity of the issues and principles is that the progression of the EFSBC's involvement should so closely parallel that of Elizabeth Fry and the Ladies' Committee a century earlier. Elizabeth Fry, motivated by her religious convictions, began her work with acts of kindness intended to mitigate the harsh conditions of incarceration. She eventually looked to more complex solutions, such as the training and employment of inmates. Fry's recommendations reflected her understanding of the often economic causes of women's crime and the futile effects of punishment as the method of reform. Her "caring" thus led to the active promotion of policies, procedures and programs to satisfy the still human needs of individuals in prison, and to enable them to make constructive choices when they were released.

This same process characterizes the history of the Elizabeth Fry Society of British Columbia nearly one hundred years later. The members of the Society sought initially to beautify the unpleasant surroundings of the provincial prison, to cheer its female inmates with magazines and cigarettes, and, on Sundays, to comfort them with prayers. However, like the first Elizabeth to visit prisons, the EFSBC found the inmates in need of improved facilities and more meaningful ways to spend their time. The Fry Society initiated craftwork, job training, education, and a library for the women in the provincial prison, in the hope that these programs would be administered, permanently, by the prison authorities. The Society became involved in the submission of proposals to governments, and briefs to Royal Commissions to urge changes to correctional policies.

The Society's concern for women in conflict with the law meant not only a commitment to an active role in their rehabilitation, but also to preventive and after-care. By its twenty-fifth year of service, the Elizabeth Fry Society had expanded its activities to provide a direct treatment resource in the form of a group home for teenage girls who were on the brink of delinquency. In 1965, this facility was an innovative step in preventive care. It was, however, consistent with two beliefs held by the Society. Firstly, that it was the responsibility of the community to be involved with all aspects of the justice system; secondly, that a secure home environment and healthy familial relationship provided the best socialization for young people. These themes, relating to the role of the voluntary sector and the preservation of the family, underlie much of the work of the EFSBC. This activity represents, perhaps, an extension of Elizabeth Fry's interest in the Newgate mothers and their children's education.

A long-held ambition of the EFSBC to provide a residence for women after their release from custody became a reality in 1970. This, too, paralleled the efforts of Elizabeth Fry who had recognized the importance of a support system for the inmate discharged from prison.

Thus from 1939 to 1989, the principles, policies, procedures, and programs of the EFSBC could have been modelled after the example set by Elizabeth Fry in her work in the prisons in the nineteenth century. In fact, it is only the clarity of hindsight that has made these patterns so apparent. Although the stories of Fry's life and work have confirmed the legitimacy of the Society's concerns and commitment, few, if any, of its members would wish to argue that they regarded Fry's methods as a paradigm for women's prison reform in the twentieth century. Similarly, it was unlikely that the Society would have studied the reasons for Fry's declining influence, in the last fifteen years of her life, in order to take precautions against sharing the same fate. Yet the Society's strategies to remain viable appear to have been instructed by lessons from the past.

The rise of professionalism, first evident in the nineteenth century, was a recurring challenge to voluntary activity in the twentieth. After 1830, Elizabeth Fry could not find a context for her ideas in the philosophy of the new penal reformers, and her activities were dismissed as ineffectual and outmoded in the face of professional expertise.[30] However, at a critical juncture in its history, the EFSBC recognized that in order to ensure its place in the forefront of correctional change it had to employ professional workers. This decision did not displace the voluntary worker; rather, the Society strengthened its capabilities as a voluntary agency. The professional workers remain, nevertheless, accountable to the voluntary board of directors. With a record of experience and innovation the EFSBC continues to command respect for its work at all levels of the correctional process.

The prestige that has been earned by the Elizabeth Fry Society of British Columbia in its first fifty years is due also to the commitment of the volunteers to put practical service to their clients before all other personal or political agendas. In the early years, this meant counselling prison visitors to leave their Bibles and moralizing at home. In later years, the Society has recoiled from any alignment with prison activists or radical feminists. Both of these groups seek a prisonless society. Many feminists, members, in fact, of other Elizabeth Fry Societies across the country, regard women in conflict with the law as a status of women issue. They argue that the socio-economic conditions under which women live will have to be remedied before crimes committed by women can be prevented effectively.[31] The EFSBC regards these goals as impractical and potentially obstructive to its credibility within the community. Preferring to work for change from within the system, the Society strives for reform, not revolution, and seeks to avoid controversy and notoriety associated with more radical movements for social change.

The Elizabeth Fry Society of British Columbia, like the first Elizabeth and her Ladies' Committees, may be called moderate feminists and for many of the same reasons. Members active in the Society perceive that women require different treatment because they are a small, often neglected group of offenders, with needs different from men. Essentially, although not exclusively, a female organization, the EFSBC has been an effective agency within the correctional process and has made inroads for women in a field historically dominated by men. The EFSBC also believes that it has more in common with organizations in the system which deal with persons in conflict with the law than with other women's organizations involved with equality issues. It feels that to promote a strong feminist identity for the Society will result in a loss of the unique place that it has carved for itself within the justice system. Thus the guiding principles of the EFSBC, in a way that perhaps distinguishes it from other sister societies, particularly in eastern Canada, stem from the tradition of philanthropic caring, not contemporary feminist philosophy.

Alongside this tradition of caring, apparent in the work of both Elizabeth Fry and the EFSBC, stands the evidence that public attitudes towards criminal behaviour and correctional treatment often swing with pendulum regularity between the rationales of punishment and rehabilitation. Thus the humanitarian impulse faces periodic obstacles, diversions, and redefinitions in its impact on the history of corrections. The acceptance and rejection of Elizabeth Fry's ideas, between 1817 and 1835, illustrates how shifts in the ideology relating to the criminal offender can result in correctional change which may or may not have benevolence as the primary objective.

Whereas Elizabeth Fry was unable to continue her brand of volunteer work in the face of the new penal philosophy that enforced silence, isolation, and penitence, the EFSBC has been able to sustain its influence in penal reform. Amidst the fluctuations of public concern that ranged from apathy to malice, the Elizabeth Fry Society of British Columbia has tried to ensure equity for women in conflict with the law. Since 1939, the Society has not only provided services for women, it has forged new relationships between the community and the criminal justice system, and the Ministry and the voluntary sector. The women who volunteered to go to prison in British Columbia fifty years ago have ensured that the spirit and caring embodied by Elizabeth Fry would continue in the twentieth, even to the twenty-first, century, or as long as necessary.

PRESIDENTS OF THE ELIZABETH FRY SOCIETY OF BRITISH COLUMBIA

Marguerite Rines	1940 – 1950
E.A. Thomson	1950 – 1953
Hilda Collins	1953 – 1957
Lennie Price	1957 – 1960
Thelma Ayling	1960 – 1963
Margery Ottman	1963 – 1966
Maida Duncan	1966 – 1968
Marie Legg	1968 – 1970
Daphne Paterson	1970 – 1971
Betsy Bennett	1971 – 1973
Beth Weese	1973 – 1974
Pat Kelgard	1974 – 1976
Patrick Graham	1976 – 1977
Joan Sprague	1977 – 1979
Vi Roden	1979 – Feb 1980
Joan Sprague	1980 – 1982
Joan Creighton	1982 – 1985
Joan Marshall	Sept – Dec 1985
Maida Duncan	1986 – 1987
Susan McKechnie	1987 – 1990
Sally Lambert	1990 –

EXECUTIVE DIRECTORS

Ethel Allardice, MSW	1965 – 1977
Dru Anderegg, MSW	1978 – Mar 1980
Jean Simmons	1980 – 1981
Sandra Simpson, MSW	1981 – Aug 1988
Mary McDonald, MSc	1988 –

TABLE 1
USE OF ALCOHOL AND DRUGS BY WOMEN SENTENCED TO OAKALLA 1922-38

YEAR	TOTAL FEMALE INMATES	DRUGS	ALCOHOL
1922-23	134	12 Charged 24 Self-confessed Addicts	Liquor Act: 12 Intoxicated 5 Selling Indian Act: 42 Intoxicated
1923-24	Report missing		
1924-25	123	9 Charged 23 Self-confessed Addicts	Liquor Act: 15 Intoxicated 14 Selling Indian Act: 24 Intoxicated
1925-26	83	6 Charged 21 Self-confessed Addicts	Liquor Act: 7 Intoxicated 12 Selling Indian Act: 24 Intoxicated
1926-27	99	5 Charged 41 Self-confessed Addicts	Liquor Act: 7 Intoxicated 4 Selling
1927-28	85	4 Charged 22 Self-confessed Addicts	Liquor Act: 14 (total)
1928-29	91	2 Charged 10 Self-confessed Addicts	Liquor Act: 16 Intoxicated 6 Selling Indian Act: 18 Intoxicated
1929-30	226	6 Charged 19 Self-confessed Addicts	Liquor Act: 30 Intoxicated 13 Selling
1930-31	132	1 Charged 3 Self-confessed Addicts	Liquor Act: 54 Intoxicated 16 Selling
1931-32	114	0 Charged 13 Self-confessed Addicts	Liquor Act: 39 Intoxicated 14 Selling
1932-33		Report not presented	
1933-34	91	0 Charged 3 Self-confessed Addicts	Liquor Act: 4 Intoxicated 7 Selling 3 other
1934-35	93	3 Charged 4 Self-confessed Addicts	Liquor Act: 5 Intoxicated 2 Selling 3 other
1935-36	92	2 Charged 7 Self-confessed Addicts	Liquor Act: 3 Intoxicated 6 Selling 0 other
1936-37	98	8 Charged 21 Self-confessed Addicts	Liquor Act: 6 Intoxicated 5 Selling 1 other
1937-38	91	7 Charged 6 Self-confessed Addicts	Liquor Act: 4 Intoxicated 0 Selling 4 other

SOURCE: From unpublished Annual Reports 1922-1938 of the Superintendent of Gaols found in the unpublished Clerk's Papers of the British Columbia Legislative Assembly.

TABLE 2

USE OF ALCOHOL BY SENTENCED FEMALE POPULATION IN B.C. 1965-1966

USE OF ALCOHOL	1965	PERCENT	1966	PERCENT
Abstainers	78	6%	56	4%
Temperate	249	20%	233	19%
Intemperate	911	74%	965	77%
TOTALS	1238	100%	1254	100%

SOURCE: Annual Reports of the B.C. Director of Corrections, 1965, 1966. EFSBC records.

TABLE 3

USE OF NARCOTICS BY SENTENCED FEMALE POPULATION IN B.C. 1965-1966

USE OF NARCOTICS	1965	PERCENT	1966	PERCENT
Abstainers	1020	82%	1032	82%
Infrequent User	19	2%	44	4%
Habitual User	199	16%	178	14%
TOTALS	1238	100%	1254	100%

SOURCE: Annual Reports of the B.C. Director of Corrections, 1965, 1966. EFSBC records.

TABLE 4
ETHNICITY OF ADMISSIONS OF SENTENCED FEMALE POPULATION IN B.C. 1965-1966

DESCRIPTION	1965	PERCENT	1966	PERCENT
White	535	43%	591	47%
Coloured	4	.5%	2	.1%
Indian	698	56%	656	52%
Asiatic	1	.08%	5	.3%
TOTALS	1238	100%	1254	100%

SOURCE: Annual Reports of the B.C. Director of Corrections, 1965, 1966. EFSBC records.

TABLE 5
PREVIOUS ADMISSIONS: 1965-1966

NUMBER OF PREVIOUS ADMISSIONS	1965	PERCENT	1966	PERCENT
Nil	317	26%	293	23%
1	145	12%	138	11%
2	109	9%	110	9%
3	87	7%	76	6%
4-10	269	21%	311	25%
11	311	25%	326	26%
TOTALS	1238	100%	1254	100%

SOURCE: Annual Reports of the B.C. Director of Corrections, 1965, 1966. EFSBC records.

TABLE 6
TOTAL SENTENCED FEMALE POPULATION IN B.C. 1959-1966

	1959-60	1960-1	1961-2	1962-3	1963-4	1964-5*	1965-6*
Totals	893	965	1084	1168	1185	1238	1254
Daily average	93	96	106	124	133	134	141
Highest	103	140	123	159	163	167	177
Lowest	53	79	85	84	107	101	110

SOURCE: Annual Reports of the B.C. Director of Corrections, 1959-1966. EFSBC records.
NOTE: Years 1960-1964 for Oakalla.* Includes Oakalla, Matsqui and Twin Maples.

TABLE 7
OFFENCES FOR WHICH WOMEN WERE SENTENCED IN B.C. 1959-1966

Offence	1959-60	1960-1	1961-2	1962-3	1963-4	1964-5	1965-6
Crimes against Persons	11	20	9	12	15	17	31
Crimes against Property	111	137	163	138	96	146	107
Crimes against Morals and Public Decency	57	2	6	41	64	89	81
Crimes against Public Order & Peace	686	721	882	946	986	973	1013
Other Offences	28	85	24	31	24	13	22
TOTAL	893	965	1084	1168	1185	1238	1254

SOURCE: Annual Reports of the B.C. Director of Corrections, 1959-1966. EFSBC records.
NOTE: Crimes against persons included: Abduction, Abortion, Assault, Bodily Harm, Murder, Rape, Suicide, Child Neglect, etc. Crimes against property included: Arson, Robbery, Forgery, Fraud, Theft, Receiving stolen goods, etc. Crimes against morals and public decency included: Indecent exposure, Incest, Inmates and frequenters of houses of ill fame, Keeper of bawdy house, Perjury, Prostitution, etc.

TABLE 8
BREAKDOWN OF CRIMES AGAINST PUBLIC ORDER AND PEACE
(FOR WHICH WOMEN WERE SENTENCED 1959-1966)

Crimes	1959-60	1960-1	1961-2	1962-3	1963-4	1964-5	1965-6
Breaches of Government Liquor Act	381	380	479	758	829	783	826
Breaches of Narcotic & Drug Act	76	58	52	64	65	71	89
Breaches of Bylaw (no BLCA)	1	1	-	1	4	2	1
Breaches of Motor Vehicle Act	6	16	29	9	13	11	10
Possession of Offensive Weapon	-	-	10	2	6	4	3
Breach of Recognizance	-	7	5	5	16	13	18
Impaired Driving	4	7	3	18	21	21	11
Escaping	2	7	5	4	-	-	-
Failing to Stop at Scene of Accident	-	-	7	-	-	2	-
Obstructing Officer	2	2	-	-	9	5	3
Breach of Excise Act	-	-	148	29	1	-	-
Selling or Giving Liquor to Indians	173	145	68	17	-	5	-
Unlawful Shooting	-	-	-	-	-	-	1
Vagrancy	17	74	59	14	5	22	19
Causing Disturbance	24	24	17	25	17	34	32

SOURCE: Annual Reports of the B.C. Director of Corrections, 1959-1966. EFSBC records

TABLE 9
TOTAL SENTENCED FEMALE POPULATION IN B.C. AND THEIR OFFENCES, 1941-1971

Offence	1940-1	1950-1	1960-1	1970-1*
Crimes against Persons	3	12	20	34
Crimes against Property	15	84	137	277
Crimes against Morals and Public Decency	21	61	2	74
Crimes against Public Order & Peace	149	450	721	254
Other Offences	4	20	85	39
TOTAL NUMBER WOMEN SENTENCED	192	627	965	678

SOURCE: Annual reports of the B.C. Director of Corrections, 1941-1971. * Includes women in the Lower Mainland Centre (Oakalla) and Twin Maples Farm.

TABLE 10
PERCENTAGE DISTRIBUTION OF ADMISSIONS BY CHARGE
FOR PROVINCIAL INDUSTRIAL SCHOOL FOR GIRLS 1955-1956

TYPE OF CHARGE	PERCENT OF ADMISSIONS
Incorrigibility	44.1
Unsatisfactory probation	25.7
Intoxication	12.85
Sexual immorality	7.1
Theft	5.5
Vagrancy	2.85
Breaking and entering	1.4

SOURCE: Report of Winifred Urquhart, superintendent of Provincial Industrial School for Girls in Report of B.C. Inspector of Gaols 1955-56.
NOTE: There were 70 girls admitted to the Industrial School for Girls in 1955-56. Recidivists counted for 20 percent of the admissions.

TABLE 11
AGES OF GIRLS ADMITTED TO
PROVINCIAL INDUSTRIAL SCHOOL FOR GIRLS 1955-1956

YEAR OF BIRTH	AGE AT ADMISSION	PERCENT OF TOTAL
1937	18	4.20
1938	17	27.00
1939	16	22.80
1940	15	18.53
1941	14	15.70
1942	13	10.00
1943	12	1.40

SOURCE: Report of Winifred Urquhart, superintendent of Provincial Industrial School for Girls in Report of B.C. Inspector of Gaols 1955-56.

ORGANIZATIONAL CHART 1
ORGANIZING STRUCTURE
ELIZABETH FRY SOCIETY OF BRITISH COLUMBIA – 1965

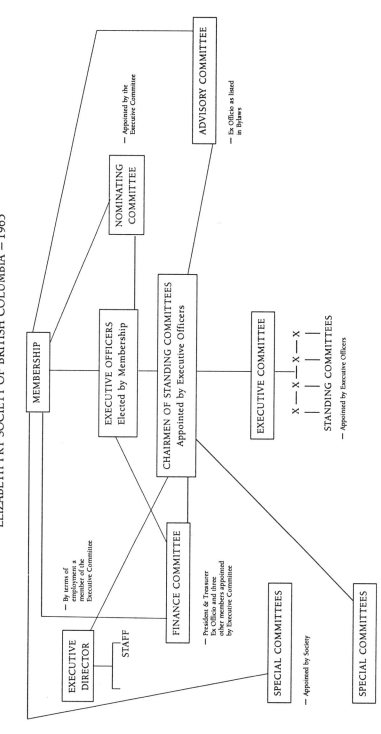

MEMBERSHIP

EXECUTIVE OFFICERS
Elected by Membership

NOMINATING COMMITTEE
— Appointed by the Executive Committee

ADVISORY COMMITTEE
— Ex Officio as listed in Bylaws

CHAIRMEN OF STANDING COMMITTEES
Appointed by Executive Officers

EXECUTIVE COMMITTEE

STANDING COMMITTEES
— Appointed by Executive Officers

EXECUTIVE DIRECTOR
— By terms of employment a member of the Executive Committee

STAFF

FINANCE COMMITTEE
— President & Treasurer Ex Officio and three other members appointed by Executive Committee

SPECIAL COMMITTEES
— Appointed by Society

SPECIAL COMMITTEES
— Appointed by the Executive Committee

ORGANIZATIONAL CHART 2
ORGANIZING STRUCTURE
ELIZABETH FRY SOCIETY OF BRITISH COLUMBIA – 1967

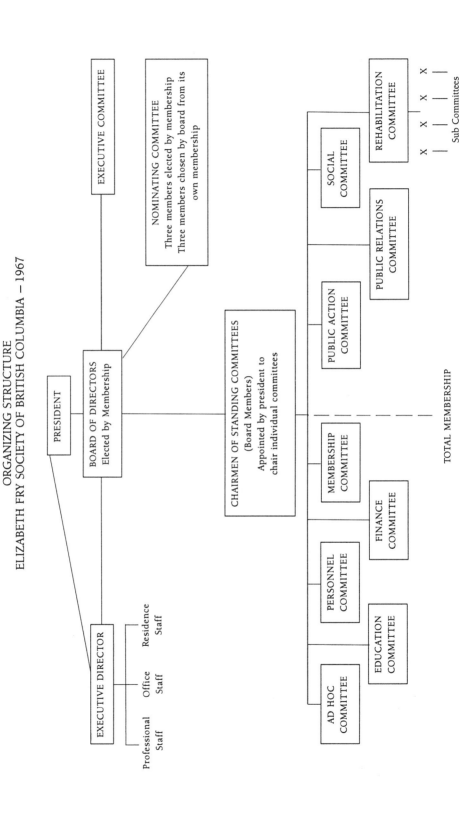

ORGANIZATIONAL CHART 3
ORGANIZING STRUCTURE
ELIZABETH FRY SOCIETY OF BRITISH COLUMBIA – 1985

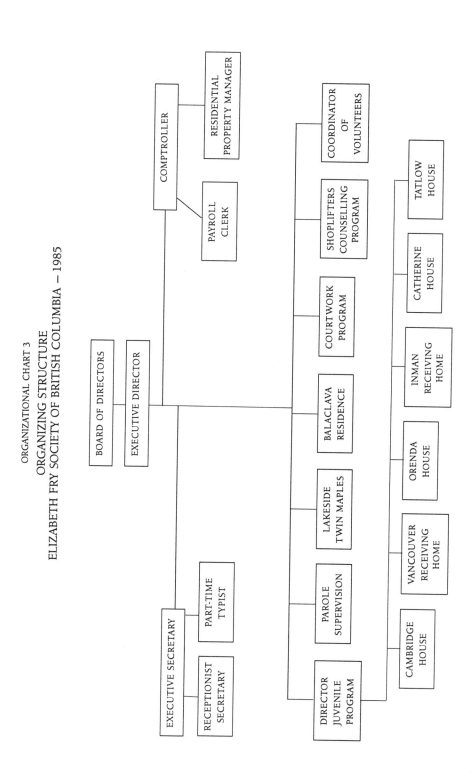

ORGANIZATIONAL CHART 4
ORGANIZING STRUCTURE
ELIZABETH FRY SOCIETY OF BRITISH COLUMBIA – 1992

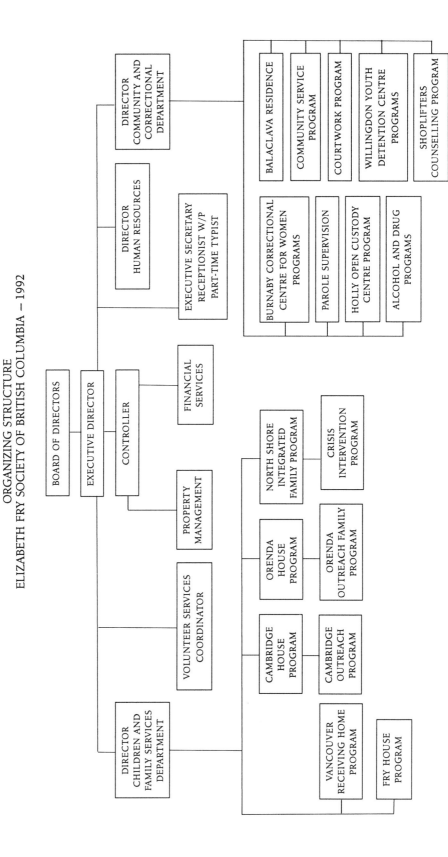

CHAPTER NOTES

Chapter 1

1   Taped interview with author, Lee Stewart, and Elizabeth Fry
    volunteer Marie Legg. November 9, 1987.

2   Although the Society has undergone several name changes since
    1939, the most recent being in 1989 to the "Elizabeth Fry
    Society of Greater Vancouver," for clarity and consistency all
    references will be to the "Elizabeth Fry Society of British
    Columbia," the title used throughout the majority of the first
    fifty years covered by this history.

3   Although Canada's first female M.P. and advocate of penal
    reform, Agnes Macphail, is often thought to be the founder of
    this organization in Canada, Macphail called for the
    establishment of an Elizabeth Fry Society in Toronto in 1951,
    eleven years after the first Society was formed in Vancouver.
    The EFSBC's research suggests the Vancouver Society was the
    first anywhere to use Fry's name.

4   EFSBC correspondence with P. Walker, December 1954; Beryl
    Fry, n.d.; Michael Fry, 1982.

5   Michael Fry donated $200 to the EFSBC which presented it to
    the CAEFS Bursary Fund established by Grace Black, on her
    retirement as president of CAEFS.

6   Elizabeth Fry Ellis and her son John Ellis.

7   Eaton developed a social conscience in her early years as a
    child growing up in the mining community of Springhill,
    Nova Scotia. She attended Acadia University and was active in
    the women's undergraduate society; after graduating, Eaton
    came to British Columbia where she married another Acadia
    alumnus, Rex Eaton. In B.C., Eaton helped organize a
    self-help group for unemployed women in the 1930s and in
    1942 she was appointed director of the Women's Division of
    the National Selective Service Agency to oversee recruitment
    of labour. Eaton also established daycare services for women
    during the war. Eaton was active in the Local Council of

Women; president of the Provincial Council of Women,
1951-53; and president by acclamation of the National Council
of Women, 1956. She was appointed to the B.C Labour
Relations Board, 1953-54. Eaton was awarded the Garnett
Sedgwick Award for outstanding contribution to furtherance of
civil liberties in B.C. in 1954 and an LLD from UBC in 1958.

8 See Gareth Morgan, *Images of Organization* (Beverly Hills: Sage
Publications, 1986), pp. 136-9.

9 The significance of the Elizabeth Fry story to current societies is
evident also in the recent biography researched and written
by a past president of the Hamilton Elizabeth Fry Society. The
publication of Eunice M. Smillie, *Elizabeth Fry* (Maple,
Ontario: Belsten Publishing, 1980) was sponsored by the
Provincial Council of Elizabeth Fry Societies to commemorate
the 200th anniversary of Fry's birth (1780-1980).

10 For example, Elizabeth Fry and her Ladies' Committee hired
and paid a matron to supervise all aspects of prison life.
Smillie, p. 24.

11 Smillie, p. 28.

12 Estelle B. Freedman, *Their Sisters' Keepers: Women's Prison
Reform in America, 1830-1930* (Ann Arbor: University of
Michigan Press, 1981), p. 14. Freedman explores the history
of women's prison reform in the United States and briefly
examines the impact of Fry's ideas on the movement for
separate women's prisons.

13 In England it was legal to force prisoners to spend ten hours a
day on the treadmill. John Kent, *Elizabeth Fry* (New York:
Arco Publishing, 1963), p. 120.

14 Smillie, pp. 22-3.

15 This term refers to the nineteenth century cultural ideal of
woman that emphasized her piety, purity, and
submissiveness, which was cultivated in her separate
domestic sphere. See Barbara Welter, "The Cult of True
Womanhood, 1820-1860," *American Quarterly* 18 (Summer
1966), pp. 150-74.

16 Smillie, p. 23.

17 Smillie, p. 35.

18 Kent, p. 74.

19 Kent, p. 114.

20 A reference to the radicals who moved Britain toward
democratic government. See Kent, p. 118.

21 In the 1830s two models of penitentiaries developed in the United States. The Pennsylvania, or separate and silent system, and the Auburn System from New York which allowed prisoners to work and eat together but still in total silence. England tried to adopt the Auburn model in prisons not designed for it. Instead of flogging the men who talked, English authorities reduced their food allotments. In Canada, the provincial penitentiary in Kingston, Ontario, was built in 1835 to house both men and women and implemented the Auburn System. On the Canadian prison see: Peter Hennessy, "The Prison at Kingston, Canada West: 'So Irksome and So Terrible'" *The Beaver*, February/March 1991, pp. 12-20.

22 The Report on Newgate, by the newly appointed Prison Inspectors in 1836, was critical of all the conditions and procedures at the jail but, unlike previous reports, was uncomplimentary to Fry and the Ladies' Committee. In particular, the report accused Fry and the Ladies' Committee of having exceeded the slight authority given to them, and claimed their presence tended "to dissipate reflexion, to diminish the necessary gloom of a prison, and to mitigate the punishment which the law has sentenced the prisoner to undergo." Kent, p. 124.

23 Kent, 129.

24 In her study of women's prison reform in America, Freedman argues that Fry's ideas, in combination with feminists' "separate but equal" political strategies, resulted in women becoming "their sisters' keepers" in their own prisons.

25 John W. Ekstedt and Curt T. Griffiths, *Corrections in Canada: Policy and Practice* (Toronto: Butterworths, 1984), p. 15.

Chapter 2

1 EFSBC minutes, annual meeting, March 27, 1947. President: Marguerite (Mrs. Alfred) Rines; Honorary vice-president: Fraudena (Mrs. Rex) Eaton; Secretary: E.A. (Mrs. F.J.) Thomson.

2 See Elsie Gregory MacGill, My Mother the Judge (Toronto: Peter Martin Associates, 1981).

3 *Ibid.*

4 *Ibid.*

5 MacGill's influential friends were many, for example, Mary Ellen Smith, first female MLA, and Evlyn Farris, founder of the University Women's Club, and her husband, J. W. de B. Farris, K.C., the Attorney General and Minister of Labour.

6 The name was changed first informally by the new superintendent and officially in 1909. See Diane L. Matters, "The Boys' Industrial School: Education for Juvenile Offenders," in J. Donald Wilson and David C. Jones, eds., *Schooling and Society in 20th Century British Columbia* (Calgary: Detselig Enterprises, 1980), pp. 53-70.

7 Vancouver Local Council of Women, minutes, February 1911.

8 *Ibid.*, April 1911. Because Ravenhill was a noted proponent of the teaching of Domestic Science to girls and women, it is likely that she envisioned these facilities to be well equipped kitchens in which the delinquent girls might learn the occupation of domestic service. See also, Alice Ravenhill, *Memories of an Educational Pioneer* (Toronto: J.M. Dent, 1951).

9 Phyllis Reeve, *The History of the University Women's Club of Vancouver, 1907-1982* (Vancouver: University Women's Club, 1982), p. 15.

10 MacGill, p. 154.

11 *Ibid.*, pp. 175-5.

12 Indiana Matters, "Sinners or Sinned Against?: Historical Aspects of Female Juvenile Delinquency in British Columbia," in Barbara K. Latham and Roberta J. Pazdro, eds., *Not Just Pin Money* (Victoria: Camosun College, 1984), p. 268.

13 *Ibid*

14 Reeve, p. 14. UWC minutes, 1913.

15 MacGill, p. 141.

16 *Ibid.*, pp. 141-2.

17 *Ibid.*, p. 142.

18 Reeve, p. 41.

19 In the early years of the twentieth century, the Fullum Street Prison in Montreal and the Mercer Reformatory in Toronto were women's institutions. See D. Owen Carrigan, *Crime and Punishment in Canada, A History* (Toronto: McClelland and Stewart Inc., 1991), p. 460.

20 John W. Ekstedt and Curt D. Griffiths, *Corrections in Canada: Policy and Practice* (Toronto: Butterworths, 1984), p. 47. For

an historical account of the penitentiary see also, Peter Hennessy, "'So Irksome and So Terrible'" *The Beaver*, Feb/Mar 1991, pp. 12-20.

21 Michael D. Wittingham, *The Role of Reformers and Volunteers in the Advance of Correctional Reform in Canada since Confederation.* No. 1984-70 (Ottawa: Ministry of the Solicitor General of Canada, 1984), p. 7.

22 For more about Agnes Macphail see Margaret Stewart and Doris French, *Ask No Quarter: A Biography of Agnes Macphail* (Toronto: Longmans, Green, 1959).

23 Ekstedt and Griffiths, p. 47.

24 *Ibid.*, p. 49.

25 Jean B. Wilton, May I Talk to John Howard? *The Story of J.D. Hobden – A Friend to Prisoners.* n.p. 1973, p. 78.

26 Coral W. Topping, *Canadian Penal Institutions* (Toronto: Ryerson, 1929).

27 See Wilton.

28 *Ibid.*

29 Reeve, p. 42.

Chapter 3

1 Hilda (Mrs. H.C.) Collins, president of the Elizabeth Fry Society of British Columbia, 1953-1957, in a letter reflecting on her involvement with the Society, June 16, 1980.

2 Kingston EFS formed 1949 with assistance from EFSBC. EFSBC minutes, May 4, 1949. Toronto EFS formed 1952 at urging from Agnes Macphail through First Unitarian Congregation of Toronto.

3 The custom of patrons was discontinued by the 1970s, but from 1940 a number of influential women agreed to be patrons of the EFSBC and added credibility to the fledgling organization. Some of the patrons included: Dr. Phyllis Ross, C.B.E.; Mrs. W.A. Akhurst; Mrs. Robert Bonner; Mrs. Rex Eaton, O.B.E.; Mrs. L. Haggen, MLA; Mrs. E. W. Hamber; Mrs. G. Hobbs, MLA; Mrs. F. Hume; Mrs. John B. MacDonald; Mrs. W. G. Rathie; Mrs. Sidney G. Smith; Mrs. Austin Taylor; Prof. C.W. Topping; Mrs. Charles N. Woodward; Mrs. Camille Mather, MLA; Mrs. Jack Wood.

4   The social gospel rested on the premise that Christianity was a
    social religion concerned with the quality of human relations
    on this earth. This ideology formed the basis of the social
    reform movement in Canada from 1890-1920.

5   Jean B. Wilton, *May I Talk to John Howard? The Story of J.D.
    Hobden – A Friend to Prisoners* (Vancouver: n.p., 1973).

6   Collins, op cit.

7   The first officers of the Elizabeth Fry Society were: Marguerite
    (Mrs. Alfred) Rines, president Elizabeth Fry Society 1940-50;
    (Mrs. Thomas) Bingham, first vice-president; Fraudena (Mrs.
    Rex) Eaton, second vice-president; Helen Douglas (Mrs.)
    Smith, honourary vice-president; Miss Hazel Van Buren,
    secretary; (Mrs. J.L.) Ballantyne, treasurer; (Mrs. H.G.) Morris,
    finance committee; (Mrs. Arthur F.) Mercer, rehabilitation
    committee; (Mrs. T.E.) Pierce, education committee;
    (Mrs. W.A.) Ackherst, program committee.

    Marguerite Rines was active in the Provincial Council of
    Women.

    Fraudena Eaton was active in the Local Council of Women, the
    Provincial Council of Women and president by acclamation
    of the National Council of Women in 1956. See chapter one,
    note 7.

    Helen Douglas Smith was president of the New Westminster
    Council of Women, the Provincial Council and vice-president
    of the National Council; the second woman in B.C. elected to
    the Legislature (1933-41). Smith held numerous other
    positions on boards of directors during her lifetime in
    addition to her work with the EFSBC.

8   The preamble read as follows: "Believing that women sentenced
    to a term in prison need special aid and assistance in the
    hope that they will return to normal and happy existence,
    certain women interested in Philanthropy, Religion, Education
    and Social Reform have determined to organize a Society for
    this purpose and to that end. . . ." EFSBC records.
    Constitution, pre-1953.

9   In this paragraph and occasionally elsewhere in the text, the
    term "girls" instead of "women" when discussing female inmates
    is used in keeping with the historical usage of the term.

10 The Borstal institutions were first established in England as an
    alternative to prison for young male first offenders. They
    offered vocational and educational training in a more relaxed
    setting and emphasized rapport between the youth and the

staff. The Borstal Home ran on the honour system and provided a support system after release.

11 The Doukhobors are a religious sect that fled Russia in the nineteenth century and settled in western Canada where they envisioned freedom from religious persecution and governmental interference. Early in the twentieth century a group known as the Sons of Freedom, who recognized no authority other than God, moved to British Columbia; for several decades they came into conflict with government authorities when they resisted conformity to certain laws in their efforts to establish communities independent from government control. Doukhobor women expressed their displeasure with government authorities by disrobing and setting fire to buildings. To cope with the numbers of Doukhobors convicted of nude protest and arson in 1932, a special federal facility at Piers Island, B.C., was opened where they served their three-year sentences. The prison was closed in 1935 after the remaining inmates were either discharged or transferred to Oakalla.

12 Wilton, pp. 120-127.

13 The *Province*, November 23, 1940, p. 10.

14 *Ibid.*

15 Arts and Crafts, Convener's report, 1948-49

16 EFSBC minutes Nov 27, 1947 and Mar 11, 1948.

17 Report by Miss B.E. Maybee, former director of Women's Correctional Centre, "Prison and Society," EFSBC records.

18 *Ibid.*

19 *Ibid.*

20 EFSBC interview with Constance Girling, 1985.

21 The prison library was first started by appeals from J.D. Hobden in 1932 to the public for used texts. See Wilton.

22 From a report of the prison librarian to EFSBC, 1951.

23 *Ibid.*

24 *Ibid.*

25 Report of Inspector of Gaols, 1952-53.

26 Report of Inspector of Gaols, 1953-54.

27 Maybee, op cit.

28 Wilton, p. 141

29 Maybee, op cit.

30 Wilton, op. cit.

31 Report of Inspector of Gaols, 1953-54.

32 Report of Inspector of Gaols, 1954-55.

33 Author's interview with Marie Legg, November 9, 1987.

34 Author's interview with Zoe Carter, October, 1987.

35 Ibid.

36 Interview with Constance Girling, 1985.

Chapter 4

1   Report on Visit of Delegation from Elizabeth Fry Society of
    British Columbia to Girls' Industrial School, 800 Cassiar
    Street, Vancouver, January 18, 1954.

2   Ibid.

3   Report of [provincial] Committee Enquiring into Operations of
    the Provincial Industrial Schools, September 15, 1954.

4   Interview wiht EFSBC volunteer Constance Girling, 1985.

5   Ian D. Parker, "Simon Fraser Tolmie: The Last Conservative
    Premier of British Columbia," in W. Peter Ward and Robert
    A.J. McDonald, eds., British Columbia: Historical Readings
    (Vancouver: Douglas & McIntyre, 1981), p. 522.

6   Report of the Provincial Industrial School for Girls, March 31, 1956.

7   Author's conversation with EFSBC volunteer Grace Black, 1987.

8   Also, as Fraudena Eaton's reputation increased, her connections
    with the EFSBC aided the Society's causes. Eaton was
    president of the Provincial Council of Women, 1951-53;
    appointed to the B.C. Labour Relations Board in 1953; won
    the Garnett Sedgwick Award for her outstanding contribution
    to the furtherance of civil liberties, in March 1954; and in
    June 1966, Eaton was elected president of the National
    Council of Women of Canada by acclamation.

9   "Canadian Training Schools Statement of Philosophy and
    Objectives," EFSBC records.

10 The Vancouver Province. November 16, 1960. p. 4.

11 Annual report of committee, 1956-57.

12 "Rules for Visitors," EFSBC records.

13 Interview with EFSBC volunteer Constance Girling, 1985.

14 Interview with EFSBC volunteer Judith Babb, October 1987.

15 Interview with EFSBC volunteer Constance Girling, 1985.

16 Interview with EFSBC volunteer Grace Bollert, 1987.

17 Interview with EFSBC volunteer Judith Babb, October 1987.

18 Interview with EFSBC volunteer Judith Babb, October 1987.

19 Interview with EFSBC volunteer Grace Bollert, 1987.

20 Interview with EFSBC volunteer Constance Girling, 1985.

21 Interview with EFSBC volunteer Judith Babb, 1987.

22 *Ibid.*

23 Interview with EFSBC volunteer Constance Girling, 1985.

24 Letters from former inmates of the girls' training school to Fry volunteers.

Chapter 5

1 EFSBC brief to City Council re. purchase of house to establish a group home, October, 1964.

2 Reports of the Working Boys' Home Committee, April 1954 and 1957. EFSBC records.

3 The EFSBC termed this a "hostel committee" because a hostel was initially the form of residence that was envisioned. However the committee would investigate various types of accommodation for both girls and women in accordance with their needs.

4 See Ekstedt and Griffiths, *Corrections in Canada*; Curt T. Griffiths, John F. Klein and Simon N.Verdun-Jones, *Criminal Justice in Canada*; (Western Canada: Butterworth & Co., 1980); Herbert Callison, *Introduction to Community-Based Corrections*, (New York: McGraw Hill, 1983); Belinda Rodgers McCarthy, Bernard J. McCarthy, *Community-Based Corrections* (Monterey: Brooks/Cole, 1984).

5 Maida Duncan reported hearing this from many people involved with boys' homes who were uninterested in providing a home for girls.

6 Special house committee meeting, July 12, 1961. EFSBC records.

7   Correspondence, EFSBC records.

8   Major Pike and Major Richardson to Grace Bollert. EFSBC
    Records.

9   Annual report of the hostel committee, 1961. EFSBC records.

10 *Ibid.*

11 Correspondence, EFSBC records.

12 EFSBC minutes, March 6, 1963.

13 Hostel committee report, March 1963.

14 Appeal letter, May 1, 1964.

15 Meeting held at Children's Aid Society June 1964 in
    connection with Elizabeth Fry Society's proposed
    pre-delinquent home. EFSBC records.

16 *Ibid.*

17 EFSBC minutes, July 9, 1964.

18 EFSBC minutes, May 11, 1965.

19 EFSBC minutes, July 9, 1964.

20 EFSBC report on history of group homes. EFSBC records.

21 *Ibid.*; EFSBC minutes, August to October 1964.

22 EFSBC brief to City Council regarding purchase of 1986 W.
    14th Avenue to establish a group home. October 19, 1964.

23 The *Province* and the *Vancouver Sun*, October 24, 1964.

24 Report of hostel committee, October 1964, EFSBC records.

25 The *Vancouver Sun*, March 27, 1965.

26 The *Vancouver Sun*, letters to the editor, April 14, 1965.

27 Newspaper clipping, April 3, 1965, EFSBC scrapbook.

28 Newspaper clipping, dated April 1965, EFSBC scrapbook. All
    quotes this paragraph from this article.

29 "Funding formulas for Elizabeth Fry Society Residences" by
    Maida Duncan.

30 EFSBC newsletter, May 1965.

31 "What is a G.L.H.?" EFSBC records. Group homes.

32 *Ibid.*

33 Duncan, "Funding formulas. . . . "

34 These qualities outlined in *The Communicator*, newsletter of the
    EFSBC, June 1974.

35 EFSBC minutes, September 16, 1965.

36 House committee minutes, June 25, 1965.

37 EFSBC newsletter, May 1965.

38 EFSBC annual report, 1965.

Chapter 6

1 Ruth Conlin, "Review of the EFSBC," 1970.

2 Tape recorded interview with Ethel Allardice and members of the EFSBC history committee, June 26, 1984.

3 Cited by Lynn Clarke in "Remarks to a joint meeting of the finance and house committee . . . ," November 25, 1965. EFSBC records.

4 *Ibid.*

5 *Ibid.*

6 Maida Duncan, "Notes on the organization of the Society," EFSBC records.

7 "Notes for Mrs. M. R. Duncan for the puposes of her remarks upon the resignations of Mesdames McCall and Ottman," December 1966; letter to Mrs. Duncan from David Tupper of Bull, Housser, & Tupper, Barristers & Solicitors, December 8, 1966; EFSBC records.

8 Letter to Mrs. Duncan from Stella McCall, November 18, 1966. EFSBC records.

9 Duncan, "Notes on the organization. . . . "

10 Tape recorded interviews with Judith Babb, October 1987, and Grace Bollert, October 1987.

11 Tape recorded interview with Judith Babb.

12 Henry Mintzberg, *Power In and Around Organizations* (Englewood Cliffs: Prentice Hall, 1983), p. 287, points out that a strong organizational ideology requires an egalitarianism that can be incompatible with status differences inherent in various forms of expertise. The EFSBC's hiring of Allardice, who was well connected to the Society's ideology, reduced the potentially divisive effect of bringing in a professional to work alongside the volunteers.

13 For the role of ideology in preserving organizational character see Henry Mintzberg, *Designing Effective Organizations* (Englewood Cliffs: Prentice Hall, 1983), p. 294.

14 Explanations for women's work for social reform, in the period to 1920, point out that volunteer work afforded women their only opportunity to work outside the home, or for social change, in a social climate that denied women both paid employment and the vote. See Linda Kealey, ed., *A Not Unreasonable Claim: Women and Reform in Canada 1880s-1920s* (Toronto: Women's Press, 1979).

15 The characteristics of the EFSBC volunteers in this and following paragraphs are based on an analysis of the membership files and the interviews compiled for this study.

16 Interview with Maida Duncan, September 1987.

17 This and following three paragraphs from interviews with Maida Duncan, Zoe Carter, Marie Legg, Beth Weese, Grace Black, Daphne Patterson, and Judith Babb.

18 Letter from Rose Rally to Kay Elliott, n.d.

19 These conclusions drawn from author's discussions with EFSBC volunteers interviewed for this history.

20 Interview with Maida Duncan, September 1987; Margo Lamont, "Hanging in There: Maida Duncan's Long Service to the Society. Part 3: From Prison Cells to Boardrooms." News[letter] of Elizabeth Fry, Autumn 1985.

21 Interview with Marie Legg.

22 The Honourable Barbara J. McDougall, PC, MP, Minister of Employment and Immigration, Address to the Elizabeth Fry Society of Greater Vancouver at its Fiftieth Anniversary Gala Dinner at the Hotel Vancouver, September 28, 1989.

23 EFSBC scrapbook, newspaper clipping, September 1969.

24 Interviews with Beth Weese, Marie Legg, and Grace Black.

25 Interview with Marie Legg.

26 Interview with Zoe Carter.

27 Interview with Grace Black.

28 In the early years of visiting at Oakalla women's unit, the inmates wore uniforms.

29 Interview with Marie Legg.

30 Interview with Zoe Carter.

31 Interview with Marie Legg.

32 "Record of Visits Made to Oakalla and Requests of Inmates November 1973 - November 1974," EFSBC records.

33 Interviews with Grace Black and Marie Legg.

[34] Interview with Zoe Carter.

[35] Member of EFSBC visiting committee, n.d. EFSBC records.

[36] Interview with Connie Girling, 1985.

[37] Interview with Ethel Allardice, Grace Black, Maida Duncan, Daphne Patterson, June 16, 1984.

[38] Interview with Beth Weese.

[39] Interview with Zoe Carter, October 1987, and discussion with Barbara Eacrett, September 28, 1989.

[40] Interview with Zoe Carter.

[41] Summary of EFSBC volunteers' workshop, 1972.

[42] *Ibid.*

[43] Interview with Maida Duncan.

[44] *Ibid.*

Chapter 7

[1] EFSBC records, Summary of Achievements and Objectives, 1970.

[2] Culhane regards the abolition of the prison system as one facet of the struggle to abolish the whole capitalist system and the struggle to build "a free and open society." See Claire Culhane, *Barred From Prison: A Personal Account* (Vancouver: Pulp Press, 1979), p. 217; and *Still Barred From Prison* (Montreal: Black Rose Books, 1985). See also Estelle Freedman, *Their Sisters' Keepers: Women's Prison Reform in America, 1830-1930* (Ann Arbor: University of Michigan Press, 1981), pp. 155-7 for discussion of contemporary feminist views. Also, in 1983 the Canadian Association of Elizabeth Fry Societies suggested a more politically feminist critique of the causes of female crime be included in CAEFS statement of its philosophy. EFSBC voiced its objections and the statement was tempered. See correspondence to Christie Jefferson from EFSBC, October 26, 1983, EFSBC records.

[3] See Griffiths, Klein and Verdun-Jones, *Criminal Justice in Canada*, p. 26. These authors suggest that the move towards more highly formalized conflict resolution mechanisms as represented by complex bureaucratic structures within the

criminal justice system can be seen as a consequence of the eclipse of the community.

4   Maida Duncan, "Funding Formulas for Elizabeth Fry Society Residences," EFSBC records, 1979.

5   "Delinquency Worst in B.C." The *Vancouver Sun*, n.d., EFSBC scrapbook, 1966.

6   Duncan, "Funding Formulas. . . . "

7   In Toronto, the Junior League helped set up the Elizabeth Fry House for women recently released from prison and created a lectureship in corrections at the University of Toronto's School of Social Work. See Cathy Kennedy and Chris Stirling, *The Junior League of Toronto, Diamond Jubilee 1926-1986* (Toronto: 1986) cited in Alison Prentice, Paula Bourne, Gail Cuthbert Brandt et al., *Canadian Women: A History* (Toronto: Harcourt Brace Jovanovich, 1988), p. 334.

8   "Report of the Committee Charged with Looking into the Application of the Elizabeth Fry Society for Membership in the United Community Services," January 14, 1969.

9   Mamie Maloney, the *Vancouver Sun*, September 15, 1967.

10   The *Vancouver Sun*, February 8, 1966. EFSBC scrapbook.

11   Simma Holt, "'Incorrigible' Tag Traced to Parents," the *Vancouver Sun*, n.d., EFSBC scrapbook, 1966.

12   Author's interviews with several EFSBC volunteers.

13   EFSBC Annual Report, 1953.

14   Committee members included Betsy Bennett, Zoe Carter, Margaret Campbell, Maida Duncan, Barbara Denman, Joan Greenwood, Lois Horan, Margaret Glass, Jean Hawksworth, Marie Legg, and Peggy Wainborn. Hostel committee minutes, March 6, 1968. EFSBC records.

15   Minutes of EFSBC board, December 12, 1968.

16   Minutes of EFSBC board, February 19, 1970.

17   Bill 101: An Act to Amend Various Enactments Relating to Courts of Justice. Passed April 4, 1968.

18   In fact, this committee was called the "hostel committee" but in this chapter will be referred to as the "residence committee" to avoid confusion with the former hostel committee (see chapter five) that initiated the group homes. EFSBC hostel committee minutes, May 15, 1968.

19   Founded in Vancouver in 1967-8, the Indian Post-Release Centre, later to become X-Kalay, was the first self-help residence in

Canada. From 1967 the Nasaika Lodge Society offered a home to Native girls wanting a life away from skid road.

20 EFSBC hostel committee minutes, May 15, 1968.

21 The first St. Leonard's Society House for men released from prison opened at Windsor, Ontario, in 1962. This halfway house for men released from Oakalla and the B.C. Penitentiary opened in Vancouver in 1967. See the *Vancouver Sun*, November 12, 1966.

22 EFSBC hostel committee minutes, March 12, 1968; May 15, 1968.

23 *Ibid.*

24 The hope was that in coming to the EFSBC office to pick up their cheques the girls might gain confidence and become interested in employment opportunities suggested by the Fry. Ethel Allardice, "Report of the Executive Director," November 24, 1966.

25 At least four of the committee members held executive offices in the EFSBC and were therefore members of the board.

26 Marie Legg in discussion with the author, November 23, 1989.

27 Report on discussions with Department of Social Planning for Vancouver. EFSBC hostel committee.

28 See executive director's report, in *The Communicator*, newsletter of the EFSBC, October 1973.

29 Duncan, "Funding Formulas. . . . "

30 Author's interviews with volunteers on the residence (hostel) committee.

31 Minutes of the board, April 22, 1971.

32 Evaluation of EFSBC women's residence. EFSBC records.

33 Executive director's report, *The Communicator*, October 1973.

34 "Case histories of residents accommodated in EFSBC residence," 1972, EFSBC records.

35 Letters from former residents. Residence files.

36 "Marg B." in EFSBC newsletter, May 1972. Fell resigned after her husband died in 1976.

37 See "Forward" to Pauline Fell, *From the Heart and Kitchen of a Vancouver Housemother* (Vancouver: n.p., n.d.).

38 Interview of the author and Beth Weese, September 1988.

39 Excerpts below from letters from residents, EFSBC records, residence files.

40 Fell, "Preface," *From the Heart.* . . .

41 Previously men had been sentenced in this manner but not women. S. 151 stated: Every court in B.C. before which any person apparently under the age of twenty-two years is convicted of an offence punishable by imprisonment for three months or longer, may sentence such person to imprisonment for a term of not less than three months, for an indeterminate period thereafter of not less than two years less a day.

42 Letter re: Elizabeth Fry Residence to Peter Battison, Drug and Alcohol Program Coordinator, Department of Education, Parliament Buildings, Victoria from W.H. Mulligan, warden, Lower Mainland Regional Corrections Service, B.C. Corrections Service. June 29, 1973.

43 Originally, the Kiwanis Club offered to buy a house and rent it to the EFSBC. Although the Society welcomed this significant vote of support, its experience had demonstrated that ownership was preferable and reasonable with the help of CMHC mortgages.

44 Maida Duncan in discussion with Lee Stewart, November 23, 1989.

45 Duncan, "Funding Formulas. . . . "

46 A reference to Oakalla.

47 See Griffiths, Klein, Verdun-Jones, *Criminal Justice in Canada*, p. 249.

48 *Ibid.*, p. 239. Report of the Commission of Inquiry into Events at B.C. Penitentiary June 9-11, 1975. Ottawa: Solicitor General of Canada.

49 Author's interview with Marie Legg.

50 EFSBC records, minutes of meeting to discuss a national association, June 11, 1969. A Sister Giselle Baily from Quebec was also present but the records do not show if she was representative of any association.

51 EFSBC minutes 1968-1971; Daphne Paterson, president's annual report to CAEFS, 1971.

52 *Ibid.*

53 CAEFS annual reports to 1989.

54 Paterson was president of the EFSBC in 1970-1.

55 The award to Allardice was made the year following her death.

56 "Notes for CAEFS Awards, 1988." EFSBC records.

57 Delegates were: from Ashcroft: Sharon Bach, Doris Bruno; from

Kamloops: Deirdre Bartlett, Enid Janzen, Elaine Mutrie; from Kelowna: Marnie McCall, Audrey Wildman; from Prince George: Ursula Morris; from Vancouver: Joan Sprague, Maida Duncan.

58 Minutes, EFSBC provincial meeting, Kamloops, May 4, 1985.

59 Minutes, EFSBC provincial committee, March 26, 1987.

60 Members of courtwork study group: Pat Kelgard, Joan Greenwood, Evelyn Robb, Carol Ward-Hall, Maida Duncan, Linda Spearin, Ethel Allardice, Carol St. Pierre, and the chair, Betsy Bennett. Minutes of court study group, April 14, 1969.

61 EFSBC operating statement, May 1977.

62 Over the years, the Koerner Foundation allowed the EFSBC to complete or enhance its projects with small grants unavailable from other sources. For example, in 1982 a Koerner grant allowed the EFSBC to put an evaluation component in place in its parenting program at the Lakeside Correctional Centre; money given to the women's residence allowed the women to take part in community activities; in 1985 a grant was given to the Child Care Counsellor Training Program.

63 Statistics from court clerk's office cited by Martha Robinson, "City clinic treats women shoplifters" in the Vancouver Sun, November 1973.

64 Studies have shown that although the "professional criminals" account for the theft of a greater percentage of goods in value, they only represent in numbers about five to fifteen percent of all shoplifters. The majority of shoplifters are "amateurs" having a "non-criminal" orientation. See M. O. Cameron, The Booster and the Snitch, Glencoe, N.Y.: The Free Press, 1964; B. Curtis, Security Control: External Theft, New York: Chain Store Age Books, N. Y., 1971; T.C.N. Gibbens & J. Prince, Shoplifting, London: Institute for the Study and Treatment of Delinquency, 1962. Cited in Mary Russell, "Groups for Women who Shoplift: An Evaluative Study of a Group Treatment Program for Women under the Auspices of the EFSBC," November 1976, EFSBC records.

65 Mary Russell, "Groups for Women who Shoplift: An Evaluative Study of a Group Treatment Program for Women Under the Auspices of the EFSBC," November 1976, EFSBC records.

Chapter 8

1 Barbara Kilbourn, president CAEFS. "Letter to all member societies," November 19, 1979. EFSBC records. CAEFS file.

2 In 1964 there were ten times more men than women charged with criminal code offences. See: National Advisory Committee on the Female Offender, *The Female Offender– Selected Statistics: Statistical Appendix to the Report of the National Advisory Committee on the Female Offender*, Canada: Solicitor General, 1977, p. 7.

3 The Lynda Williams House accommodated ten women and the Graham Street House, four. The EFSBC was asked at a later date to take over the operations of Graham House in Victoria but declined when capital was not forthcoming to raise it to EFSBC standards.

4 *The Female Offender– Selected Statistics*, p. 7. The number of women charged with criminal code offences from 1964 to 1974 increased 176 percent. See Tables 6, 7, and 9 for provincial increase.

5 These reports were the findings of Royal Commissions or Parliamentary Committees of Inquiry.

6 EFSBC brief to the Royal Commission on the Incarceration of Female Offenders, 1978.

7 EFSBC minutes of board meetings, e.g., April 22, 1976; May 20, 1976; June 17, 1976.

8 *Ibid.*, May 20, 1976.

9 Miss B. Maybee, matron of the Oakalla women's unit from 1948 to 1972, retired due to poor health.

10 See: Estelle B. Freedman, *Their Sisters' Keepers: Women's Prison Reform in America, 1830-1930* (Ann Arbor: University of Michigan Press, 1981).

11 See recommendation 27, EFSBC brief to the B.C. Royal Commission on the Incarceration of Female Offenders (1978), EFSBC records.

12 The *Vancouver Province*, October 26, 1977.

13 The *Province*, July 11, 1974; February 22, 1978; the *Vancouver Sun*, March 4, 1978; *The Province*, February 10, 1978.

14 EFSBC minutes of board, January 15, 1976.

15 EFSBC minutes of board, August 19, 1976.

16 A person accused of a misdemeanor in prison would be brought before the prison warden's court.

17 EFSBC minutes of board, April 21, 1977.

18 EFSBC minutes of board, August 18, 1977.

19 Oakalla committee report to EFSBC board, August 1977.

20 The Honourable Madam Justice Patricia M. Proudfoot, Justice of the Supreme Court of British Columbia, Commissioner, *Report of the British Columbia Royal Commission on the Incarceration of Female Offenders*, (Hereafter, Proudfoot Report) British Columbia, April 1978, p. 2.

21 Proudfoot was born in Saskatchewan in 1928 and graduated from UBC's law school in 1952 before setting up a private law practice in Vancouver. She was the first woman appointed judge of the Provincial Court–Criminal Division in October 1971, first woman appointed judge of the County Court of Vancouver in March 1974, and had received an Honourary Doctor of Law from SFU in May 1977 before her appointment to the Supreme Court in September 1977. She currently sits in the Court of Appeal.

22 Proudfoot Report, pp. 3-6.

23 *Ibid.*, Section 1.

24 Robert Martinson, "What works? Questions and Answers About Prison Reform" in David M. Petersen and Charles W. Thomas, eds., *Corrections: Problems and Prospects.* 2nd edition. (Englewood Cliffs: Prentice-Hall, 1980), pp. 11-44. (Article originally published in 1974.)

25 John W. Ekstedt, Commissioner of Corrections, "Brief Presented to the Royal Commission on Incarceration of Female Offenders," February 8, 1978; p. 1.

26 *Ibid.*, pp. 1-5.

27 Proudfoot Report, p. 8.

28 *Ibid.*, pp. 8-10.

29 Proudfoot Report, p. 11.

30 *Ibid.*, pp. 14-16.

31 *Ibid.*, p. 10.

32 *Ibid.*, See recommendations nos. 9; 1, 2, 3, 11, 12, 19, 20, 21, 23, 24, 32, 36, 51, 52; 10, pp. 171-4.

33 *Ibid.*, nos. 22, 23, 25, 26, 27, 28, 30.

34 EFSBC brief to the Royal Commission on Female Offenders, 1978.

35 *Ibid.*, pp. 157-8.

[36] *Ibid.*, p. 158.

[37] *Ibid.* For historical perspective see: Freedman.

[38] Proudfoot, p. 156.

[39] Author's interview with Zoe Carter.

[40] EFSBC, "Brief to the B.C. Royal Commission on Female Offenders, 1978." See Recommendation 40.

[41] *Ibid.*

[42] See: Clare Culhane, *Barred From Prison: A Personal Account,* (Vancouver: Pulp Press, 1979.) Also see Proudfoot Report.

[43] Discussion paper prepared for information systems and statistics division of the Ministry of the Solicitor General, "Trends in the Federal Female Inmate Population and Issues Related to the Future of the Prison for Women," January 1978, p. 35.

[44] Proudfoot Report, pp. 164-5.

[45] See "Historical Development" in Lorraine Berzins and Sheelagh Dunn, "Federal Female Offender Program: Progress Report, 1978," Ottawa: Female Offender Program, 1978.

[46] Berzins and Dunn, "Progress Report."

[47] The Report of the Inspectors of the Penitentiary, November 2, 1835, captured the attitude towards female offenders that still predominates: "It is to be observed that the sentencing of females to the penitentiary causes some inconvenience." The remark was prompted by the arrival of the first female prisoner in August 1835. This anecdote appeared in an address to the EFSBC on April 4, 1968 by John Braithwaite, Director of Corrections Planning. EFSBC records.

[48] Berzins and Dunn, Progress Report, "Historical Development."

[49] *Ibid.*

[50] *Ibid.*

[51] *Ibid.*

[52] *Ibid.*

[53] Public Affairs Division of the Canadian Penitentiary Service and the National Parole Service, Solicitor General's Office. Report of the National Advisory Committee on the Female Offender, Spring 1977, p. 15.

[54] *Ibid.*, p. 9.

[55] Owing to the pressure of other work, the CASCW did not respond to the NPCFO until September 1978, too late to be included in the first draft of the report. "Report of the

National Planning Committee on the Female Offender," p. 14.

56 Letter from ASCSW, vice-president Sue Findlay to Solicitor General A.F. Lawrence, October 24, 1979.

57 Report of the National Planning Committee on the Female Offender, pp. 53-4.

58 Although the executive directors of the EFSBC and the Toronto EFS, Allardice and Haslam, were appointed to the National Advisory Committee on the Female Offender in 1974, they were appointed as individuals. In 1978, the Toronto EFS was invited to provide a representative to the Joint Committee.

59 The current and former coordinators of Female Offender Programs, Sheelagh Dunn and Lorraine Berzins, respectively, and André Frommer, Special Projects Division, assisted the steering committee with their expertise.

60 EFSBC, *Report on B.C. Federal Women: An Alternative Proposal*, June 1979, Appendix B; minutes of a meeting held at the Hotel Vancouver on Monday January 29, 1979, p. 3.

61 EFSBC, *Report on B.C. Federal Women*, June 1979, pp. 2-4.

62 See Curt Taylor Griffiths and Margit Nance, eds., *The Female Offender: Selected Papers from an International Symposium*, (Criminology Centre: Simon Fraser University, Burnaby, B.C., 1980).

63 The participants on the trip to visit U.S. institutions included: Joan Sprague, Maida Duncan and Dru Anderegg who were, respectively, the president, treasurer and executive director of the EFSBC. They were accompanied by Jim Murphy, Pacific Region director general, CSC; Pat Drew, director of Twin Maples, Minimum Security Institution, B.C. Corrections; John Stonoski, director of Mission Security Institution, CSC; Sara Breault, executive director Ottawa E. Fry; and Jean Simmons, Canadian Penitentiary Services Staff member, assigned as resource person to EFSBC. (Simmons later replaced Anderegg as EFSBC executive director.) These delegates visited institutions in Lexington, Kentucky; Nashville, Tennessee; Memphis, Tennessee; and in Pleasanton, California. See Appendix F, EFSBC report on B.C. Federal Women.

64 EFSBC report on B.C. Federal Women, pp. 9-10.

65 *Ibid.*, p. 11.

66 *Ibid.*, p. 15-16.

67 *Ibid.*, p. 17.

68 *Ibid.*, pp. 18-19.

[69] *Ibid.*, pp. 22-27.

[70] Letter from EFSBC president Vi Roden, and executive director Dru Anderegg, to Solicitor General Allan Lawrence, dated October 10, 1979. Original underlining (italics) for emphasis.

[71] Solicitor General Jean-Jacques Blais had announced in December 1978 the building of nine new prisons and the expansion and renovation of nine existing prisons. This was contrary to the recommendations of the parliamentary subcommittee; and numerous other groups opposed the construction of new and larger prisons, including the EFSBC.

[72] Notes of the CAEFS executive meeting with the solicitor general of Canada, October 23, 1978, Ottawa. EFSBC records.

[73] *Ibid.*

[74] By October 1979, the CACSW had reversed its stand on the retention of the P4W after noting the recent agreement between Quebec and the federal government.

[75] See *Creating Choices: The Report of the Task Force on Federally Sentenced Women*, April 1990. Confidential advance copy, p. 100.

[76] *Creating Choices.*

[77] Margaret Shaw, "The Federal Female Offender: Report on a Preliminary Study," Solicitor General of Canada, June 1989, cited in *Creating Choices*, p. 80.

Chapter 9

[1] The Honourable Barbara McDougall, "Speaking Notes for the 50th Anniversary Meeting of the EFSBC," September 28, 1989. EFSBC records.

[2] *Ibid.*

[3] *Ibid.*

[4] A biography of Fry to commemorate the 200th anniversary of her birth was written by a member of the Ontario Provincial Council of Elizabeth Fry Societies, Eunice M. Smillie, *Elizabeth Fry* (Maple: Belsten Publishing, 1980) and circulated among members of the EFSBC.

[5] EFSBC minutes, annual meeting, March 27, 1947.

[6] Taped Interview. Maida Duncan and Susan McKechnie,

September 17, 1989. Also from discussion with McKechnie and the author, December 1989.

7   Maida Duncan interview with Theresa Citterelle, 1989.

8   Discussion with Marie Legg and author, November 1990.

9   In fact, women's prisons held larger consequences for non-offenders who found expanded opportunities for the employment of women beyond the domestic sphere.

10 The EFSBC did not maintain membership in the umbrella organizations of the Council of Women or the University Women's Club.

11 For example, the John Howard Society of Canada formed in 1962 and the Association des Services de Rehabilitation Sociale formed in Quebec as a federation of all agencies in that province, including the John Howard Society of Quebec. See Task Force on the Role of the Private Sector in Criminal Justice, *Community Involvement in Criminal Justice*, (Ottawa: Supply & Services, 1977), pp. 14-16.

12 Informal discussion about a national association began in 1969 and CAEFS was incorporated in 1978.

13 See Alison Prentice, Paula Bourne, Gail Cuthbert Brandt et al., eds., *Canadian Women: A History*, pp. 344-49; Nancy Adamson, Linda Briskin, Margaret McPhail, *Feminist Organizing for Change: The Contemporary Women's Movement in Canada* (Toronto: Oxford University Press), pp. 42-64.

14 The EFSBC was and continues to be very selective of the women's issues that it supports. For example, the EFSBC declined to participate in any official capacity in the action groups established in 1971 in the wake of the Report of the Royal Commission on the Status of Women because these groups were "quite dissociated from the Society's area of concern." Barbara J. McDougall, "Report on Conference Concerning the Royal Commission on the Status of Women," February 18, 1971, EFSBC records.

15 Taped interview with Sandy Simpson and author, January 30, 1988.

16 Author's interview with Beth Weese and letter from former resident in EFSBC records.

17 Taped interview by author with Selwyn Rocksborough Smith, former Director of Corrections and Chief Probation Officer for British Columbia, January 19, 1988.

18 Taped interview with Sandy Simpson and author, January 30, 1988. Simpson stated that all aspects of the women's

residence underwent changes as a result of a tragic incident that occurred in a halfway house in Ottawa. A young staff member was killed by a parolee.

[19] The Vancouver Receiving Home provided emergency 24-hour residential care for adolescents for periods up to six weeks. The Society administered the receiving home for the city after 1983 but it was formerly the EFSBC's third group home.

[20] In recent years, in addition to volunteer coordinators the Society employed an arts and crafts instructor and two lifeguards to work at Willingdon.

[21] Minutes, EFSBC executive, September 29, 1975.

[22] A few men were originally invited to serve on the EFSBC board in the 1970s in response to external criticism that men were illogically excluded. Male volunteer Patrick Graham served as president of the EFSBC in 1976-77.

[23] Taped interview with Sandy Simpson by author, January 30, 1988.

[24] Fry House is a specialized resource for six boys and girls, aged thirteen to seventeen years. The program provides individual long-term treatment for youths who are experiencing difficulty in their home, school, or community. The maximum stay at Fry House is two years.

[25] Sandy Simpson in taped interview.

[26] EFSBC minutes, December 4, 1985. Ware had been a Fry board member, chaired the Lakeside Advisory Board and had been president of the John Howard Society.

[27] J. Laurine Greig, S.W., "Historical Report of the Elizabeth Fry Society 1939-1970." EFSBC records.

[28] Joan Driedger in the EFSBC newsletter, December 1968.

[29] Jane Roberts Chapman, "The Treatment of Convicted Female Offenders in the Criminal Justice System," in *The Female Offender: Selected Papers from an International Symposium*, eds. Curt T. Griffiths and Margit Nance (Burnaby: Simon Fraser University, 1979), p. 197.

[30] The prison inspectors' definition of the purpose of imprisonment showed how fundamentally different were the views of these new reformers with Elizabeth Fry's. The report stated "the object of imprisonment is to deter from crime by the endurance of hardship and privation, and to dispose the prisoner, by seclusion and meditation, to return to an honest life." Kent, p. 126.

[31] CAEFS Philosophy Statement 1983, draft copy, EFSBC records.

PRIMARY SOURCES

From 1939, a variety of documents, organized by subject, have been kept by the Elizabeth Fry Society of British Columbia (EFSBC) in its office at 2412 Columbia Street, Vancouver, B.C., V5Y 3E6. The majority of primary sources that formed the basis of the research for this history are cited, generally, as EFSBC records except those that are listed below.

EFSBC Records

EFSBC Annual Reports
EFSBC Correspondence
EFSBC Minutes of Annual Meetings
EFSBC Minutes of the Board
EFSBC Minutes of Executive Committees
EFSBC Newsletters
EFSBC Scrapbooks

Interviews

Allardice, Ethel. Taped interview with Grace Black, Maida Duncan, Daphne Patterson, Marie Legg, Beth Weese, June 16, 1984.

Babb, Judith. Taped interview with Lee Stewart, October 1987.

Black, Grace. Taped interview with Lee Stewart, November 1987.

Bollert, Grace. Taped interview with Lee Stewart, October 1987.

Carter, Zoe. Taped interview with Lee Stewart and Maida Duncan, October 1987.

Carter, Zoe. Taped interview with Marie Legg, Maida Duncan, n.d.

Citterelle, Theresa. Taped interview with Maida Duncan, 1989.

Duncan, Maida. Taped interview with Lee Stewart, September 21, 1987.

Eacrett, Barbara. Discussion with Lee Stewart, September 28, 1989.

EFSBC History Committee: M. Duncan; M. Legg; G. Black; B. Weese. Taped interview with Lee Stewart, August 24, 1987.

Girling, Constance. Taped interview with Maida Duncan, Marie Legg, Grace Black, 1985.

Legg, Marie. Taped interview with Lee Stewart, September 1987; November 9, 1987.

Legg, Marie. Discussion with Lee Stewart, November 1990.

McKechnie, Susan. Taped interview with Maida Duncan, September 17, 1989.

McKechnie, Susan. Discussion with Lee Stewart, December 1989.

Simpson, Sandy. Taped interview with Lee Stewart, January 30, 1988.

Smith, Selwyn Rocksborough. Taped interview with Lee Stewart and Marie Legg, January 19, 1988.

Weese, Beth. Taped interview with Lee Stewart, September 1988.

Newspapers

Vancouver Province
Vancouver Sun
Victoria Times

Reports and Discussion Papers

Berzins, Lorraine and Dunn, Sheelagh. *Federal Female Offender Program: Progress Report, 1978.* Ottawa: Female Offender Program, 1978.

British Columbia Legislative Assembly, Clerk's Papers. *Reports of the Inspector of Gaols*, 1938-1961.

EFSBC. *Report on B.C. Federal Women: An Alternative Proposal*, June 1979.

National Advisory Committee on the Female Offender. *The Female Offender - Selected Statistics: Statistical Appendix to the Report of the National Advisory Committee on the Female Offender*, Canada: Solicitor General, 1977.

Proudfoot, The Honourable Madam Justice Patricia M., Justice of the Supreme Court of British Columbia, Commissioner. *Report of the British Columbia Royal Commission on the Incarceration of Female Offenders*, British Columbia, April 1978.

Solicitor General's Office. Discussion Paper prepared for Information Systems and Statistics Division, Ministry of the Solicitor General. Trends in the Federal Female Inmate Population and Issues Related to the Future of the Prison for Women, January 1978.

_____ . *Creating Choices: The Report of the Task Force on Federally Sentenced Women*, April 1990.

_____ . Discussion Paper on the Relationship of the Ministry of the Solicitor General with the Voluntary Sector, 1987.

_____ . Public Affairs Division of the Canadian Penitentiary Service and the National Parole Service. *Report of the National Advisory Committee on the Female Offender*, Spring 1977.

_____ . *Report of the Commission of Inquiry into Events at B.C. Penitentiary June 9 - 11, 1975*.

Task Force on the Role of the Private Sector in Criminal Justice. *Community Involvement in Criminal Justice*. Ottawa: Supply & Services, 1977.

Wittingham, Michael D. *The Role of Reformers and Volunteers in the Advance of Correctional Reform in Canada Since Confederation*. No. 1984-70. Ottawa: Ministry of the Solicitor General of Canada, 1984.

SECONDARY SOURCES (ARTICLES and BOOKS)

Adamson, Nancy; Briskin, Linda; McPhail, Margaret. *Feminist Organizing for Change: The Contemporary Women's Movement in Canada*. Toronto: Oxford University Press, 1988.

Backhouse, Constance. *Petticoats & Prejudice: Women and Law in Nineteenth-Century Canada.* Toronto: Women's Press, 1991.

Callison, Herbert. *Introduction to Community-Based Corrections.* New York: McGraw Hill, 1983.

Carrigan. D. Owen. *Crime and Punishment in Canada, A History.* Toronto: McClelland & Stewart, 1991.

Chapman, Jane Roberts. "The Treatment of Convicted Female Offenders in the Criminal Justice System." In *The Female Offender: Selected Papers from an International Symposium,* eds., Curt T. Griffiths and Margit Nance. Burnaby: Simon Fraser University, Criminology Centre, 1979.

Culhane, Claire. *Barred From Prison: A Personal Account.* Vancouver: Pulp Press, 1979.

_____ . *Still Barred From Prison.* Montreal: Black Rose Books, 1985.

Ekstedt, John W. and Griffiths, Curt T., eds. *Corrections in Canada: Policy and Practice.* Toronto: Butterworths, 1984.

Fell, Pauline. *From the Heart and Kitchen of a Vancouver Housemother.* Vancouver: n.p; n.d.

Freedman, Estelle B. *Their Sisters' Keepers: Women's Prison Reform in America, 1830-1930.* Ann Arbor: University of Michigan Press, 1981.

Griffiths, Curt T.; Klein, John F.; and Verdun-Jones, Simon N. *Criminal Justice in Canada.* Western Canada: Butterworth & Co., 1980.

_____ and Nance, Margit, eds. *The Female Offender: Selected Papers from an International Symposium.* Burnaby: Simon Fraser University, Criminology Centre, 1980.

Hennessy, Peter. "The Prison at Kingston, Canada West: 'So Irksome and So Terrible,'" *The Beaver.* February/March, 1991: pp. 12-20.

Kealey, Linda, ed. *A Not Unreasonable Claim: Women and Reform in Canada 1880s-1920s.* Toronto: Women's Press, 1979.

Kent, John. *Elizabeth Fry.* New York: Arco Publishing.

Lachance, André. "Women and Crime in Canada in the Early Eighteenth Century, 1712-1759." In *Lawful Authority: Readings on the History of Criminal Justice in Canada.* Mississauga: Copp Clark Pitman, 1988.

McCarthy, Belinda Rodgers and McCarthy, Bernard J. *Community-Based Corrections.* Monterey: Brooks/Cole, 1984.

MacGill, Elsie Gregory. *My Mother the Judge.* Toronto: Peter Martin Associates, 1981.

Macleod, R.C. ed. *Lawful Authority: Readings on the History of*

Criminal Justice in Canada. Mississauga: Copp Clark Pitman, 1988.

Martinson, Robert. "What works? Questions and Answers About Prison Reform." In *Corrections: Problems and Prospects,* 2nd edition. eds., David M. Petersen and Charles W. Thomas. Englewood Cliffs: Prentice-Hall, 1980.

Matters, Diane L. "The Boys' Industrial School: Education for Juvenile Offenders." In *Schooling and Society in 20th Century British Columbia,* eds., J. Donald Wilson and David C. Jones. Calgary: Detselig Enterprises, 1980, pp. 53-70.

Matters, Indiana. "Sinners or Sinned Against?: Historical Aspects of Female Juvenile Delinquency in British Columbia." In *Not Just Pin Money,* eds., Barbara K. Latham and Roberta J. Pazdro. Victoria: Camosun College, 1984, pp. 265-77.

Mintzberg, Henry. *Power In and Around Organizations.* Englewood Cliffs: Prentice Hall, 1983.

Mintzberg, Henry. *Designing Effective Organizations.* Englewood Cliffs: Prentice Hall, 1983.

Morgan, Gareth. *Images of Organization.* Beverly Hills: Sage Publications, 1986.

Parker, Ian D. "Simon Fraser Tolmie: The Last Conservative Premier of British Columbia." In *British Columbia: Historical Readings,* eds., W. Peter Ward and Robert A.J. McDonald. Vancouver: Douglas & McIntyre, 1981, pp. 517-32.

Prentice, Alison; Bourne, Paula; Brandt, Gail Cuthbert; et al., *Canadian Women: A History.* Toronto: Harcourt Brace Jovanovich, 1988.

Ravenhill, Alice. *Memories of an Educational Pioneer.* Toronto: J.M. Dent, 1951.

Reeve, Phyllis. *The History of the University Women's Club of Vancouver, 1907-1982.* Vancouver: University Women's Club, 1982.

Rose, June. *Elizabeth Fry.* London: Macmillan, 1980.

Smillie, Eunice M. *Elizabeth Fry.* Maple, Ontario: Belsten Publishing, 1980.

Stewart, Margaret and French, Doris. *Ask No Quarter: A Biography of Agnes Macphail.* Toronto: Longmans, Green, 1959.

Topping, Coral W. *Canadian Penal Institutions.* Toronto: Ryerson, 1929.

Welter, Barbara. "The Cult of True Womanhood, 1820-1860," *American Quarterly* 18 (Summer 1966).

Wilton, Jean B. *May I Talk to John Howard? The Story of J.D. Hobden – A Friend to Prisoners.* n.p., 1973.

INDEX

Salvation Army, *18, 31, 60, 101*
Sancta Maria House, *102*
School of Home Economics, UBC, *43*
School of Social Work, UBC, *17, 34*
school subjects, *40*
Scott, Frank R., *17*
Second World War, *17, 20, 23, 42, 80*
separate prisons for females, *9*
sexual misconduct, *119, 121*
sexual offences, *6 – 7*
shoplifting, *113 – 114, 153*
Simpson, Sandy, *149, 152*
Smith, Helen Douglas, *19, 22, 84*
Smith, Marjorie, *34*
Smith, Mary Ellen, *12, 15*
social gospel, *21*
Solicitor General, *110 – 111, 134, 136 – 138*
solitary confinement, *5*
Spofford, Anne, *12*
Sprague, Joan, *111*
St. Leonard's House, *102*
St. Pierre, Carol, *113*
status of women and children, *12*
Stratton, Jocelyn, *113*
Study – Alternatives for Housing, *132*

T

Tatlow House, *151*
Topping, Dr. Coral W., *17, 34*
Townley, Alice, *12*
training schools, *68*
transition homes, *1*
treatment of prisoners, *7*
treatment programs, *42*
Twin Maples Correctional Centre, *1, 117 – 118, 124 – 125, 149*

U

United Community Services, *97*
University Women's Club (UWC), *11 – 12, 15, 18, 147*
Urquhart, Winifred M., *58, 62 – 63*

V

Vancouver Foundation, *104, 113*
Vancouver Law Foundation, *113*
Vancouver Local Council of Women, *13*
Vancouver Receiving Home, *96*
vandalism, *48*
Victorian Order of Nurses (VON), *11*
vocational training, *41, 44, 46*
voluntary societies, *12*
volunteer workers, *1, 11, 33, 50 – 52, 56, 79, 81, 84, 87, 92, 112, 144 – 145, 148*

W

Webster, Jack, *120 – 121*
Weese, Beth, *xi, xiv, 90, 105, 146*
Willingdon Detention Centre, *1*
Willingdon School for Girls, *47 – 48, 56, 59, 61 – 63, 68, 70, 80, 83, 85, 110, 149 – 150, 153*
Willingdon Training School, *58*
Willingdon Youth Detention Centre, *150*
Wilton, Jean, *21, 31 – 32*
Women's Christian Temperance Union (WCTU), *11 – 12, 14, 25*
women's clubs, *11, 20*
women's crimes, *6, 156*
women's culture, *10, 147*
women's jail – Prince George, *30*
women's philanthropic organizations, *11*
women's prisons, *147*
Women's Probation Officer, *31*
women's residence, *99, 102, 110, 116, 149 – 150*
Woodsworth, J.S., *21*
Woodward's, *64, 71*
Woodward, Rosemary, *64*

Y

Young Offenders' Unit – Oakalla, *43*
Young Women's Christian Association (YWCA), *11, 35*